357 -

Bernard

St. James's, Renfrew.

26ᵗʰ Oct. 1960.

# THE SPIRITUALITY OF
# THE MASS

# THE SPIRITUALITY
# OF
# THE MASS

*In the Light of Thomistic Theology*

BY

Rev. ADOLPH DOMINIC FRENAY, O.P., Ph.D.

B. HERDER BOOK CO.
15 & 17 SOUTH BROADWAY, ST. LOUIS 2, MO.
AND
33 QUEEN SQUARE, LONDON, W. C.
1953

IMPRIMI POTEST

T. S. McDermott, O.P., S.T.Lr.,

Prior Provincialis

NIHIL OBSTAT

Right Rev. Msgr. John J. Hayes

Censor Librorum

IMPRIMATUR

✠ Henricus J. O'Brien, D.D.

Episcopus Hartfordiensis

Hartford, Conn. die 30. Januarii 1952

Second Printing

Library of Congress Catalog Card Number: 52-10737

Vail-Ballou Press, Inc., Binghamton and New York

## ACKNOWLEDGMENTS

With the permission of Benziger Brothers, Inc., the publishers and copyright owners, the quotations from the *Summa theologica* of St. Thomas are taken from the American edition; the Communion Prayers of St. Thomas are taken from the *Blessed Sacrament Book* by Father Lasance, likewise with the same permission.

# Foreword

IN THE SPIRITUALITY OF THE MASS IN THE LIGHT OF THOMISTIC THEOLOGY Father Frenay has given us a book rich in source material from the prayers of the Mass and complete and scholarly in commentary upon these prayers. The fifty chapters of his book take their inspiration from the approximately fifty prayers which make up the Ordinary and the Canon.

The value of such a work is immediately evident. The many prayers of the Mass are recited by the priest each day but always in the space of a half-hour. Under such conditions it is impossible for him to savor the full beauty and significance of each prayer. Consequently it has long been a priestly custom to meditate before and after Mass on the spiritual significance of the various prayers. In order to assist the priest in this laudable and pious practice the present author puts into his hand a manual bringing out the wealth of meaning and thought of each prayer in the Roman Missal.

As the title of the book indicates, the author is chiefly concerned with a study of the Thomistic tract on the Eucharist in the *Summa theologica*. He has spared himself no time or labor in accomplishing this purpose. In some two hundred eighty quotations from the *Summa* the mind of the incomparable Thomas on this subject is laid before us. St. Thomas is the great theologian of the Blessed Sacrament, and the pages of the present work glow with the love and insight and inspiration of the Angelic Doctor to whom God Himself said, "Thou has written well of Me, Thomas." Incidentally, the author ranges very widely through the whole corpus of the *Summa* in finding passages which apply to a better understanding of the Mass. For example, in commenting upon the prayer "Libera nos, quaesumus Domine ab omnibus malis" the whole Thomistic doctrine on the problem of good and evil is philosophically explained. Every section of the *Summa* contributes to the illustration of the depth and beauty of the Ordinary of the Mass. The new publication, indeed, in the course of thoroughgoing commentaries on the Mass, provides a most interesting and inspiring outline of one's philosophical and theological studies. They are all very gracefully and easily tied in with the Sacrifice of the Mass which should be the center of the priest's learning as well as the center of his life.

After the theological aspect of the various prayers has been presented, the author asks himself (and us) the following question: How far does all this apply to our own spiritual life? From his own long and varied experience in the priesthood, the author guides the soul of the reader, calling attention to spiritual pitfalls and dangers. He frequently concludes with eloquent and moving appeals to the love of a priestly soul for its divine Lord and Master. He aims to arouse in the heart sentiments of gratitude for our priestly vocation and a determination to spend ourselves for the glory and the advancement of the kingdom of God on earth.

Finally, of course, as any treatise on the Mass must be, Father Frenay's book is full of the Scriptures. From the Old Testament and from the New, in rich profusion and with remarkable apposite and pertinent force, the noble words of Holy Writ adorn these pages to the great benefit of the reader. It will be the rare priest indeed who will not find herein new approaches to an understanding of the Mass. For all these reasons I am glad to recommend the following pages to the use of the clergy. It has been for Father Frenay a labor of love to bring all these things together between the covers of one book; to read all this attentively and carefully may well be the beginning for anyone of us of a deeper love of God. May it be so!

Henry J. O'Brien, D.D.<br>Bishop of Hartford

# Contents

# THE SPIRITUALITY OF
# THE MASS

# CHAPTER 1

## *At the Foot of the Altar*

P. In nomine Patris et Filii et Spiritus Sancti. Amen.
Introibo ad altare Dei.

S. Ad Deum qui laetificat juventutem meam.

### Psalm 42

P. Judica me, Deus, et discerne causam meam de
gente non sancta: ab homine iniquo et doloso erue me.

S. Quia tu es, Deus, fortitudo mea: quare me repulisti
et quare tristis incedo, dum affligit me inimicus?

P. Emitte lucem tuam et veritatem tuam: ipsa me de-
duxerunt, et adduxerunt in montem sanctum tuum, et in
tabernacula tua.

S. Et introibo ad altare Dei: ad Deum qui laetificat
juventutem meam.

P. Confitebor tibi in cithara, Deus, Deus meus: quare
tristis es, anima mea, et quare conturbas me?

S. Spera in Deo, quoniam adhuc confitebor illi: salutare vultus mei, et Deus meus.

P. Gloria Patri et Filio et Spiritui Sancto.

S. Sicut erat in principio et nunc et semper: et in saecula saeculorum. Amen.

P. Introibo ad altare Dei.

S. Ad Deum qui laetificat juventutem meam.

P. Adjutorium nostrum in nomine Domini.

S. Qui fecit caelum et terram.

WHEN the priest enters the sacred precincts of the altar,
should there be any doubt that he does so "in the name of the

1

Father and of the Son and of the Holy Ghost"? For, every prayer is begun with the sign of the cross, every sacrament is administered in the name of the triune God. The sign of the cross is a profession of faith. By this sign we are delivered from the evil of sin, and the same sign is the blessed signal which ushers us into the holy of holies where the great Sacrifice of the Mass is celebrated.

"I will go unto the altar of God: unto God who giveth joy to my youth." This antiphon gives us the key to the fundamental thought, to the liturgical and mystical understanding of the psalm that follows. Standing at the foot of the altar, the priest is reflecting on what he is about to do. He is to enter the holy of holies to perform the great mystery of the New Covenant. He is to ascend the steps of the altar, to stand at the table of the Lord, to offer the Lamb of God to the divine Majesty, to the Father in heaven.

Every priest, saying this verse, is reminded of the days of his youth, when he stood for the first time in his life on the steps of the altar. The palms of his hands were still moist with the holy oil with which, at his ordination, he was anointed by the bishop, after which he celebrated his first Mass. What a joy made his heart beat faster! What spiritual gladness filled his soul! What supernatural delights enraptured his whole being! The desires of his youth had been fulfilled. After years of longing and striving, after a life of work and worries, after a decade or two of studies and struggles, and, finally, after a week spent in retreat and earnest prayer, at last he stood in the sanctuary of the Lord. The goal of his youth had been attained. How his young heart was overflowing with spiritual gladness and what sentiments of gratitude to his Blessed Lord ascended to the heights of heaven! How he was consumed by the fires of spiritual zeal! How his youthful being was inflamed with devotion, acts of piety, and love of God! The joys of youth brightened his countenance. Since then, long months and years have passed. But ever since then, this antiphon, said in his daily Mass, has reminded the priest of his ordination and rekindled the flames of love in his priestly heart. Ever since, it has revived enthusiasm and pure joy in his priestly soul. The antiphon brings back the same sentiments of happiness, the happiness of celebrating once more the mystery of religion, of offering with renewed zeal the obligation which does not grow old or morose, the sacrifice which is, and remains forever, the source of his priestly vigor and strength.

The days of his ordination and of his first Mass have long passed, but the memories of his blessed ascent unto the sacred hill of divine worship have not vanished. These memories are still here. The past has become the present; the days of old are renewed. His service at the altar has gone on, has continued, and has come down to the present day. And when the daylight breaks, he, the priest, once more proceeds from the sacristy to take his place at the altar. And now that he stands again at the foot of the altar of God, he stops to recollect himself and he reminds himself of the intention that was in his mind and is still, and he says the words of the inspired singer, the verse of the Psalmist, "Judica me, Deus."

"Judge me, O God." I, your priest, O God, am Thy legitimate servant. I am the lawful minister of Thy divine worship. "Judge me, O God." Thou, O Lord, vindicate my rights. "Distinguish my cause from the nation that is not holy." Distinguish me from false prophets, from pretenders, from the ministers of heresy and schism. I, Thy priest, belong to Thy nation, to Thy holy nation, to Thy holy generation, to Thy holy people, redeemed by the blood of Thy beloved Son, Jesus

Christ. Ordained to the priesthood, I, though unworthy, trust in Thy goodness, O Lord, and I dare to approach once more the altar of the Lord. "Deliver me from the unjust and deceitful man." Save me from the persecutions of the unholy and from the snares of the evil one. "For Thou, O God, art my strength." For, indeed, "the Lord is my firmament, my refuge, and my deliverer." [1] For, in truth, "the Lord is the strength of His people and the protector of the salvation of His anointed." [2]

Though trusting in the Lord of heaven and confiding in His never-failing help and support, the priest is encompassed by temptations that deprive him of the feeling of security. And while he struggles with the evil one, with the powers of darkness; while his soul feels abandonment, he cries out to heaven: "Why hast Thou cast me off? And why go I sorrowful whilst my enemy afflicteth me?" Though feelings of despair struggle to overpower his soul, he does not yield. He fights the good fight, battling against temptations and praying for spiritual help. "Send forth Thy light and Thy truth." Give me Thy grace. And again he wins the victory over sin and despair. As in the past, so now Thy light and Thy truth, Thy divine graces, "have led me and brought me unto Thy holy hill, and into Thy tabernacles." Strengthened and fortified by Thy never-failing hand, I take courage and "I will go in unto the altar of God; unto God, who giveth joy to my youth." The priest's soul is inflamed with joy. St. Thomas tells us that joys are "the delights of the soul," [3] that "joy denotes pleasure of the soul." [4] As the priest stands at the altar, he does not think

[1] Ps. 17:3.
[2] Ps. 27:8.
[3] *Summa theol.*, Ia IIae, q.31, a.3 ad 1.
[4] *Ibid.*, a.6, ad 1.

of the pleasures of the body, but only of the joys of his soul. Being a rational creature and endowed with an intellectual will or appetite, he is inflamed and he burns with the joys of his soul. Filled with this joyful spirit, he continues to praise his God and Lord in the words of the Psalmist: "I will praise Thee upon the harp, O God, my God." "I will praise the name of God with a canticle: and I will magnify Him with praise." [5] "Praise ye the name of the Lord: O you His servants, praise the Lord: you that stand in the house of the Lord, in the courts of the house of our God." [6]

A certain sadness suddenly overshadows the soul of the priest while he is still singing the glories of heaven. What has befallen him? With an eye trained to discern the mysteries of faith, the priest gazes into the past and there he beholds Christ making ready for the great sacrifice of Calvary. He sees our Lord in the upper chamber of Jerusalem and, while listening attentively to every syllable from the Savior's mouth, he hears Him say: "Now is My soul troubled." [7] And then the priest leaves the Last Supper room and follows the Lord to the Garden of Gethsemane, where the priest hears Him uttering similarly mournful words: "My soul is sorrowful, even unto death." [8] And Christ's sadness burdens the soul of the priest, who exclaims: "Why art thou sad, O my soul, and why dost thou disquiet me?" The altar is Mount Calvary and the Mass is the renewal, in an unbloody manner, of the Sacrifice of the Cross. It is not difficult to see that the prayer of the priest at the foot of the altar resembles the Savior's last discourse in the upper room at Jerusalem and the agony in the Garden of

[5] Ps. 68:31.
[6] Ps. 134:1 f.
[7] John 12:27.
[8] Matt. 26:38.

Gethsemane. In those places the sadness of Christ at the beginning of His sacred passion; here the disquieted soul of the
priest at the foot of the altar.

But as our Lord in His agony in the Garden was strengthened by an angel, so the voice of the prophet admonishes the
priest to have hope and courage: "Hope thou in God, for I will
yet praise Him." God in heaven will be praised by something
far more worthy than the words of praise spoken by the priest.
God the Father will be praised in the most perfect and sublime
manner by the sacrifice of His only-begotten Son, Jesus Christ.
And while, by the sacrifice of the body and blood of our Lord
Jesus Christ, God the Father in heaven is infinitely praised,
glorified, and adored, the blood of the Savior is mystically shed
for my benefit and for "the salvation of my countenance." And
since, during the celebration of the Sacrifice of the Mass,
Christ is really present on the altar, with His body and blood,
with His sacred humanity and His divinity, the priest ador-
ingly exclaims: Deus meus!

All will be done and is done in the name of the Blessed
Trinity. "Glory be to the Father and to the Son and to the Holy
Ghost. As it was in the beginning, is now, and ever shall be,
world without end. Amen." With the help of the triune God,
the priest gathers his strength and courage to advance toward
the altar. "I will go in unto the altar of God. Unto God, who
giveth joy to my youth." Not by his own daring. "Our help is
in the name of the Lord, who made heaven and earth."

# CHAPTER 2

# The Priest Confesses His Sins

P. Confiteor Deo omnipotenti, beatae Mariae semper Virgini, beato Michaeli Archangelo, beato Joanni Baptistae, sanctis Apostolis Petro et Paulo, omnibus Sanctis, et vobis, fratres, quia peccavi nimis cogitatione, verbo et opere: mea culpa, mea culpa, mea maxima culpa. Ideo precor beatam Mariam semper Virginem, beatum Michaelem Archangelum, beatum Joannem Baptistam, sanctos Apostolos Petrum et Paulum, omnes Sanctos et vos fratres, orare pro me ad Dominum Deum nostrum.

S. Misereatur tui omnipotens Deus, et dismissis peccatis tuis, perducat te ad vitam aeternam.

P. Amen.

S. Confiteor . . . tibi pater . . . te pater. . . .

P. Misereatur vestri omnipotens Deus, et dismissis peccatis vestris, perducat vos ad vitam aeternam.

S. Amen.

P. Indulgentiam, absolutionem, et remissionem peccatorum nostrorum tribuat nobis omnipotens et misericors Dominus.

S. Amen.

AFTER reciting psalm 42, the priest becomes more conscious of his unworthiness. Confessing his sins and begging forgiveness, he bows down in sorrow, and with a contrite heart he says: "I will declare my iniquity: and I will think for my sin." [1] "Confiteor Deo omnipotenti." "I confess to almighty God." For it is wise and prudent to follow the counsel of the

[1] Ps. 37:19.

7

inspired writer and to "justify not thyself before God, for He knoweth the heart. . . ." [2] "Be not ashamed," says the same sacred writer, "to confess thy sins. . . ." [3] And the royal singer chants in the psalms: "I have acknowledged my sin to Thee, and my injustice I have not concealed. I said I will confess against myself my injustice to the Lord: and Thou has forgiven the wickedness of my sin." [4] And as emphatically as the prophets in the Old Testament, St. John, in the New Covenant, recommends the confession of sins; for we read in his First Epistle: ". . . the blood of Jesus Christ, His Son, cleanseth us from all sin." "If we confess our sins, He is faithful and just, to forgive us our sins, and to cleanse us from all iniquity." [5]

The priest confesses his faults to the Lord, not merely privately and in secret, but openly and publicly. He acknowledges his wickedness to the whole Church of God, to the Church triumphant as well as to the Church militant. He confesses to the Queen of heaven, "the Blessed Mary ever Virgin," to the prince of the celestial courts, "blessed Michael the archangel," to the leader among the prophets of the Old Testament, "the blessed John the Baptist," to the princes of the new dispensation of God on earth, "the holy apostles Peter and Paul," to all the saints "in heaven" and "to the brethren," his fellow men and members of the mystical body of Christ on earth. As "we have fellowship one with another," [6] the priest heeds the words of St. James, who admonishes us to "confess . . . your sins one to another: and pray one for another, that you may be saved." [7]

[2] Ecclus. 7:5.
[3] Ecclus. 4:31.
[4] Ps. 31:5.
[5] I John 1:7, 9.
[6] I John 1:7.
[7] Jas. 5:16.

"That I have sinned exceedingly." For "who can say: My heart is clean, I am pure from sin?" [8] ". . . in many things, we all offend." [9] For is it not true, that "if we say that we have no sin, we deceive ourselves"? [10] Or, as St. Paul has expressed it, "For I am not conscious to myself of anything, yet am I not hereby justified. . . ." [11]

I have sinned in thought, word, and deed.

In thought. The Psalmist rightly asks: "Who can understand sins? From my secret ones cleanse me, O Lord . . ." [12] "for the imagination and thought of man's heart are prone to evil from his youth. . . ." [13] And the Book of Proverbs assures us that "evil thoughts are an abomination to the Lord. . . ." [14]

In word. "Let no evil speech proceed from your mouth," wrote St. Paul to the Ephesians.[15] "Shun profane and vain babblings, for they grow much towards ungodliness," [16] the same apostle wrote to Timothy.

In deed. "All iniquity is sin," [17] says the beloved disciple. "The countenance of the Lord [is] upon them that do evil things." [18]

Considering his evil thoughts, his sinful words, and his wicked deeds, the priest now strikes his breast three times while saying: "Through my fault, through my fault, through my most grievous fault." Anyone, when saying these words is reminded of the publican who "standing afar off, would not

[8] Prov. 20:9.
[9] Jas. 3:2.
[10] I John 1:8.
[11] I Cor. 4:4.
[12] Ps. 18:13.
[13] Gen. 8:21.
[14] Prov. 15:26.
[15] Eph. 4:29.
[16] II Tim. 2:16.
[17] I John 5:17.
[18] I Pet. 3:12.

so much as lift up his eyes towards heaven, but struck his breast, saying: O God, be merciful to me a sinner." [19]

The *mea culpa* forms the central idea of this prayer. In the first part of the Confiteor, the priest professes his fault; in the second part he begs heaven and earth to intercede for him. Hence we may rightly ask: What is a fault, or what does fault consist in? St. Thomas Aquinas, in his *Summa theologica,* tells us that a "fault itself consists in the disordered act of the will." [20] He gives two other definitions. He writes: "the nature of guilt consists in a voluntary aversion from God." [21] And again "the evil which consists in the subtraction of the due operation in voluntary things has the nature of a fault." [22] This is short, but to the point. Fault or guilt is the transgression of the eternal law considered from the point of view of the sinner. We use the word "sin" when we consider a moral evil in itself or with respect to God, the eternal Lawgiver, whose ruling has been transgressed or whose eternal will has been offended by a willful act of the sinner; we use the word "fault" or "guilt" to denote this same moral evil or sin, but with respect to the transgressor. The willful disregard of the eternal law leaves attached to the soul of the offender a certain blame, opprobrium, or shame; this stigma resulting from the commission of a sin is called "fault" or "guilt." Hence, when acknowledging that he sinned "in thought, word, and deed through his most grievous fault," the priest confesses that his sinful action was his own doing, his own evil deed or wrongdoing.

Continuing his prayer, the priest, in the second part of the Confiteor, invokes the saints and his brethren and beseeches them to intercede for him before the throne of God.

[19] Luke 18:13.
[20] *Summa theol.,* Ia, q.48, a.6.
[21] *Ibid.,* IIa IIae, q.34, a.2.
[22] Ia, q.48, a.5.

Now that he has repented of his sins, the Church puts the *Misereatur* into the mouth of the priest: "May almighty God have mercy upon thee, forgive thee thy sins, and bring thee to life everlasting." The mercy of God is invoked. Due to God's mercifulness, the sins of the penitent priest are forgiven, with the happy result that life everlasting may be obtained.

Having made the sign of the cross, the priest begins the *Indulgentiam:* "May the almighty and merciful God grant us pardon, absolution, and remission of our sins." The words "pardon," "absolution," and "remission" are not merely a play on words or an expression to emphasize the mercifulness of God. The threefold enumeration analyzes the elements of sin. For, sin is, first, an offense directed against God. This offense results, secondly, in the guilt of the sinner, and thirdly, draws some punishment upon him. Accordingly, God in His infinite mercy "remits" the sins, by which man rebelled against His laws, "absolves" the guilt incurred by the sinner, and "pardons," either completely or partially, the punishment man so justly deserved.

The order of the threefold act of divine forgiveness is not without significance. The least of the three evils is the punishment, and this is most easily forgiven and therefore first pardoned. Of graver concern than the punishment is, in the eyes of eternal truth, the guilt of the sinner, and this guilt is consequently absolved less readily. But the sin itself, the act provoking the justice of God, is the greatest of all evils, and is, therefore, remitted with the least speed, only after due consideration. Hence the order: pardon, absolution, and remission. Thus almighty God reveals, in this prayer, the depth of His mercy and the extent of His charity.

What is, we may ask, the value of these three prayers: the *Confiteor*, the *Misereatur*, and the *Indulgentiam?* The last two are prayers in the deprecatory form ("May God be merciful, may God grant us pardon"), a form distinct from the indicative way of speech. The difference between the two constitutes, according to St. Thomas, the mark between the judicial absolution of the sacrament of penance and the imploring prayer or petition of a sacramental. The efficacy of these three prayers is *ex opere operantis*. They contribute toward the freeing from venial sin provided the priest is really repentant of his transgressions. These prayers, says St. Thomas, "conduce to the remission of venial sins." [23]

Let us now, for a moment or two, take our attention away from these prayers and look at the Mass as a whole. As we know, the Mass is a sacrament. As a sacrament, it has, as St. Thomas teaches, "the power to forgive venial sins." [24] The Angelic Doctor declares: "This sacrament is received under the form of nourishing food. But nourishment from food is requisite for the body to make good the daily waste caused by the action of natural heat. But something is also lost daily of our spirituality from the heat of concupiscence through venial sins, which lessen the fervor of charity . . . and therefore it belongs to this sacrament to forgive venial sins. Hence Ambrose says [25] that this daily bread is taken as a remedy against daily infirmity." [26] St. Thomas, furthermore, points out the fact that "the reality of this sacrament is charity, . . . which is kindled in this sacrament, and by this means venial sins are forgiven." [27] This sacrament, the Angelic Doctor teaches, can even effect the forgiveness of mortal sin, "when received by one in mortal sin of which he is not conscious and

23 *Ibid.*, IIIa, q. 87, a. 3.
24 *Ibid.*, q. 79, a. 4.
25 *De sacram.*, V.
26 *Summa theol.*, IIIa, q. 79, a. 4.
27 *Ibid.*

for which he has no attachment; since possibly he was not sufficiently contrite at first, but by approaching this sacrament devoutly and reverently he obtains the grace of charity, which will perfect his contrition and bring forgiveness of sin." [28]

Now, since the inner working of this Eucharistic sacrament liquidates sin, will it not be wise and prudent to follow the advice of Mother Church and to elicit, at the very beginning of Mass, an act of perfect contrition? Hence let us say the *Confiteor*, the *Misereatur*, and the *Indulgentiam* in the spirit of a heart filled with sorrow for all sins. And God will be merciful to us and will remit sins and stains of which we may still be guilty. Happy, indeed, the priest who, with a clear and good conscience, in the state of sanctifying grace, ascends the steps of the altar.

[28] *Ibid.*, a. 3.

# CHAPTER 3

# *The Ascent to the Altar*

P. Deus, tu conversus vivificabis nos.
S. Et plebs tua laetabitur in te.
P. Ostende nobis, Domine, misericordiam tuam.
S. Et salutare tuum da nobis.
P. Domine, exaudi orationem meam.
S. Et clamor meus ad te veniat.
P. Dominus vobiscum.
S. Et cum spiritu tuo.
P. Oremus.
P. Aufer a nobis, quaesumus, Domine, iniquitates nostras: ut ad Sancta sanctorum puris mereamur mentibus introire. Per Christum Dominum nostrum. Amen.

Oramus te, Domine, per merita Sanctorum tuorum, quorum reliquiae hic sunt, et omnium Sanctorum: ut indulgere digneris omnia peccata mea. Amen.

AFTER the priest has confessed his sins and besought, in the *Confiteor, Misereatur,* and *Indulgentiam,* the pardon of heaven, he is more confident of the mercy of God. While the consciousness of sinfulness has not yet entirely left his spirit, the priest begins to say two verses of the eighty-fourth psalm: "Thou wilt turn, O Lord, and bring us to life." The priest asks God, according to the words of St. Thomas, "to move his soul by turning it to Himself." [1] This being done, the priest continues in the words of the Psalmist. "And Thy people will rejoice in Thee." The ways of divine grace and love quicken and gladden the heart of man. "Show us, O Lord, Thy mercy," and

[1] *Summa theol.,* Ia IIae, q. 113, a. 4.

all that the mercy of God brings to humanity; "and grant us Thy salvation." Then the priest recites the second verse of psalm 101: "O Lord, hear my prayer." Confidence in the goodness of God now fills the soul of the priest, and he addresses the Christian salutation to the faithful, and they respond: "The Lord be with you." "And with thy spirit." Inviting them to join him in his prayers, with a sincerely felt *Oremus,* the priest dares to ascend the steps of the altar. "Take away from us our iniquities, we beseech Thee, O Lord." He wishes, in all purity and worthiness, to climb the hill on which the altar of the New Testament stands, "that being made pure in heart we may be worthy to enter into the holy of holies, through Christ our Lord. Amen."

The Christian altar was foreshadowed by the holy of holies in the temple on Mount Sion, for here stood the Ark of the Old Covenant. The holy of holies was separated by a heavy veil from the holy place into which the priests of the Old Testament could enter. Into the holy of holies, however, only the high priest was permitted to enter, once a year, on the feast of Atonement. For the holy of holies was the sacred spot where the God of Israel dwelt. The ark which stood here was made of precious wood and covered inside and outside with gold. At the ends of it were statues of two cherubim, the only two angelic figures permitted in Israel, lest the people be exposed to the temptation of falling into idolatry. Moses had placed in the ark the two stone tablets on which were inscribed the Ten Commandments. Next to them in the ark was preserved the staff of Aaron and a vessel filled with manna. The holy of holies was the most sacred spot of Israel. It was, too, a prefigure of the altar of the New Covenant.

Now the priest ascends the steps of the altar, of which the holy of holies in the Old Covenant was but a shadow, a type.

He himself is, indeed, a priest more privileged than the high priest of the Old Law, for he is permitted to enter the holy of holies daily.

While the center of the worship of the Old Covenant was passing away with the destruction of the Temple of Jerusalem, there arose another sanctuary, dipped in the blood of martyrs. From Mount Sion the thoughts of the priest fly to the city of the seven hills, where Christianity descends and finds refuge in the catacombs. Here, over the relics of the martyrs, the bread of life was broken and the contents of the chalice consumed. The catacombs, sacred to the memory of the Church, are reconstructed in every Christian church, where the relics of martyrs and confessors are enshrined in the altar. The knowledge of touching such a sacred spot fortifies the spirit of the priest, and he sends the following prayer to heaven: "We beseech Thee, O Lord, by the merits of Thy saints whose relics are here, and of all the saints, that Thou wouldst vouchsafe to forgive me all my sins. Amen." In his trust in the mercy of God, the priest is sure that the martyrs and confessors, especially those over whose earthly remains he is going to celebrate the Sacrifice of the Mass, will intercede for him before the throne of God and obtain for him the remission of his sins.

The Christian altar is, indeed, a place of sacred fear. More blessed are its precincts than were those of the holy of holies on Mount Sion. Sanctified is the altar by the relics of the saints, consecrated by the holy oils when blessed by the bishop. An awe-inspiring table, for here the Sacrifice of the Mass is celebrated. Here in the tabernacle dwells the Eucharistic Lord. "How terrible is this place! This is no other but the house of God, and the gate of heaven." [2]

[2] Gen. 28:17.

Our daily entrance into this holy place should, indeed, not breed in us a spirit of irreverence. Clean should be the soul whenever drawing near the holy table of the Lord. "Keep thy foot, when thou goest into the house of God," warns the preacher.[3] For remember "there is undoubtedly in that place a certain power of God. For He that hath His dwelling in the heavens, is the visitor, and protector of that place. . . ."[4]

[3] Eccles. 4:17.
[4] II Mach. 3:38 f.

# CHAPTER 4

# The Introit

HAVING confessed his sinfulness and unworthiness, at the foot of the altar, the priest, imploring help from above, ascends the steps and kisses the saints' relics embedded in the altar stone. Now he stands at the altar and is ready to begin the sacred function. What should he do to set his mind and heart in readiness to perform so great an act? How should he infuse into his soul thoughts and affections of devotion? How should he elicit from his heart acts of love and adoration? What is more natural at this particular moment, at the beginning of Mass, than that he should turn to the word of God, to the reading of passages from the psalms of King David or from other inspired writers of the Old or the New Testament? Accordingly he begins with the reading of the Introit, which consists of an antiphon, a psalm-verse, and a *Gloria Patri*.

This Introit does not yet, strictly speaking, belong to the sacrificial action, but leads up to it. Such sacrificial action, as sacred as that contained in the Mass, necessitates a worthy preparation in the spirit of prayer. "Since the whole mystery of our salvation," remarks St. Thomas, "is comprised in this sacrament, therefore it is performed with greater solemnity than the other sacraments." And, since it is written [1] "Keep thy foot when thou goest into the house of God," and [2] "Before prayer prepare thy soul," the celebration of this mystery is

[1] Eccles. 4:17.
[2] Ecclus. 18:23.

18

preceded by a certain preparation that we may worthily perform what follows. The first part of this preparation is divine
praise and consists of the Introit, "The sacrifice of praise shall
glorify me; and there is the way by which I will show him the
salvation of God"; [3] and the Introit is taken for the most part
from the psalms, or, at least, is sung with a psalm because, as
Dionysius [4] quotes: "The psalms comprise by way of praise
whatever is contained in Sacred Scripture." [5]

Can we think of anything more befitting than prayer to
serve as a worthy introduction to the sacrificial action? Prayer
is the sweet incense veiling the altar of the Lord and ascending
to the heights of heaven. St. Paul wrote the following exhortation to the Philippians: ". . . in everything, by prayer and
supplication, with thanksgiving, let your petitions be made
known to God." [6] If this is to be true in everyday life, how
much more appropriate is prayer to serve as the keynote, nay,
the basis, of the sacrificial action. Throughout the history of
men prayers accompanied sacrifices. With prayer our Blessed
Lord sanctified His life and blessed His sacrifice on the cross.
Correspondingly, prayer should begin, accompany, and end
the sacrifice of the New Testament.

Though the Introit is a relatively short prayer, it is marked
by a few characteristics worthy of our attention. The antiphon
and the psalm-verse, which besides the *Gloria Patri* compose
the Introit, are selected according to the liturgical seasons or
in conformity with the purpose for which a particular Mass is
said. Hence almost every day during the ecclesiastical year
we are led into the holy courts of the Sacrifice through
new porticoes, a practice that renders the reading always

[3] Ps. 49:23.
[4] *Eccl. Hier.*, 3.
[5] *Summa theol.*, IIIa, q.83, a.4.
[6] Phil. 4:6.

interesting and stimulating to devotion and to reflections.

Since the Introit is short, all that could lead to fatigue is absent. By its very brevity the Introit arouses our prompt attention. Like an aspiration, it is breathed forth from the breast of the celebrant. Like a short knock at the gates of heaven, it opens the doors to the sacrifice.

In addition to conciseness, profoundness of thought is another feature of the Introit. The antiphon and the psalm-verse are the pious reflections, the deep thoughts, of the inspired writers of the Old and of the New Testament. The keen mind of the royal singer David, who most frequently strikes the first chords in the opening of readings from the Missal, ascends to the most sublime heights of religious thought. The meditations and reflections he gave to the world in the psalms are some of the best of all religious literature. Written under the guidance and inspiration of the Holy Ghost, the psalms have ever been the favored prayer book of the Church.

What a happy combination we find in this short, introductory reading to the Mass! The psalm-verse, in conjunction with the antiphon (both of them are generally taken from the Old Testament), represents the very best of the spirituality of the Old Testament. But no longer does the Old Covenant stand alone, isolated in the midst of a pagan world. No longer does the Old Law suffer the pains of a longing and anxious heart, to see only in the far-removed future the time of its fulfillment. The days of Israel have been accomplished, and the promises have been fulfilled. In the midst of the *Introit* there is erected and there stands, well-founded, strong, and immovable, like a pillar of strength, the doxology, the praise of God the Father and of God the Son and of God the Holy Ghost. For, the sum of all Christian thought, the quintessence of Christian theology, the foundation of Christianity, is the belief

in the adorable mystery of the Blessed Trinity; the unity of
essence and the trinity of persons of the one and undivided
God. Here, in the Introit, we behold the foundation of the
faith in the kingdom of God: the *Gloria Patri* surrounded by
the praise of the psalms. The best of the Old Testament is
combined with the most profound revelations entrusted to
the New Testament. The praise of the Blessed Trinity, as
chanted by Christian voices, fertilizes the venerable thoughts
of the Old Testament. The pious reflections of the ancient
prophets gain new life and new strength and become once
more invigorated by the power that proceeds from the basic
revelations of the New Testament.

Depth of thought is vested in the most beautiful forms. The
psalms are the masterpieces of religious literature. The *Gloria
Patri* is unsurpassed. Many indeed are the praises that ascend
day by day to heaven. But of all these the most comprehensive
one, and yet the one in the most concise form, is this chant
of the *Gloria Patri*. We cannot think of a more sublime praise
than that of the three divine Persons. Indeed the first part of
the *Gloria Patri* has for its author our Lord Jesus Christ Himself, when He commissioned His apostles to go into the world
and to preach and to baptize every creature in the name of
the Father and of the Son and of the Holy Ghost.[7] The second
part was composed by the early Church at the time of her
struggle against the Arian heresy. Our pious prayer is that this
glory of the three divine Persons may, as it was in the beginning, be now and forever. It is our wish to see the praise of
the divine Majesty extended from the world here below into
everlasting times.

Can there be a more beautiful beginning for the great Sacrifice the priest is going to offer? He is led into the sacred action

[7] Cf. Matt. 28:18 f.; Mark 16:15–18.

by readings from the Psalter or from other inspired writings, which of old were chanted in the halls and courts of the great Temple in Jerusalem. But as the promises of Israel became fulfilled, the sacred texts were Christianized, so to speak, and, being marked with the sign of the Blessed Trinity, they serve now the venerable task of leading the priest into the spirit of the Eucharistic liturgy.

If the Church takes such exquisite pains preparing for the worthy celebration of the Mass, should it not be the sacred duty of every priest to second the efforts of Mother Church, to enter into her spirit, to dismiss all unworthy thoughts, to set his mind and heart aright, and to concentrate his mind on the Eucharistic mystery? Let him realize that he is setting out to perform his foremost priestly duty, the greatest act on earth, to the glory and honor, praise and adoration, of the triune God, God the Father and God the Son and God the Holy Ghost, who liveth and reigneth world without end. Amen.

# CHAPTER 5

# *The* Kyrie Eleison

To THE cross was nailed an inscription written in three languages, an inscription that announced to the world Christ's sacred name and title. These languages, Latin, Greek and Hebrew, are still preserved in the liturgy of the Mass. The *Amen, Hosanna, Alleluia,* and *Sabaoth* represent the Hebrew language; the *Kyrie Eleison* is the only Greek word in the Mass. The *Kyrie Eleison,* according to St. Thomas, refers "to our present misery by reason of which we pray for mercy, saying: Lord, have mercy on us, thrice for the Person of the Father; and Christ, have mercy on us, thrice for the Person of the Son; and Lord, have mercy on us, thrice for the Person of the Holy Ghost; against the threefold misery of ignorance, sin and punishment; or else to express the circumincession of all the divine Persons." [1]

Just a few minutes ago at the foot of the altar the priest, head bent down, struck his breast as a repentant sinner, and asked God to forgive his guilt. Now that he has ascended the steps and stands at the altar, he becomes, while faced with the most profound mysteries and while called upon to perform the greatest act of religion, fully conscious of his own unworthiness, insignificance, and misery. And in the depth of his spiritual distress and anguish, the priest raises his voice and implores heaven while he cries out: "Lord, have mercy."

[1] *Summa theol.,* IIIa, q. 83, a. 4.

"Have mercy on me, O Lord. . . ." [2] "Turn to me, O Lord, and deliver my soul: O save me for Thy mercy's sake." [3]

Great indeed is human misery. Man is, in the opinion of the holy doctor, St. Thomas, afflicted with a threefold misery: the misery of ignorance, sin, and punishment.[4]

Ignorance certainly is an affliction, ever degrading the human mind since the days of Adam. Ignorance is at once a cause and an effect, for in this double way God has stricken the intelligence of man, who had wished to exalt himself above the divine command. As a cause, ignorance is the origin of many transgressions of the laws of God. As an effect, ignorance follows only too frequently a sinful life and, under this curse, man has lived since the days the gates of paradise were closed. Thousands of years were required to discover the most primitive laws in the physical order. And the transgressions that resulted from ignorance in the social and moral order are legion. Behold the utter religious confusion of paganism and of the Churches outside the true fold of Christ. And beware of the ignorance of so many, of the coolness of so many souls, and of the lack of interest of so many Christians in the face of so profound a mystery as that of the transubstantiation. Compare these effects with such sublime heights of supernatural truths as expressed by the Psalmist: "Do not become like the horse and the mule, who have no understanding." [5] Lack of comprehension of religious truth is indeed a misery.

Sin is misery. "Many are the scourges of the sinner. . . ." [6] "I will declare my iniquity. . . ." [7] ". . . I will confess against

[2] Matt. 15:22.
[3] Ps. 6:5.
[4] *Loc. cit.*
[5] Ps. 31:9.
[6] Ps. 31:10.
[7] Ps. 37:19.

myself my injustice to the Lord. . . ." [8] "To Thee only have I sinned. . . ." [9] "If Thou, O Lord, wilt mark iniquities: Lord, who shall stand it?" [10] "Who shall confess to Thee in hell?" [11] "Have mercy on me, O God, according to Thy great mercy. And according to the multitude of Thy tender mercies blot out my iniquity." [12] "Cleanse me from my sin." [13] "Thou shalt wash me, and I shall be made whiter than snow." [14] Thou "over-lookest the sins of men for the sake of repentance." [15] For "a contrite and humble heart, O God, Thou wilt not despise." [16] Such is the voice of the inspired word.

And in the footsteps of sin follows punishment. "Woe to the wicked unto evil: for the reward of his hands shall be given him." [17] "That they might know that by what things a man sinneth, by the same also he is tormented." [18] Punishment burdens the life of man. "I am become miserable," [19] confessed the Psalmist. And he adds, "I am withered like grass." [20] In its anguish, the troubled heart of man turns to his God: "Have mercy on me, O Lord, for I am weak: heal me, O Lord, for my bones are troubled." [21] "Turn not away Thy face from me . . . incline Thy ear to me." [22] "Restore unto me the joy

[8] Ps. 31:5.
[9] Ps. 50:6.
[10] Ps. 129:3.
[11] Ps. 6:6.
[12] Ps. 50:3.
[13] Ps. 50:4.
[14] Ps. 50:9.
[15] Wisd. 11:24.
[16] Ps. 50:19.
[17] Isa. 3:11.
[18] Wisd. 11:17.
[19] Ps. 37:7.
[20] Ps. 101:12.
[21] Ps. 6:3.
[22] Ps. 101:3.

of Thy salvation, and strengthen me with a perfect spirit." [23]
Great is the misery of man, but immense the mercy of God.
"The Lord is merciful and compassionate," says St. James.[24]
And the royal Psalmist confesses: "Thy mercy will follow me
all the days of my life." [25] "And His tender mercies are over
all His works." [26] "As a father hath compassion on his children,
so hath the Lord compassion on them that fear Him." [27]

Beautiful and consoling words indeed! And that misery
which displays itself at large in the universe is found concentrated and focused in the few words that the priest addresses
to the Triune God: *Kyrie Eleison.* Out of these words speaks
the depth of human misery, an acknowledgment of the priest's
own wretchedness, and a recognition of his weakness and
helplessness. Yet it is far from breathing the spirit of despair.
With humility and simplicity, with confidence and filial trust,
the priest turns to God. "Out of the depths I have cried to
Thee, O Lord: Lord, hear my voice. Let Thy ears be attentive
to the voice of my supplication." [28] Thou, O Lord and God,
". . . art my refuge. . . ." [29] Nay, even more than a harbor of
refuge. Thou, O God, art the source of my life. Thou, O God,
art, as the Psalmist rightly adds, ". . . my joy." [30]

The heart of the priest has been filled with sorrow and contrition. With a longing eye, he has turned to the triune God,
and in Him his troubled soul has found refuge, help, mercy,
pardon, life, and joy.

[23] Ps. 50:14.
[24] Jas. 5:11.
[25] Ps. 22:6.
[26] Ps. 144:9.
[27] Ps. 102:13.
[28] Ps. 129:1–2.
[29] Ps. 31:7.
[30] Ps. 31:7.

It is no wonder, then, that after the depressing acknowledgment of his own misery and distress, the priest, seeing the helpful hand of God the Father almighty extended to him, bursts out in a cry of joy and jubilant exultation and intones the *Gloria in excelsis Deo.*

# CHAPTER 6

# The Gloria

Gloria in excelsis Deo. Et in terra pax hominibus bonae voluntatis. Laudamus te. Benedicimus te. Adoramus te. Glorificamus te. Gratias agimus tibi propter magnam gloriam tuam. Domine Deus, Rex caelestis, Deus Pater omnipotens. Domine Fili unigenite, Jesu Christe. Domine Deus, Agnus Dei, Filius Patris. Qui tollis peccata mundi, miserere nobis. Qui tollis peccata mundi, suscipe deprecationem nostram. Qui sedes ad dexteram Patris, miserere nobis. Quoniam tu solus Sanctus. Tu solus Dominus. Tu solus Altissimus, Jesu Christe. Cum Sancto Spiritu in gloria Dei Patris. Amen.

*Gloria in excelsis Deo!* This jubilant song "commemorates the heavenly glory, to the possession of which, after this life of misery, we are tending, in the words, Glory be to God on high."[1]

Why, we may ask, should the glories of heaven be referred to in the Sacrifice of the Mass? To this the Angelic Doctor replies: "The Eucharist is the sacrament of the unity of the whole Church; and therefore in this sacrament, more than in the others, mention ought to be made of all that belongs to the salvation of the entire Church."[2] Not only is the Church triumphant part of the communion of saints, but also all we know of its glorious existence has come to us through divine revelation.[3]

[1] *Summa theol.*, IIIa, q.83, a.4.
[2] *Ibid.*, q.83, a.4, ad 3.
[3] Cf. *ibid.*, ad 6.

28

*Gloria.* What does this word denote? St. Thomas knows three ascending grades of distinction, namely, praise, honor, and glory. "Praise," he says, "consists only of verbal signs," or by bearing "witness to a person's goodness in reference to an end; thus we praise one that works well for an end." [4] Honor however is of a greater nature. Honor "consists of any external signs" and "bears witness to a person's excelling goodness absolutely." [5] But the highest degree of distinction is that of glory. "It is the effect of honor and praise." [6] A person's "goodness becomes clear to the knowledge of many." [7]

Glory "properly denotes that somebody's good is known and approved by many," [8] or it "denotes the display of something as regards its seeming comely in the sight of men." [9] "It consists in being well-known and praised." [10] "It is clear knowledge together with praise." [11] "To be glorified is the same as to be clarified." [12] Hence glory includes praise and honor. Glory demands that the goodness of the being become known to all men, near and far, and that it become clear in the sight of all men, thereby also evoking approval, fame, and admiration.

Accordingly we see the Holy Scriptures conferring these three titles of distinction on the name of God. Especially, the psalms abound with praise, honor, and glory to the God of heaven and earth: "O praise the Lord all ye nations: praise Him, all ye people." [13] And "Praise ye the Lord from the heav-

[4] *Ibid.*, IIa IIae, q. 103, a. 1, ad 3.
[5] *Ibid.*
[6] *Ibid.*
[7] *Ibid.*
[8] *Ibid.*, q. 132, a. 1.
[9] *Ibid.*
[10] *Ibid.*, q. 2, a. 3.
[11] *Ibid.*, q. 103, a. 1, ad 3.
[12] *Ibid.*, q. 132, a. 1.
[13] Ps. 116:1.

ens: praise ye Him in the high places. Praise ye Him, all His angels: praise ye Him, all His hosts. Praise ye Him, O sun and moon, praise Him, all ye stars and light. Praise Him, ye heavens of heavens, and let all the waters that are above the heavens praise the name of the Lord." [14]

Honor, as we have seen, goes further than a mere paying of tribute by way of words. Honor acknowledges, completely and absolutely, God's exceeding goodness, by external signs. The inspired writers desire man to give honor to God by his noble deeds; nay, by his whole life, for in the Book of Proverbs we read: "Honor the Lord with thy substance. . . ." [15] And "He that oppresseth the poor, upbraideth his Maker: but he that hath pity on the poor, honoreth Him." [16] "Honor thy father and thy mother." [17] This commandment certainly requires on the part of the child, something more than a few good words. It demands the virtues of obedience, submission, and respect. We honor God by an upright life. We further God's honor by our virtues, and we honor God by good and noble deeds. Where the song of praise and a holy life are combined, there God is glorified. "Do all to the glory of God." [18] And where God's name, power, goodness, and magnificence of His works become known to His creatures, there His name is glorified. "Bring to the Lord glory and honor: bring to the Lord glory to His name: adore ye the Lord in His holy court." [19] "Glory to God in the highest; and on earth peace to men of good will." [20] This was the jubilant chant sung by the celestial choirs over the silent fields of Bethlehem. These were

[14] Ps. 148:1–5.
[15] Prov. 3:9.
[16] Prov. 14:31.
[17] Exod. 20:12.
[18] I Cor. 10:31.
[19] Ps. 28:2.
[20] Luke 2:14.

the words that announced to a world veiled in sleep and sin the birth of the Word incarnate. These are the very words that proclaim to heaven and earth the presence of the Eucharistic Lord in the Sacrament of the Altar, whenever the ritual of the Mass has a festival character. And the glories of the courts of heaven will be reflected on earth in the blessings of peace among men of good will, for, where is there greater happiness on earth than where real and lasting peace rules? "May He grant us joyfulness of heart, and that there be peace in our days in Israel forever." [21]

And now that the priest has intoned the "Hymn of the Angels," God's goodness and majesty are proclaimed and praised in the great and most beautiful doxology: "We praise Thee, we bless Thee, we adore Thee, we glorify Thee." "Blessed be the Lord the God of Israel, from everlasting to everlasting: and let all the people say: So be it, so be it." [22] "We give thanks to Thee for Thy great glory, O Lord God, heavenly King, God the Father Almighty." "Praise the Lord, for He is good: for His mercy endureth forever." [23] "Now to the king of ages, immortal, invisible, the only God, be honor and glory forever and ever, Amen." [24]

Next to the glory of God the Father, praise is given to His only beloved Son. "O Lord Jesus Christ, the only-begotten Son, O Lord, Lamb of God, Son of the Father, who takest away the sins of the world, have mercy on us. Who takest away the sins of the world, receive our prayers. Who sitteth at the right hand of the Father, have mercy on us." Certainly the nature and mission of Christ is here set forth in concise, but significant and jubilant, words: Christ, the incarnate Word, the Re-

[21] Ecclus. 50:25.
[22] Ps. 105:48.
[23] Ps. 135:1.
[24] I Tim. 1:17.

deemer, the triumphant Savior; in brief, the whole Christology is here proclaimed.

And now that the greatness and goodness of God the Father are honored, and the work of the Word incarnate is glorified, the great doxology ends in a praise to the triune God. "For Thou only art holy, Thou only art the Lord, Thou only, O Jesus Christ, together with the Holy Ghost, art most high in the glory of God the Father, Amen."

CHAPTER 7

# *The* Oratio

AFTER the Gloria, the priest, having kissed the altar stone, turns toward the people and salutes them in the words with which the archangel Gabriel, at the Annunciation, greeted the blessed Mother: *Dominus vobiscum,* "the Lord [is] with Thee." Then the priest proceeds to the Epistle side, where he reads the Collect. This is the prayer, *Oratio,* of the Mass that states the mystery, the feast, or the occasion for which this particular Mass is celebrated, and in virtue of which the Church petitions heaven to grant a corresponding favor. The *Oratio* is a short, yet comprehensive, prayer. The more ancient prayers particularly are remarkable for their beauty of language, for the Romans were masters in symmetrical construction and rhythmical phrasing.

The *Oratio* is not merely a private prayer of the priest, but the official prayer of the Church, the prayer by which the Church addresses heaven and presents her petition for the welfare of the Christian community. In this respect it differs from private prayer or the prayer of the individual. Commenting on this distinction, St. Thomas remarks: "Prayer is twofold, common and individual. Common prayer is that which is offered to God by the ministers of the Church representing the body of the faithful: wherefore such prayer should come to the knowledge of the whole people for whom it is offered: and this would not be possible unless it were vocal prayer.

Therefore it is reasonably ordained that the ministers of the Church should say these prayers even in a loud voice, so that they may come to the knowledge of all." [1] Bearing this in mind, the cry of the priest, *Oremus*, before he starts the *Oratio*, is significant, since he invites all the faithful to join him in this official prayer, for this is their prayer as well as his.

What do the priest and people do when prayers are said? Prayer is not merely something like a pious sentiment or a religious feeling. Prayer is, as Damascene says, "the raising up of the mind to God." [2] Prayer is "an act of reason," [3] or, according to Cassiodorus, "spoken reason." [4] It is an act of the most noble faculty of the human being, of his "intellective power." [5] Correspondingly, Dionysius says: "When we call upon God in our prayers, we unveil our minds in His presence." [6]

When praying, the mind of man transcends all things earthly, ascends to the most sublime heights an intellectual being is capable of reaching, and unites itself with God our Lord and Creator. Destined to meet his Maker in eternity, man, when praying, already here below leaves all earthly forms and, following the dictates of his inclination, tends toward his natural destination, his God and Maker. When praying, the soul seeks rest and happiness, refuge and courage in the bosom of its good and loving Father and Creator, God in heaven.

Having placed ourselves in the presence of God, we present to the Divinity the acts of homage, worship, and adoration that are due the Supreme Being. Recognizing God as the

---

[1] *Summa theol.*, IIa IIae, q. 83, a. 12.
[2] *Ibid.*, a. 1, ad 2.
[3] *Ibid.*, a. 1.
[4] *Ibid.*
[5] *Ibid.*
[6] *Ibid.*, a. 1, ad 2.

author and giver of all good things, we unfold our concerns in His presence. We petition God to grant us His blessings. "We ask becoming things of God." [7] Man "subjects himself to God and, by praying, confesses that he needs Him as the author of his goods." [8]

Here we may advance the following objection: Why should we petition God who, in His omniscience, knows from all eternity the things that we need? In His infinite wisdom He has decreed, long before the world was made, what is best for us. In our prayers are we not asking God for things He has already decided to give us, or do our prayers change the eternal plans of God? To this, the Angelic Doctor gives the following reply: "our motive in praying," he says, "is not that we may change the divine disposition, but that, by our prayers, we may obtain what God has appointed." [9] For "we pray, not that we may change the divine disposition, but that we may impetrate that which God has disposed to be fulfilled by our prayers, in other words, that by asking, men may deserve to receive what almighty God from eternity has disposed to give, as Gregory says." [10] Hence "we need to pray to God, not in order to make known to Him our needs or desires, but that we ourselves may be reminded of the necessity of having recourse to God's help in these matters." [11]

"God bestows many things on us out of His liberality, even without our asking for them; but that He wishes to bestow certain things on us at our asking, is for the sake of our good, namely, that we may acquire confidence in having recourse to God and that we may recognize in Him the author of our

[7] *Ibid.*, a. 1.
[8] *Ibid.*, a. 3.
[9] *Ibid.*, a. 2, ad 2.
[10] *Ibid.*, dial. 1, q. 83, a. 2.
[11] *Ibid.*, q. 83, a. 2, ad 1.

goods. Hence Chrysostom says . . . 'Think what happiness
is granted thee, what honor bestowed on thee, when thou con-
versest with God in prayer, when thou talkest with Christ,
when thou askest what thou wilt, whatever thou desirest.' " [12]

In prayer, we communicate with God. We raise our minds
above all things earthly, ascend to things spiritual, place ourselves in the presence of God and communicate to Him the
inmost thoughts, concerns, and wants of our heart. What a
wonderful thing to be able to communicate with the Divinity!
How we should enjoy this privilege! We should frequently
make use of this ability of ours. Think how easy and inex-
pensive it has become, during the past few decades, to communicate with those dear to us, regardless of the distance. We
think of them, and instantly a phone call, a wire, a letter, a
radio message communicates our thoughts, our feelings, and
our wishes. Communication with anyone to whom we wish to
speak, at any distance, at very low cost, with great facility,
when we please: this is the accomplishment of the modern
age. At the same time, incredible and contradictory as it may
sound, communication with the very best Friend of our soul,
with our greatest Benefactor and Protector, our Father in
heaven, seems to be something burdensome to us, something
we do not indulge in frequently and voluntarily. We claim to
be too busy, to have little time for prayer. Yet, look at the
saintly priests who are accomplishing great things and who
are occupied day and night. These are the very priests who
spend much time in prayer, who kneel long hours before the
tabernacle. We think we are active and busy, when in truth
a certain restlessness has set in, a nervosity that keeps us always active, so that we occupy ourselves with endless minor
affairs. We run hither and thither and, after all, accomplish

[12] *Ibid.,* ad 3.

little for our dear Lord. Despite the activity of a priest, if he neglects prayer, his work will not draw the blessings of God, for he disregards the Lord's advice that "we ought always to pray, and not to faint. . . ." [13] Work never supplants prayer. A priest who puts little value in prayer deprives himself and those entrusted to his care of many graces. He misses many an opportunity to do something for our Lord. Graces and spiritual values can never be acquired by earthly labors or material works. The material side of a parish may at times claim the full attention of the pastor. But, if the finances and repairs absorb all his attention, crowd out and set aside his spiritual cares, he will, in the course of time, fail as a priest. A priest, after all, is not an agent, or a manager, or a superintendent, but a man of God. He is a spiritual man, one whose very office is that of being a mediator between God and man, but there is no mediatorship except by prayer. Here, in the Mass, the priest exercises this office of mediator, when he presents to almighty God, in the *Oratio,* the prayers of the Christian community.

Let us carry this spirit of being a mediator from the altar into practical life. Let us pray for those dear to us, for those entrusted to our care, for those who recommend themselves to our prayers. Let us remind ourselves that many things in life, perhaps even our priestly vocation itself, we owe to the good prayers of someone. Now that our spiritual benefactors are gone, the duty devolves on us to pray for others as they prayed for us. Let us prove to be real priests, for, to be a priest means to intercede before God for our fellow men, for those who may expect our prayers. [14]

[13] Luke 18:1.
[14] As the principles and considerations that govern the *Oratio* are practically identical with those ruling the *Secreta* and the Post Communion, no special chapter will be devoted to the latter two.

# CHAPTER 8

# *The Epistle*

THE Epistles are readings from the books of the Old and the New Testaments, the four Gospels and the Psalms excepted. Thus, the apostles, through their Epistles, and the prophets, through their writings, speak to us. It may be asked, why does the holy Mass contain readings from the Scriptures? Is it not true that the Mass is a sacrifice and, as such, does not the Mass rather call for ritual prayers than for the reading of lessons? We may reply that these lessons are intended as instruction for the faithful. In these lessons, the reasons are given for the celebration of the Eucharistic Sacrifice, for as St. Thomas says: "This Sacrament is a mystery of faith." [1] "Now this instruction," the Angelic Doctor adds, "is given dispositively." [2] The prophetic lessons and the readings from the Epistles of the apostles incline us to receive willingly and worthily the word of God as announced in the Gospels by Jesus Christ Himself. Not that the truths taught us in the Epistles are of an inferior grade or of less importance. We are called upon to believe the truths laid down in the Epistles as firmly as the Gospel truth itself. But, since the Epistles are the words of the apostles and the prophets, the Epistles precede the Gospel, which is the word of Christ. For in the Mass the lessons are arranged according to dignity, demanding that the lesser ones precede those of greater dignity.

[1] *Summa theol.,* IIIa, q.83, a.4.
[2] *Ibid.*

38

What do the Epistles represent? They are revealed truth. They were written by divine inspiration. They are the word of the Holy Ghost; and, being divine lessons, they were composed for our spiritual benefit. "For what things soever were written, were written for our learning: that through patience and the comfort of the Scriptures, we might have hope." [3] In brief, the Epistles, together with the rest of the Holy Scriptures, are part of the whole economy of salvation.

Though divine, on account of being inspired by the Holy Ghost, the Epistles contain also some human features. They present to us the solicitude, the anguish, the cares, the worries, the labors, and the strenuous efforts of Saints Paul, Peter, John, James, and Jude in ministering to the sheep entrusted to their care. When not actually engaged in the work of preaching, organizing new congregations, or in the work of the ministry, the apostles would not consider themselves free or at ease. At all times, their zeal to spread the kingdom of God was great. When they had finished their work with those in their immediate surroundings, their hearts, solicitude, and care would go out to those afar. They wished to be all to all. "For out of much affliction and anguish of heart, I wrote to you with many tears, not that you should be made sorrowful: but that you might know the charity I have more abundantly towards you." [4] Should this not be an example to us? Let the Epistle we read daily while celebrating Mass be a lesson of apostolic zeal to us. "In carefulness not slothful. In spirit fervent. Serving the Lord." [5]

Writing may be the means to extend the kingdom of God. Letters may be the instruments of apostolic labors. The ministry may use the pen to do the works of charity. The

[3] Rom. 15:4.
[4] II Cor. 2:4.
[5] Rom. 12:11.

written word may supplement the word that comes from the mouth.

The apostles wrote Epistles to congregations and to individuals alike. The practice of the apostles is continued in the encyclical letters of the popes and in the pastoral letters of the bishops. But the simple priest, too, may do a great deal of good by employing his pen, for, by his contributing to our Catholic magazines and newspapers, the kingdom of God is advanced. This is priestly work. Articles in the Catholic press are products of apostolic labor, and Catholic papers are in need of the help of zealous priests. We preach once a year on the importance of Catholic literature. We see that our people subscribe to the diocesan paper. We recommend the leading Catholic periodicals of the country. These publications come to our own rectory. They await us on the desk in our study and we pass pleasant hours with them. Let us be leaders! Let us lead in thought and action! Let us be the intellectual leaders of our congregation!

Why not reach out for the pen and note down a few ideas? Why not work out a problem with the pen in your hand, or on the typewriter? Do not wait for inspirations, literary or poetical moods, or hours of leisure. All writings are the product of much pain. All Catholic papers are the result of real apostolic labor. It is a fallacy to pursue only the things that produce visible results. A writer, so to speak, is in the dark regarding the far-reaching results of his labors. He seldom harvests the fruits of his pen. Such fruits are gathered by the invisible hands of the angels. But what is produced in much pain and anguish will be of a lasting nature! Remember the Latin proverb: "*Verba volant, Scripta manent!*" Spoken words pass away, but the written word remains.

You may dislike publicity. Nevertheless you should put

your lonely hours to profit. Send a message of encouragement, of consolation, of advice, of instruction to a lonely soul far away. Charity is not limited by space. Zeal is not curtailed by border lines. Read the letters of St. Jerome, St. Bernard, St. Francis de Sales. Admire the wisdom and charity that are reflected in their works. How much good may be accomplished by a written message! Think of the many forgotten souls, and the delight with which the message from a pious priest is received by these souls. Do not leave anything undone to press pen or typewriter into the service of the ministry. Extend and advance the kingdom of God on earth by using all means at your disposal, and you will be a true ambassador of Christ.

CHAPTER 9

# The Intermediary Chant

### The Gradual, Tract, and Sequence

HAVING finished the reading of the Epistle, the priest reflects on the lesson received. Almost spontaneously he gives expression to his feelings. Now that God, through the mouth of the inspired writer, has spoken to man; man, on his part, in the intermediary chant, speaks to God. Man's immediate reaction is that of praising and of thanking the Divinity.

The spirit of the *Gradual* and of the verses and hymns read after the Epistle is mostly joyful and happy, praising and thanking God for benefits received. But during Lent, when the Epistles recall the sinfulness of man, the mind of the priest, while reading the Tract, turns sorrowful. Even then the language is noble and elevating, and all the thoughts and feelings of the priest are expressed in poetry and song. The verses of the intermediary chant are always highly artistic in nature. Since these verses are of such a nature, it is not difficult to see why the Church has set these verses into rhyme and music, to be sung by the choir, together with the Introit, the Offertory, and the Communion, whenever High Mass is celebrated.

Poetry, song, and music, as part of the divine service, are as old as religious worship. When King David organized the service in the Temple, he did so in a grand and magnificent style. He employed every means to make the religious service of Israel as solemn as humanly possible. To this end, he made use of the best in arts and in crafts. Everything had to serve this one end: to make the worship of Jehovah the most solemn and the most dignified on earth. The best in poetry, song, and music, he dedicated to the Temple. Of the Levites, David selected four thousand singers, "singing to the Lord with the instruments, which he had made to sing with." [1] He appointed no less than two hundred and eighty-eight teachers to instruct the people in the song of the Lord. [2] At all times, he exhorted his people and his priests to "sing . . . to the Lord a new canticle." [3] He ordered them to praise the Almighty's name in choir with the timbrel and the psaltery. [4] He admonished them "to sing to our God upon the harp." [5] "Praise ye Him, all His angels: praise ye Him, all His hosts." [6] "Shout with joy to God, all the earth, sing ye a psalm to His name: give glory to His praise." [7] "O clap your hands, all ye nations: shout unto God with the voice of joy. . . ." [8] Yes, King David called upon the choir of his singers and musicians to praise the name of the Lord: "Praise Him with sound of trumpet: praise him with psaltery and harp. Praise Him with timbrel and choir: praise Him with strings and organs. Praise Him on high sounding cymbals: praise Him on cymbals of joy: let every spirit praise the Lord. Alleluia." [9]

What a grand religious function the service in the Temple must have been! The Book of Paralipomenon records the solemnity of the bringing of the Ark of the Covenant into the Temple, in words as these: "Both the Levites and the singing

[1] I Par. 23:5.
[2] I Par. 25:7.
[3] Ps. 149:1.
[4] Ps. 149:3.
[5] Ps. 146:7.
[6] Ps. 148:2.
[7] Ps. 65:1, 2.
[8] Ps. 46:2.
[9] Ps. 150:3–5.

men . . . clothed with fine linen, sounded with cymbals, and
psalteries, and harps, standing on the east side of the altar,
and with them a hundred and twenty priests, sounding with
trumpets. So when they all sounded together, both with
trumpets, and voice, and cymbals, and organs, and with divers
kinds of musical instruments, and lifted up their voice on
high: the sound was heard afar off, so that when they began to
praise the Lord, and to say: Give glory to the Lord for He is
good, for His mercy endureth forever; the house of God was
filled with a cloud." [10]

Indeed, Jehovah was worshiped in Israel in becoming and
solemn fashion. Poetry, song, and music were part of the religious rites. The example set by David was followed on even
a larger scale by his son, Solomon; but, as time went on, the
interest in these functions dwindled, and the priests and
Levites showed less zeal. During the Babylonian captivity,
music and song could not be maintained, and sorrow and sadness were seen where joy and happiness had once reigned.
However, the memory of music and of song was not completely lost, and two hundred singers were found among those
returning from Babylon. A revival of the old spirit took place,
though it was not carried out with the former magnificence
and grandeur. Yet it has to be said that till the walls of the
Temple crumbled A.D. 70, the priests and Levites had been
faithful in the liturgical service of Jehovah.[11]

Did our Lord Jesus Christ sing religious songs? We know
that He joined the annual processions to Jerusalem and that
the pilgrims sang the psalms and sacred hymns. On the

[10] II Par. 5:12–13.
[11] For further information see Dr. Michael Seisenberger, *Practical Hand-
book for the Study of the Bible and of Bible Literature*, chapters on "The
Temple," pp. 80–90, and "Music and Singing," pp. 134 ff.; and Rev. F. E.
Gigot, *Outlines of Jewish History*, chapters: "The Tabernacle and its Ministers," pp. 84–88; and "Return from the Exile," pp. 310–23.

Sabbath day, in the synagogues, the psalms were sung. Our Lord, taking part in these functions, must have joined the people. When celebrating the Pasch, certain psalms were prescribed to be sung by the father of the house. Who would not have liked to listen when our Lord, with a clear, rich, melodious, and expressive voice, sang the psalms at the occasion of His Last Supper?

It is evident that St. Paul approves of singing in church, for in his Epistle to the Ephesians he says: ". . . be ye filled with the Holy Spirit. Speaking to yourselves in psalms, and hymns, and spiritual canticles, singing and making melody in your hearts to the Lord. . . ." [12] In a similar tone he speaks to the Colossians.[13]

The first Christians, assembled for the celebration of the mysteries of the faith, could not have sung with a loud voice, if at all, for, during the persecutions, any sound would have betrayed their hiding places. But as soon as that period of bloodshed had passed, voices and melodies began to enrich the Christian cult. Organs were set up in the churches as early as the fourth century, to accompany the singers, and, from then on, every age and every country contributed new methods and new ways to beautify and to solemnize the cult of the Christian Church.

Some of the most outstanding pieces of literature of all times are the Sequences. They are read by the priest, and sung by the choir. Depth of thought and a wealth of spiritual feeling are combined with beauty of expression and poetical power. All that is good and animating vibrates through the verses of the Sequences. Is there a song where the Easter spirit is reflected with greater force and with more profound senti-

[12] Eph. 5:18–19.
[13] Col. 3:16.

ments than in the *Victimae paschali?* Is there a prayer more
ardent and more touching than the *Veni Sancte Spiritus,* calling down upon men the gifts of the Holy Ghost? Is there a
more beautiful Eucharistic chant, is there a more eloquent
composition in honor of the hidden Lord in the Blessed Sacrament, than the *Lauda Sion?* Where is the deep sorrow of a
mother's heart more forcefully brought forth than in the
*Stabat Mater?* And does not the *Dies Irae* stir the heart of all
men, while it calls forth reflections that penetrate to the very
depth of life and death?

Great indeed is the poetical language of the Church. And
equally majestic and inspiring are the compositions of music
and song. The melodies of ecclesiastical composers are supreme. In these melodies the human voice and the sound of
instruments find their earthly perfection and glorification.

The praise, honor, and glory of God is the first and primary
object of liturgical solemnity. But there is a secondary purpose, which must not be overlooked. Poetry, song, and music
are intended to stir the soul of man and to evoke from that
soul feelings of piety and devotion. Having this in mind, St.
Thomas commends: "The praise of the voice is necessary in
order to arouse man's devotion towards God. Therefore whatever is useful in conducting to this result is becomingly
adopted in the divine praises. Now it is evident that the
human soul is moved in various ways according to various
melodies of sound. . . . Hence the use of music in the divine
praises is a salutary institution that the souls of the faint-
hearted may be the more incited to devotion. Wherefore Augustine says: 'I am inclined to approve of the usage of singing
in the church, that so by the delight of the ears, the weaker
minds may rise to the feeling of devotion.' " [14] And he says

[14] *Conf.,* X, 33.

of himself: "I wept in Thy hymns and canticles, touched to the quick by the voices of Thy sweet-attuned Church." [15]

In the field of church music, any priest has ample opportunity to further the glory of God. Even non-Catholics are frequently attracted by a well performing choir. Catholics, too, are known to travel a considerable distance to hear good music in church. But, when complaints are heard about the poor attendance at High Mass on Sundays, would it not be better to improve the performances of the choir? In order to have an accomplished choir, the priest himself does not need to be a talented musician. In any parish there are to be found good voices ready to lend their services. The priest's task consists rather in supervising the choir. He is required to stand guard that there be no inordinate solos or causes for disharmony among the singers.

Remember, a good church choir accrues to the credit of both pastor and parish.

[15] *Summa theol.*, IIa IIae, q.91, a.2.

# CHAPTER 10

## *The Gospel*

Munda cor meum, ac labia mea, omnipotens Deus,
qui labia Isaiae Prophetae calculo mundasti ignito: ita
me tua grata miseratione dignare mundare, ut sanctum
Evangelium tuum digne valeam nuntiare. Per Christum
Dominum nostrum. Amen.
Jube, Domine benedicere.
Dominus sit in corde meo, et in labiis meis: ut digne
et competenter annuntiem Evangelium suum. Amen.

AFTER the apostles or the prophets, in the Epistle just read,
have prepared the way of the Lord, the Gospel, the word of
God as announced by Jesus Christ, is read by the priest.

As the mission of Christ was to be prophet, priest, and king,
so we find in the Mass the threefold offices of the Savior reflected. The solemn moment, when Christ exercises His
priestly office in a mystical way, centers around the Consecration. In Holy Communion He becomes leader of His people
and king of our hearts. When the Gospel is read, the mystical
Christ re-enacts His office as prophet and teacher.

Christ came into this world to bring the manna of heavenly
truth to a confused and agnostic world. Scarcely had He left
the barren grounds of the desert when he "began to
preach. . . ." [1] He "went out through the whole country.
And He taught in their synagogues. . . ." [2] And He was

[1] Matt. 4:17.
[2] Luke 4:14–15.

"preaching the gospel of the kingdom of God. . . ." [3] And the people glorified God, saying: "A great prophet is risen up among us. . . ." [4] "This is of a truth the propet, that is to come into the world." [5] Of Himself, the Eternal Word testified: "For this was I born, and for this came I into the world; that I should give testimony to the truth." [6]

This mission of Christ did not cease with His ascension into heaven. Christ commissioned His apostles to go into the whole world and to preach the gospel to every creature. In this undertaking He promised His everlasting assistance. And while the word of God is brought to the whole world and dispensed in the highways and byways of all countries, should it be lacking when the Christian world assembles to worship? Should the mystical Christ, who sacrifices in the Mass and who nourishes His flock in Holy Communion, be silent at this particular time? Should the life-giving waters from the fountain of eternal truth cease, during the Holy Sacrifice, to refresh and bring new life to those who assemble in His own name?

No. Christ, who since His ascension is enthroned in heaven, does not cease to speak to men on earth. The Gospel is, as St. Augustine expresses it, "the mouth of Christ." [7] Here, in the Gospel, He continues His office of prophet and teacher; hence the greatest solemnity surrounds the reading of the Gospel. For the Lord Himself speaks. Christ's own word is announced to us. The gospel truth is the word of eternal life. The message of Christ is "the law of faith." [8] The reading of the Gospel is "the power of God unto salvation. . . ." [9] And as the Holy

[3] Mark 1:14.
[4] Luke 7:16.
[5] John 6:14.
[6] John 18:37.
[7] *Sermo* 85, no. 1.
[8] Rom. 3:27.
[9] Rom. 1:16.

Scriptures pronounce, so the Church ever taught. "The teaching of the Gospel," St. Thomas declares, "is the doctrine of perfection." [10] And on another occasion the same Angelic Doctor states: "The people are instructed perfectly by Christ's teaching contained in the Gospel." [11]

Since the Gospel is the word of God, its reception in the hearts of men requires preparation. For this reason the priest prays when he recites the two introductory prayers, "Cleanse my heart and my lips, almighty God, who didst cleanse the lips of the prophet Isaias with a burning coal: vouchsafe of Thy gracious mercy, so to cleanse me, that I may be worthy to proclaim Thy holy Gospel. Through Christ our Lord, Amen."; and "The Lord be in my heart and on my lips, that I may worthily and in a becoming manner announce His holy Gospel. Amen."

The Fathers of the Church advise us repeatedly to prepare ourselves for the worthy reception of the word of God, as proclaimed in the Gospel, in the same way as we cleanse our hearts from sin for Holy Communion.

That seems almost ridiculous in a time such as ours, when it is so easy to attend Mass and when we hear the Gospel read so frequently. Yet the Lord Himself warns us lest we hear and understand not.[12] Are there not many men outside the Church who have read through the whole Bible, but have not received its truth in their hearts? Is it not sometimes surprising to hear someone else explain the deep meaning of some Gospel truth that we thought we knew so well? Yet this is the mystery of the Gospel, that at the same time it is so simple yet descends to the greatest depth of wisdom and knowledge.

[10] *Summa theol.*, IIa IIae, q.56, a.1, ad 2.
[11] *Op. cit.*, IIIa, q.83, a.4.
[12] Cf. Matt. 13:14; Mark 4:12; Luke 8:10.

The gospel truth is so simple that even the immature mind
of a child can grasp its meaning.

In a few words, written in the form of parables, an amount
of heavenly wisdom is found that is not contained in the pon-
derous volumes of the world.

The gospel truth is so beautiful that it never fatigues the
listener. The most brilliant poetry has never surpassed it. It
is always new and fascinating, no matter how often it has been
heard. Compare it with the best folklore, the best of oratory,
the best of human wisdom, and the gospel truth always excels.

The Gospel's depths are never reached; its profundity is
never exhausted. Students have explained it 101 times. Preachers have expounded it. Scholars have searched the depths of
its mysteries, and yet it is never exhausted. It is always new
and enlightening.

Such is the word of God proclaimed to us in each reading
of the Gospels. What security the word of God gives to our
whole aspect of life! How well the Gospel penetrates the
mystery of death and of the life beyond! Now the smallest
child, who listens attentively to it, is better equipped to answer the foremost questions of life than the wisest philosophers of ancient Greece and of Rome.

What a grace to know what can be expected beyond the
grave! We, who are born in the Catholic faith, can scarcely
realize the struggle of a soul searching for truth. As the grow-
ing tree stretches and twists its branches to reach the light,
so the soul of man longs for truth. And yet, so fierce is the
struggle of the human heart and mind in penetrating the darkness of ignorance and in overcoming the obstacles of prejudice
born far back in history, prejudice bequeathed to us as our
heritage: prejudices of a national or racial nature; prejudices

resulting from family or social relationships; prejudices
breathed into us with our mother's milk and fostered by all
the arts of education and training; prejudices that darken
the prospects for the future; prejudices tearing asunder friend-
ships of life; and prejudices endangering our very status, or
position in life, and threatening the daily bread of our dear
ones. Is truth really to be found in that Church so cold and
stiff, so fanatical and fantastic, so unsympathetic and so dogmatic? Has the freedom of one's mind, the liberty of one's
spirit, one's very own self, to be chained and to be enslaved,
in order to find and conquer the truth?

It is easy to understand that the world, rather than undergo
this struggle, throws itself incessantly from one amusement
into another. And whosoever does not find satisfaction in the
distraction of the senses is still driven on, as though by a rest-
less impulse from within, to search, to investigate, to study
the great problems of the day, the questions of philosophy and
of science, in both the material and the immaterial order. To
whom can one turn in the troubles of the soul? Friends and
family wave their hands and beg one not to worry foolishly
over nothing. Yes, it is bordering on bad taste to bring up a
question of any religious nature within the circle of friends.
Somebody's feelings may be hurt. Turn to books, to the philosophy of old. They are superseded. Turn to the philosophers
of today. What a confusion! "What fools these mortals be!"
Disagreement on the very first questions of life: strife over
the first principles of philosophy. Is it to be wondered that
many a heart becomes finally embittered against everything
and anything that the mind has not conquered? Discourage-
ment sets in. The desire to give up forever, to declare as incapable of solution the questions of life, gains the upper hand.

Agnosticism begins to reign. And the century-old question is once more repeated: "What is truth?" [13]

How happy indeed are we who possess the truth! We scarcely realize the confusion in the hearts of so many struggling souls. We have only a faint idea of the many trials of those who seek the truth. Let us implore the Father of all to give His grace of light and truth to those who are in error. Let us pray for the conversion of souls, and let us be always willing and helpful to those who approach us in an endeavor to find enlightment and understanding. Our priestly zeal may direct us to go even out of our way to make converts. An understanding of the difficulties and trials of our converts will draw upon us the blessings of heaven. We do not need to dream of what we could do in foreign countries; right here in our own parish we have ample occasion to spread among our fellow men the kingdom of truth, which is the kingdom of God.

[13] John 18:38.

# CHAPTER 11

# *The Sermon*

CHRIST commissioned His priests to preach. Consequently the priest, in virtue of his ordination, is invested with the office of a preacher. In the Mass he executes this office when he reads the Epistle and Gospel, and when he mounts the pulpit to preach. Hence the sermon is not, as people sometimes erroneously think, an interruption of the Mass, but is joined to the liturgy of the Mass. For, when the priest delivers to the people the word of God, the priest executes, in its completeness, Christ's preaching mission entrusted to him. Sermons, it is true, may be preached outside Mass, but the canonical way is to have a homily preached at Mass.

Much has been said about sermons and preaching, and any priest who takes his apostolic work seriously has ample opportunity to perfect himself in the art of preaching. What we intend to do in this chapter is to see whether, from the writings of the Angel of the Schools, we may derive some benefits for ourselves as preachers and teachers.

One accustomed from childhood to see the pastor or curate or any priest ascend the pulpit is undoubtedly taken by surprise when first he reads in the *Summa theologica* of St. Thomas that "to teach, i.e., to expound the Gospel, is the proper office of a bishop." [1] That this is not merely a passing remark of the saint, reflecting the conditions of his own time,

[1] *Summa theol.*, IIIa, q. 67, a. 1, ad 1.

but his theological conviction and teaching, becomes evident a few pages later, where in most determined and distinct language he formulated the following thesis: "The instruction in the profound mysteries of faith, and on the perfection of Christian life: this belongs to bishops ex officio—in virtue of their office." [2] Just as the Eastern Church has conceded to all priests the privilege of administering the sacrament of confirmation, so the Roman Church permits the priest to enjoy the episcopal prerogative of preaching. Do we priests, when mounting the pulpit, become mindful that we are permitted to assume an episcopal prerogative? Let us priests always remember that preaching is an episcopal privilege. Let us, indeed, ascend the pulpit only after a most painstaking preparation, and let us deliver our sermons with dignity and unction.

We wish to call attention to the fact that the Angelic Doctor designates as the episcopal office "the instruction in the profound mysteries of faith and on the perfection of Christian life." [3] He distinguishes very markedly between this instruction, which he says belongs to the bishop, and the instruction in the rudiments of the faith, which one must have for the reception of the sacraments which is designated as the office of the priest. [4]

And following the mind of the Angelic Teacher in his reflections on preaching, we find that he wishes that the preachers not merely skim the surface, but enter the depth of the mysteries of our holy faith. He expects the preachers to expound not the beginnings, but the perfections of the Christian life. For "to teach, i.e., to expound the Gospel, is the proper office of a bishop, whose action is to perfect . . . and to perfect is

[2] Ibid., q.71, a.4, ad 3.
[3] Ibid.
[4] Cf. ibid.

the same as to teach." [5] To perfect the faith of the people in the mysteries of our holy religion and to perfect the life of virtue: this is the task of the preacher. The perfection of Christian life: this is the real object of all our sermons. How is this aim to be attained? The *Summa* gives us the answer. "Now," says St. Thomas, "no one should take up the office of preacher unless he be already cleansed and perfect in virtue." [6] Begin with yourself. Your words are worthless unless put into practice by yourself. To translate this into biblical language, we may say with St. Paul: "Thou therefore, that teachest another, teachest not thyself: thou, that preachest that men should not steal, stealest . . . thou, that abhorrest idols, committest sacrilege." [7] "But I chastise my body, and bring it into subjection: lest perhaps, when I have preached to others, I myself should become a castaway." [8] ". . . Be thou an example of the faithful in word, in conversation, in charity, in faith, in chastity." [9]

The preacher will have to accomplish this. By what means may the priest sanctify himself and preach "perfection of Christian life"? St. Thomas knows the dangers that confront a preacher who is constantly before the public. He knows, too, that one who is ever busy and ready to spend himself in all things and wishes to be all to all, is in peril of becoming confused mentally, as well as physically and spiritually exhausted. Therefore, St. Thomas makes a strong appeal to the preachers, placing before them the example of Christ Himself. "Christ's action," he says, "is our instruction. And therefore, in order to teach preachers that they ought not to be forever before

[5] *Ibid.*, q.67, a.1, ad 1.
[6] *Ibid.*, q.41, a.3, ad 1.
[7] Rom. 2:21–22.
[8] I Cor. 9:27.
[9] I Tim. 4:12.

the public, our Lord withdrew Himself sometimes from the crowd." [10]

There is still another point that the Angelic Doctor emphasized in his great work for the benefit of the preacher. Let us quote it in its full length: "It was fitting," he pointed out, "for Christ to lead a life of poverty in this world. First, because this was in keeping with the duty of preaching, for which purpose He says that He came. 'Let us go into the neighboring towns and cities, that I may preach there also, for to this purpose am I come.' [11] Now in order that the preachers of God's word may be able to give all their time to preaching, they must be wholly free from the care of worldly matters, which is impossible for those who are possessed of wealth." [12]

The rare advice St. Thomas occasionally gives in the course of his *Summa,* deserves the attention of every preacher. It is as up to date now, in the twentieth century, as it was during the twelfth and thirteenth.

During the last two or three decades, preaching, on the whole, has lost much of its flare for the rhetorical, and, instead, the truth is stated in straightforward terms. In some ways this trend is for the better because we now speak to the point and use simple and plain language. It is gratifying to see that, in this respect, matters have improved. But let us priests be mindful that it is our duty, as pastors and shepherds of souls, to place before our people spiritual food, that is, instruction full of nourishment for the soul. Having been busy all week with the cares of a parish, it is no easy task to prepare a spiritual talk that expounds and enters into what St. Thomas called "the profound mysteries of the faith" and "the perfection of Christian life." Instead of decrying the shortcomings

[10] *Op. cit.,* IIIa, q.40, a.1, ad 3.
[11] Mark 1:38.
[12] *Op. cit.,* IIIa, q.40, a.3.

of our people, let us instruct the faithful, in a practical way, on the life of virtue, on Christian perfection, on grace, and on the life of union with God. People nowadays are hungry for spiritual food; they are longing for positive and profound instruction. Hence, we should do our best. Let us instruct to the best of our ability and to the capacity of our people. For this is the advice of the Council of Trent: "Pastors should preach to the flock, entrusted to their care, sermons which they can easily understand." [13] And an easily and well understood sermon is the accomplishment of a good preacher.

[13] The Latin text reads as follows: [Parochi] "plebes sibi commissas pro sua et earum capacitate pascant salutaribus verbis" (Sess. 5, c. 2, "De ref.").

# CHAPTER 12

# *The Credo*

Credo in unum Deum, Patrem omnipotentem, factorem caeli et terrae, visibilium omnium, et invisibilium. Et in unum Dominum Jesum Christum, Filium Dei Unigentum. Et ex Patre natum ante omnia saecula. Deum de Deo, lumen de lumine, Deum verum de Deo vero. Genitum, non factum, consubstantialem Patri: per quem omnia facta sunt. Qui propter nos homines, et propter nostram salutem descendit de caelis. Et incarnatus est de Spiritu Sancto ex Maria Virgine; et homo factus est. Crucifixus etiam pro nobis: sub Pontio Pilato passus, et sepultus est. Et resurrexit tertia die, secundum Scripturas. Et ascendit in caelum: sedet ad dexteram Patris. Et iterum venturus est cum gloria judicare vivos et mortuos: cuius regni non erit finis. Et in Spiritum Sanctum, Dominum, et vivificantem: Qui ex Patre Filioque procedit. Qui cum Patre, et Filio simul adoratur, et conglorificatur: qui locutus est per Prophetas. Et unam, sanctam, Catholicam et apostolicam Ecclesiam. Confiteor unum baptisma in remissionem peccatorum. Et exspecto resurrectionem mortuorum. Et vitam venturi saeculi. Amen.

AFTER the Gospel has been read, frequently the Creed is said or intoned by the priest.

Whether we consider the Symbol as the last prayer of the Mass of the catechumens, or as the first prayer of the faithful, its position is most appropriate. For, it forms the crowning piece of the mystery of faith, which catechumens are striving for, and it is the foundation stone of the mystery that is about to take place in the Mass of the faithful.

In the Gospel, the word of God has been read and proposed to the faithful. In the Creed, the priest and the faithful accept this divine message, and solemnly confess its acceptance. Or, to express the same idea in the words of the Angelic Doctor: "After the Gospel has been read," he says, "the Creed is sung, in which the people show that they assent by faith to Christ's doctrine." [1]

In another place in his *Summa*, the great doctor explains the reasons for the Symbol, when he says: " 'He that cometh to God, must believe that He is. . . .' [2] Now a man cannot believe, unless the truth be proposed to him that he may believe it. Hence the need for the truth of faith to be collected together, so that it might the more easily be proposed to all, lest anyone might stray from the truth through ignorance of the faith." [3] St. Thomas continues in favor of the symbol of faith, when he says: "The truth of faith is contained in Holy Writ, diffusely, under various modes of expression, and sometimes obscurely, so that, in order to gather the truth of faith from Holy Writ, one needs long study and practice, which are not attainable by all who are required to know the truth of faith, many of whom have no time for study, being busy with other affairs. And so it was necessary to gather together a clear summary from the sayings of Holy Writ, to be proposed to the belief of all." [4]

Finally, the Angelic Doctor shows how it came about that the Symbol was composed. "The same doctrine of faith," he

1 *Summa theol.*, IIIa, q. 83, a. 4.
2 Heb. 11:6.
3 *Op. cit.*, IIa IIae, q. 1, a. 9.
4 *Ibid.*, ad 1.

argues, "is taught in all the symbols. Nevertheless, the people need more careful instruction about the truth of faith, when errors arise, lest the faith of simple-minded persons be corrupted by heretics. It was this that gave rise to the necessity of formulating several symbols, which nowise differ from one another, save that on account of the obstinacy of heretics one contains more explicitly what another contains implicitly." [5]

Thus, the Symbol is, to use the words of St. Augustine, "a short yet grand norm of faith, short in so far as the number of the words is concerned, yet grand as to the depth of the propositions of faith." [6]

We may ask why the Nicene-Constantinopolitan Creed or the "Symbol of the Fathers of the Church," as it is sometimes called, was introduced into the liturgy of the Mass in preference to the Apostles' Creed, which is greater in dignity on account of its apostolic origin and authority. Historical developments, too many to enumerate in this short essay, are responsible. These historical developments are referred to by St. Thomas who, furthermore, gives a mystical reason for their occurrences. In particular, he says: "Since the symbol of the Fathers is an explanation of the symbol of the apostles, and was drawn up after the faith was already spread abroad, and when the Church was already at peace, it is sung publicly in the Mass. On the other hand, the symbol of the apostles, which was drawn up at the time of persecution, before the faith was made public, is said secretly at Prime and Compline, as though it were against the darkness of past and future errors." [7]

[5] *Ibid.*, ad 2.
[6] "Symbolum est regula fidei brevis et grandis: brevis numero verborum, grandis pondere sententiarum" (St. Augustine, *Sermo 59*, no. 1).
[7] *Op. cit.*, IIa IIae, q. 1, a. 9, ad 6.

In the Creed, the principal points of our faith are brought forth with great precision. First, we profess our belief in God the Father, the creator of all things. Then we declare our belief in the divinity of His only-begotten Son, Jesus Christ, after which the mysteries regarding His sacred humanity are stated. His passion and death, His resurrection and ascension into heaven, and His final return to judge the living and the dead, are proclaimed. Belief in the third Person of the Blessed Trinity is professed; and, finally, our faith in the Catholic Church and in the future life is declared.

Thus we see, in the Symbol, the Christian doctrine briefly stated and well defined and, at the same time, easy for people to understand. By this method the Church proves herself to be a wise teacher, an accomplished educator, and a successful pedagogue, an accomplishment which is the more remarkable when we consider the vastness of the Sacred Writings and the wealth of tradition.

The Church has repeatedly employed the same method. We do not need to point to succeeding symbols: to the Anthanasian Creed, to that of the Lateran, to the profession of faith by the Council of Trent and the Vatican Council. Outside these professions of faith, the Church uses the same method in the Catechism where, with the greatest economy of words, the immense wealth of revealed truth is set forth.

In this method the priest ought to imitate and follow the Church. The priest's words should be few, but instructive, and his sermon should not be lengthy and fatiguing, but short and pregnant with wisdom and knowledge. His lessons should be clear and enlightening, his instructions to the point. His advices and exhortations should be models of zeal, wisdom, and moderation, worded with brevity and precision. Let him give a message that is worth-while. In this present age, men are not given to long orations. Men desire the substance, the digest, the resumé.

We must master the field to supply this need. It is a fallacy for so many speakers to think they can be simple and plain in their talks and instructions without proper preparation. Only a master will be able to outline the principles. The more familiar anyone is with the sacred sciences, the better he is equipped to emphasize the high points of the immense treasure of revealed truth. An unlearned speaker is not convincing. By high-sounding phrases no one dispatches a message that persuades. It is imperative for the priest to keep in constant touch with the study of the sacred sciences. Here more than one priest may object and say: The parish priest is not a professor. What is the purpose in spending one's time and energy in an effort to penetrate the depth of the mysteries, or in trying to master the finest points of speculations? This question reflects truth and untruth. We admit that more is required from a professor of philosophy or theology than from a parish priest, but, on the other hand, it cannot be denied that a parish priest is in constant touch with the daily life of his parishioners. It is his duty to combat the current errors that are circulating among those entrusted to his care. He has to warn his people against misconceptions and the erroneous ideas of the time. He, more than anyone else, must counteract the errors confronting his parishioners. And he cannot brush aside, by a broad sweep of the hand or an empty phrase, the heretical opinions, the current misconceptions, and the erroneous teachings of the world in which he and his parishioners live. The non-Christian philosophy of the day must be answered point by point. This task devolves upon the priest, and foremost the parish priest. If we had had more learned priests, heretical views would not have made such inroads among our own people in the past. A categorical denunciation of an error does not eliminate an error. Unless our contradictions are to the point, they rather work harm, for they give rise to the frequently heard complaint that priests and the Church do not understand the spirit of the times.

Zeal for truth consumes the good priest, who spares no effort to face and battle false philosophies; who does not sleep while the enemy goes around spreading the seed of erroneous teachings. The good priest does not remain silent or timid in the face of the errors of his time, but carries the torch of truth through the lands. In order to accomplish this, and to do it effectively, he has first to equip himself, to study the problem, to be ready for attacks and counterattacks, and to uproot the sources of false doctrines. And all this is accomplished only by an ever renewed and never-ending application of the principles and foundations of philosophy and of theology. Our Lord Himself admonishes us to do this when He spoke the short, but profound word: "Search the Scriptures. . . ." [8] And, undoubtedly, St. Paul, the great foe of the errors of his own time, had this in mind when he wrote to the Colossians: "Let the word of Christ dwell in you abundantly. . . ." [9]

[8] John 5:39.
[9] Col. 3:16.

# CHAPTER 13

## *The Offertory*

THE Offertory begins the sacrificial celebration proper. Let us pause for a few moments and reflect with St. Thomas on the different parts of the Sacrifice of the Mass. "After the people," he says, "have been prepared and instructed, the next step is to proceed to the celebration of the mystery, which is both offered as a sacrifice, and consecrated and received as a sacrament; since first we have the oblation; then the consecration of the matter offered; and thirdly, its reception. In regard to the oblation, two things are done, namely, the people's praise in singing the Offertory, expressing the joy of the offerers, and the priest's prayer asking for the people's oblation to be made acceptable to God." [1]

Before considering this second part of the Mass, the sacrifice proper, it is befitting that we should clarify our ideas regarding a sacrifice. What is a sacrifice?

In the course of our cultural progress, we have almost overlooked the original meaning of certain terms. Very often we may be well acquainted with the figurative sense of a word, but can only with difficulty recall its original meaning, or in other words, we may be more familiar with the applied sense of a word than with its proper meaning. This circumstance occurs in the conceptions applicable to the word "sacrifice." We say that a mother sacrifices her sleep for her child, or that

[1] *Summa theol.*, IIIa, q. 83, a. 4.

a father makes sacrifices to send his children to a Catholic
school. Now, what does this mean? It means that the father
denies himself certain legitimate pleasures or satisfactions,
such as a higher-priced cigar, a trip, a show, and so forth, that
he may have the money necessary to defray the expenses of
a Catholic education for his children. In other words, he
waives all these things: tobacco, trips, shows, and so forth,
for the good of his children. Here we have used only the figurative sense of the word "sacrifice." Let us see what the original
meaning of this word is. We must approach this problem sys-
tematically. What is a sacrifice? What are the elements constituting a sacrifice? From the very beginning let us make it
perfectly clear that a sacrifice is something that is essentially
directed toward God. God is the aim and end of every sacrifice. There cannot be true sacrifices offered up to anyone or
anything except the Divinity. To God alone sacrifices should
be offered. "He that sacrificeth to gods shall be put to death,
save only to the Lord." [2] Thus the Mosaic Law enacted. St.
Thomas justified and defended this prescription in the following words: "We find in every country the people are wont
to show the sovereign ruler some special sign of honor, and
that if this be shown to anyone else, it is a crime of high
treason. Therefore, in the divine law, the death punishment
is assigned to those who offer divine honor to another than
God." [3] The Doctor of the Schools produces another proof
for the Divinity's being the end of all sacrifices, when he says:
"Just as to God alone ought we to offer spiritual sacrifices, so
too ought we to offer outward sacrifices to Him alone: even
so in our prayers and praises we proffer significant words to
Him to whom in our hearts we offer the things which we desig-

[2] Exod. 22:20.
[3] *Op. cit.*, IIa IIae, q. 85, a. 2.

nate thereby, as Augustine states." [4] Even though altars and churches are raised to the saints, the sacrifices, nevertheless, are offered to God alone. For thus the great Bishop of Hippo explains: "We do not raise temples and priesthoods to the martyrs, because not they but their God is our God. Wherefore the priest says not: I offer sacrifice to thee, Peter or Paul. But we give thanks to God for their triumphs, and urge ourselves to imitate them." [5] Hence it is evident that the end of all sacrifice is God's infinite supremacy. The end of the sacrifice is God, and God alone.

Let us now ask: Who offers the sacrifice? The answer is simple and distinct. The sacrificial offerer is the priest. The priest offers the sacrifice. This is the way it is, and was with every nation. The priest performs the sacrificial act or function. At the altar he stands duly appointed, representing a group of people. He functions in the name of a community or congregation. "The priests," St. Thomas remarks, "offer those sacrifices that are specially directed to the divine worship, not only for themselves but also for others." [6] Of the same mind was St. Paul, who wrote to the Hebrews: "For every high priest taken from among men is ordained for men in the things that appertain to God, that he may offer up gifts and sacrifices for sins. . . ." [7]

The next question is: What is offered? In what does the sacrificial gift consist? The sacrifice consists in a visible object, removed from the use of men, set apart as something sacred, or given to God. An article of human possession, or an object of definite value to men is dedicated in a special manner to God; is handed over to God; is made the exclusive property of

---

[4] De Civ. Dei, X, 19; Summa theol., IIa IIae, q.85, a.2.
[5] De Civ. Dei, VIII, 19; cf. Summa theol., IIa IIae, q.85, a.2, ad 3.
[6] Summa theol., IIa IIae, q.85, a.4, ad 3.
[7] Heb. 5:1.

God. An object's use is returned to God and this is accomplished by placing the gift in a state of sacrifice. "A sacrifice, properly speaking," says St. Thomas, "requires that something be done to the thing which is offered to God, for instance, animals were slain and burnt, the bread is broken, eaten, blessed. The very word signifies this, since sacrifice is so called because a man does something sacred (*facit sacrum*)." [8] This is in keeping with the words of St. Paul, who wrote to the Ephesians: "Walk in love, as Christ also hath loved us and hath delivered Himself for us, an oblation and a sacrifice to God for an odor of sweetness." [9]

Another question is: For whom are sacrifices offered, and for whose benefit is the oblation made? There is not the slightest doubt that a sacrifice is offered for the good of men. Man is conscious of his dependency on the divine Being. At the same time, he is conscious of his sinfulness and guilt, of his degradation and moral weakness. He offers a sacrifice to dispel the wrath of God, and to draw upon himself the good pleasure of the Divinity. The value of the sacrifice in reconciling man with God was pointed out by St. Paul in his Epistle to the Hebrews when he said: ". . . Without shedding of blood there is no remission." [10]

The four elements upon which a sacrifice is constituted, as we have seen, are the following: first, God, the end of the sacrifice, or He to whom it is offered; secondly, the minister of the sacrifice, or he by whom it is offered, the priest; thirdly, the sacrificial gift, or that which is offered; fourthly, the people for whom it is offered. In this enumeration we followed the lead of the Angel of the Schools who was guided by St. Augustine and who said: "There are four things to be noted in

[8] *Op. cit.*, IIa IIae, q.85, a.3, ad 3.
[9] Eph. 5:2.
[10] Heb. 9:22.

every sacrifice, to wit: to whom it is offered, by whom it is offered, what is offered, and for whom it is offered." [11]

The offering of sacrifice is in conformity with the natural law. "At all times," says the Angelic Doctor, "and among all nations there has always been the offering of sacrifices. Now that which is observed by all is seemingly natural. Therefore the offering of sacrifices is of the natural law." [12] This statement of St. Thomas is endorsed by modern anthropologists and ethnologists. Go into the wilds of Africa, the mountains of Asia, the deserts of Australia, the woods of South America, and you will see the natives following the dictates of the natural law, often to the consternation of the intruding cultured whites, who witness a sacrifice without understanding its meaning. It is true that some religions do not recognize the institution of the sacrifice. Protestantism, for the most part, denies it. But while Protestantism abolished the Sacrifice of the Mass, this same Protestantism recognizes the sacrifice of Calvary. The great religions of Asia know the sacrifice, as do the less cultivated tribes of Africa and Australia, who, as a matter of course, offer their gifts on the altar. Man, as a rule, follows the dictates of the natural law, and it has been observed by many travelers that the primitive peoples have, in many instances, clearer ideas and more fundamental conceptions in regard to the natural law, than the nations more advanced in cultural development. The natives are still closer to the aboriginal ideas. Their conceptions are aboriginal.

[11] *Summa theol.* IIIa, q.48, a.3; q.22, a.3.

St. Augustine continues his thoughts, reflecting on these four elements, and the Eucharistic Christ when he says: "That the same one true Mediator reconciling us with God through the peace-sacrifice might continue to be one with Him to whom He offered it, might be one with them for whom He offered it, and might Himself be the offerer and what He offered" (*De Civ. Dei*).

[12] *Op. cit.,* IIa IIae, q.85, a.1.

Of all the sacrificial gifts that the ancient world offered, a large percentage of them were animals. Similarly animals are sacrificed in great numbers among many aboriginal tribes. In the religion of the people of Israel, blood sacrifices were most numerous. In the ancient world, as with many aboriginal tribes, the victims slain at the altars of the nation, supplied the people with meat. The animals were first sacrificed and then given to the people for consumption at the banquet tables. The priests were also butchers for their nation, a wise provision, for in a world which was, or still is, crude and bloody, the animal world was saved from unnecessary cruelty and extinction. Now, when you place before your mind the picture of a priest of old in his bloody business of slaying the livestock of the nation, his instrument a cruel knife, his hands stained red with blood, his clothes colored with the life stream of victims, and his altar sprinkled with blood, you surely begin to understand the joy of the Scriptures singing a praise to the "pure and clean" sacrifice of the New Covenant. And you, the priest, will fall on your knees praising God for having called you, not to be butcher and priest, not to shed the blood of animals; but to be a priest of the New Testament, a priest who offers the pure and clean oblation of bread and wine.

We wish to call attention here to a feature that, it is true, is not essential to a sacrifice, but that is, nevertheless, not entirely absent. It is according to nature, that some pain is present whenever a sacrifice is made. The ancient world placed objects of great value on their altars. The farmer who anxiously awaited the first cut of his crop carried his first fruits to the priest. The shepherd who was proud of the first arrivals in his flock did not hesitate to present the first lambs at the temple. The natives of many tribes still offer their most priceless possessions. That possession which is dearest to the heart of man, or at least a part of that possession, is offered to the deity. And it was in perfect harmony with this central idea of sacrifice that in the early Christian Church, while the Offertory antiphon and verses were chanted, the faithful made an offering of bread and wine or of a similar possession. And even nowadays we are reminded of this ancient custom when, at this particular part of the Mass, the ushers begin to take up the collection. Now this giving of a coin, or, as in olden times, this parting with an object of value, that is, this depriving oneself of a possession, is an act that naturally causes some pain or discomfort to the heart of the owner. It may be that the pain caused by the loss of an object is not felt very keenly, because it is superseded by the joy arising from some virtuous motive, but, nevertheless, the parting with a certain object of possession is naturally painful to the human heart.

Let us priests remember this. We are living on the offerings and sacrifices made by the laymen. Every cent of the dollar that we priests spend, comes out of the pocket of some faithful giver. Some donor overcame his natural love for a possession of his and sacrificed it that we might live.

If we priests could only know the history of the donor of every dollar bill in the collection basket! Now these dimes were dropped into the basket by a humble servant girl, or by a poor woman, a widow, or by a sick or crippled person; and here is a dollar of a hard pressed business man. Here again, we gather the few cents given by a father of a big family. Hence, let us think twice before we go to gratify our desires. Are they really necessities, or are they luxuries?

The laymen give willingly to the support of the pastor, but what is the case in reverse? Is it hard for the business man to collect a legitimate bill at the rectory? Is it difficult for a faithful parishioner of years of good standing, when suddenly confronted with reverses, to secure certain help from a priest?

We need not multiply examples. Suffice it to say that we, as priests, know all that makes a sacrifice and we should have an appreciation for the sacrifices made by others.

# CHAPTER 14

# *The Oblation*

Suscipe, sancte Pater, omnipotens aeterne Deus, hanc immaculatam hostiam, quam ego indignus famulus tuus offero tibi Deo meo vivo et vero, pro innumerabilibus peccatis et offensionibus et negligentiis meis, et pro omnibus circumstantibus, sed et pro omnibus fidelibus Christianis, vivis atque defunctis: ut mihi et illis proficiat ad salutem in vitam aeternam. Amen.

THE disposition of the person who offers a sacrifice is of the greatest importance. This fact is evident from what we know about sacrifices as they were offered up by man from the beginning of time, for, of the sacrifice of Abel and Cain we read: "By faith," says St. Paul, "Abel offered to God a sacrifice exceeding that of Cain. . . ." [1] The heart of man renders a sacrifice pleasing or unacceptable to the divine Majesty. "The sacrifice of the just is acceptable, and the Lord will not forget the memorial thereof." [2] When the good disposition is wanting in the offerer, the Lord despises the sacrifice as an empty ceremony: "The victims of the wicked are abominable to the Lord. . . ." [3] "To what purpose do you offer Me the multitude of your victims, saith the Lord? I am full, I desire not holocausts of rams, and fat of fatlings, and blood of calves, and lambs, and buck goats." [4]

[1] Heb. 11:4.
[2] Ecclus. 35:9.
[3] Prov. 15:8.
[4] Isa. 1:11.

Let us heed this warning of the Old Testament. If then the intention of the offerer was of so paramount an importance in the offering of the sacrifices of the Old Testament, it is important that we take care to approach the great Eucharistic Sacrifice of the New Covenant in a spirit that will be pleasing to the divine Majesty. Mother Church, as a wise teacher, comes to our aid and puts into the mouth of the celebrating priest the befitting words, for the oblation prayer, *Suscipe sancte Pater*, expresses the correct intention in which the Eucharistic Sacrifice is to be offered.

Let us analyze this prayer. The *Suscipe sancte Pater* is addressed to God, to the Divine Being, to the one Supreme Being, to *"Deus."* This divine Majesty is adored and praised on account of His absolute perfections: He is *sancte, omnipotens, aeterne, vivo* and *vero*. He is the God of all perfections, of all goodness; the only being that exists in the fullness of truth and life (*vivo et vero*). But he is not a strange God, a being in heaven who does not concern us mortals. No, He is my God (*Deo meo*). He is the *Pater*. The priest who pronounces these words recognizes the absolute lordship of the Divinity. He professes God by the words *pater* and *meo* to be the *causa prima* and the *finis ultimus* of his very existence and being. In this connection the angelic teacher remarks fittingly: "A sacrifice is offered in order that something may be represented. Now the sacrifice that is offered outwardly represents the inward spiritual sacrifice, whereby the soul offers itself to God. . . . Again the soul offers itself in sacrifice to God as its beginning by creation, and its end by beatification." [5] In truth, the correct spirit when approaching the altar to offer the sacrifice is, first, to acknowledge God as the only and true Supreme Lord of heaven and earth, and as the one

[5] *Summa theol.*, IIa IIae, q. 85, a. 2.

who holds absolute dominion over all creatures and gives life (*vivo*) and truth (*vero*) to all mortals.

What is man in comparison with this all-holy and omnipotent God? Man is bound to acknowledge his own nothingness and his absolute dependence on God. *Ego indignus famulus tuus.* This is the spirit that ought to animate the celebrating priest. We are subjects of God. We are His servants. We owe to the Divinity our absolute subjection and submission. This humble spirit of submission causes man to offer up sacrifices. "Natural reason," says St. Thomas, "tells man that he is subject to a higher being on account of the defects which he perceives in himself, and in which he needs help and direction from someone above him; whatever this superior being may be, it is known to all under the name of God. Now just as in natural things the lower are naturally subject to the higher, so too, it is a dictate of natural reason in accordance with man's natural inclination that he should tender submission and honor, according to his mode, to that which is above man. Now the mode befitting to man is that he should employ sensible signs in order to signify anything, because he derives his knowledge from sensibles. Hence it is a dictate of natural reason that man should use certain sensibles, by offering them to God in sign of the subjection and honor due to Him, like those who make certain offerings to their lord in recognition of his authority. Now this is what we mean by a sacrifice." [6]

St. Thomas tells us that it is natural to man, who is conscious of his dependency upon God and of his subjection to Him, to employ certain sensible signs when signifying an object. Man wishes to give himself wholly and entirely to his sovereign Lord, yet he cannot destroy himself, since he is not lord over his life and death. In his desire to give himself to his

[6] *Ibid.*, a. 1.

absolute Lord and owner, man substitutes for himself certain sensible signs. In the Old Testament, animals and victuals were placed on the altar. The idea of the animal's being used as a substitute for the offerer was clearly expressed in the offering of an atonement sacrifice, when the priest placed his hands over the victim. In this sense, St. Thomas interprets the nature of the sacrifices of the Old Testament when he writes as follows: "The slaying of the animals signified the destruction of sins; and also that man deserved death on account of his sins; as though those animals were slain in man's stead, in order to betoken the expiation of sins." [7] In the New Dispensation, a fundamental principle of the doctrine of the Redemption is the fact that Christ, when suffering on the cross, offered Himself to His heavenly Father for the transgressions of the human race. "He was wounded for our iniquities, He was bruised for our sins. . . ." [8] "Who His own self bore our sins in His body upon the tree. . . ." [9] "In whom we have redemption through His blood, the remission of sins. . . ." [10] "Knowing that you were not redeemed with corruptible things . . . , but with the precious blood of Christ, as of a lamb unspotted and undefiled. . . ." [11]

As the Sacrifice of the Mass is substantially identical with the Sacrifice of the Cross, or, to use a Thomistic term, as the Mass is the "continuation" of the Sacrifice of the Cross, Christ, in the Mass as on the cross, substitutes Himself for us poor mortals, takes our place before the eternal judgment seat and offers Himself in our stead. Raising the paten, on which the host is placed, and holding it towards heaven, the priest has

[7] *Ibid.*, Ia IIae, q. 102, a. 3, ad 5.
[8] Isa. 53:5.
[9] I Pet. 2:24.
[10] Eph. 1:7.
[11] I Pet. 1:18–19.

this idea in mind when he says: "Suscipe . . . hanc immaculatam hostiam, quam ego . . . offero tibi. . . ." The priest offers to God this unspotted host, which is destined to be changed into the body and blood of our Lord. He presents to God the "clean oblation" of which, in the Old Testament, Malachias [12] speaks. Our Lord's body and blood, under the appearance of bread and wine, is the "sensible sign" that is offered up to God ". . . pro innumerabilibus peccatis, et offensionibus, et negligentiis meis, et pro omnibus circumstantibus, sed et pro omnibus fidelibus Christianis vivis atque defunctis. . . ." "For this is My blood of the New Testament, which shall be shed for many unto remission of sins." [13] On the cross Christ took upon Himself our guilt. On the altar, Christ offers Himself to His heavenly Father as a sacrifice of propitiation for our sins. For our sins. For our guilt.

Who does anything for us? When we are in need of something, we must pay for it in dollars and cents, and when we cannot do so we hesitate to ask for help, even from our relatives or friends. At any rate, only an intimate friend is approached for a favor. If the favor we ask, however, will cause inconvenience or trouble, how many of our intimate friends do we feel free to approach for help? Where in the whole wide world is there a single friend who is ready to answer for a fault or transgression of ours? Some may not censure us, others may excuse us, even condone and pardon us, but we will hardly find one friend that will burden himself with our guilt. A father may declare himself ready to suffer for an innocent, unfortunate child; but where under God's sun is the parent who presents himself to the judge or to the jailer to take the place of a grown son who is guilty of a crime? Such love sur-

[12] Mal. 1:11.
[13] Matt. 26:28.

passes the heights of parental love or of filial devotion. This love is almost unknown among men, yet it was known to the God-man who accomplished the impossible, who, out of love, substituted Himself for us, took upon Himself our guilt and suffered for our sins.

Let us confess our sins. I reiterate, let us priests admit our faults. The laymen speak of the priest as a "holy man," or say: "How good Father is!" They speak out of hearts filled with reverence for our vocation, yet such praise must not enter our hearts. The man that becomes convinced of his own goodness digs the grave for his downfall. Nor is it right to lessen the extent of our guilt; carloads of alibis and excuses are worthless; explanations of "intentions," "meanings" and "reasons" are worse than useless. No, Mother Church knows her sons and her priests, and it is not without intention that, in the Oblation prayer, she puts into the mouth of the priest words that admit his guilt in threefold enumeration, ". . . pro innumerabilibus peccatis et offensionibus et negligentiis meis. . . ." Anyone who assumes an air of guiltless behavior, who refuses to acknowledge his personal weaknesses and faults and has no idea of the immensity of his sins, cannot appreciate Christ's gift to him in the Redemption, nor does he realize the extent of Christ's pains and sufferings for him. The person who makes little of his own guilt, makes little, too, of Christ's Redemption. The more we realize the gravity of our sins, the better we understand Christ's redeeming work for us. The greater the remorse for our sins, the deeper the appreciation of Christ's love for us, the more profound the realization of the immensity of the love that the Savior had for us when He took upon Himself our transgressions, our sins, and our faults. If we acknowledge, as the prayer *Suscipe, sancte Pater* says, "our innumerable sins, offenses, and negligences," and offer up in the right spirit the Sacrifice of the Mass, we may be reasonably sure that "it may avail both me and them," that is, all faithful Christians, ". . . for salvation unto life everlasting. Amen."

# CHAPTER 15

# *Wine and Water*

Deus, qui humanae substantiae dignitatem mirabiliter
condidisti, et mirabilius reformasti: da nobis per hujus
aquae et vini mysterium, ejus divinitatis esse consortes,
qui humanitatis nostrae fieri dignatus est particeps, Jesus
Christus Filius tuus, Dominus noster: qui tecum vivit et
regnat in unitate Spiritus Sancti Deus: per omnia saecula saeculorum. Amen.

AFTER the offering of the host, the priest goes to the Epistle
side where he pours wine and, after blessing the water, pours
water also into the chalice. What is the significance of mingling water with wine, and why does the priest not bless the
wine, whereas he blesses the water?

"Water," says St. Thomas, "ought to be mingled with the
wine, which is offered in this sacrament. First of all on account of its institution, for it is believed with probability that
our Lord instituted this sacrament in wine tempered with
water according to the custom of that country: hence it is
written, 'Drink the wine which I have mixed for you.' [1] Secondly, because it harmonizes with the representation of our
Lord's Passion. Hence Pope Alexander I says: 'In the Lord's
chalice neither wine only nor water only ought to be offered,
but both mixed, because we read that both flowed from His
side in the Passion.'" [2] "The shedding of the blood belonged

[1] Prov. 9:5.
[2] *Summa theol.*, IIIa, q.74. a.6.

80

directly to Christ's Passion; for it is natural for blood to flow
from a wounded human body. But the flowing of the water
was not necessary for the Passion; but merely to show its
effect, which is to wash away sins, and to refresh us from the
heat of concupiscence." [3] "Thirdly, because this is adapted
for signifying the effect of this sacrament, since as Pope Julius
says: [4] 'We see that the people are signified by the water, but
Christ's blood by the wine. Therefore, when water is mixed
with the wine in the chalice, the people are made one with
Christ.' " [5] In other words, "by the mixing of the water with
wine is signified the union of the people with Christ." [6] This
significance, of the wine symbolizing Christ and of the water
symbolizing the people, is accountable for blessing only the
water. For Christ does not need man's benediction, whereas
the people are in need of divine graces and blessings.

Let us continue the thought of St. Thomas: "Fourthly,"
he says, "because this is appropriate to the fourth effect of
this sacrament, which is the entering into everlasting life:
hence Ambrose [7] says, 'The water flows into the chalice and
springs forth into everlasting life.' " [8]

Wine and water, the matter of the sacrament, are, as we
have seen, rich in symbolic significance. And listening to the
prayer "Deus, qui humanae," we wonder at the wealth, beauty,
and depth of the thought that we associate with the seemingly
simple action of pouring wine and water into the chalice.

God, in creating the human being, dignified man. In what,
we may ask, does this dignity consist? The Holy Scriptures
tell us that God made man the lord of the universe to "rule

[3] *Ibid.*, a.7, ad 2.
[4] Concil. Bracarens, III, canon 1.
[5] *Summa theol.*, IIIa, q.74, a.6.
[6] *Ibid.*, a.7.
[7] *De Sacram*, v.
[8] *Op. cit.*, IIIa, q.74, a.6.

over the fishes of the sea, and the fowls of the air, and all living creatures that move upon the earth." [9] Now the dignity of man consists, according to the inspired text, even in something more than the lordship over "all living creatures." "And God," we read in Genesis, "created man to His own image: to the image of God He created him. . . ." [10] The Angelic Doctor tells us what is meant by an "image" and what the corresponding dignity of man consists in, when he clearly explains to us the meaning of the word "image" and distinguishes it from the word "trace." "Every effect in some degree," he says, "represents its cause, but diversely. For, some effects represent only the causality of the cause, but not its form, as smoke represents fire. Such a representation is called a trace, for a trace shows that someone has passed by but not who it is." [11] Let us inject here that in all creatures there is found the trace of the Trinity. "Other effects," St. Thomas continues, "represent the cause as regards the similitude of its form, as fire generated represents fire generating and a statue of Mercury represents Mercury, and this is called the representation of image. Now the processions of the divine Persons are referred to the acts of intellect and will. For the Son proceeds as the word of the intellect, and the Holy Ghost proceeds as love of the will. Therefore, in rational creatures, possessing intellect and will, there is found the representation of the Trinity by way of image, inasmuch as there is found in them the word conceived, and the love proceeding." [12] Man, poor, sinful man, is an image of the Blessed Trinity. Surely, Mother Church is right when she prays: "O God,

[9] Gen. 1:28.
[10] Gen. 1:27.
[11] *Op. cit.*, Ia. q.45, a.7.
[12] *Loc cit.*

who in creating human nature, hast wonderfully dignified it."
And "still more wonderfully was this human nature renewed,"
after its pitiful fall into sin, in the great act of the Redemption.

Is this mixing of the water with the wine a mystery? St.
Thomas sees wonderful analogies in this specific function,
for, he thinks that "the more probable opinion is that which
holds that the water is changed into wine, and the wine into
blood." [13] And then he adds a second thought, as it were, to
make the analogy complete: "When the water is changed into
wine, it is signified that the people are incorporated with
Christ." [14]

We, the people, who are signified by the water changed into
wine, beg Thee, O God, to grant that "we may be made partakers of the divine nature of Him, who vouchsafed to become
partaker of our human nature, namely Jesus Christ, our Lord."
Can you think of a more beautiful prayer? The second Person
of the Blessed Trinity, assuming human flesh, was born of
the Blessed Virgin Mary. God became man and thus became
partaker of our human nature. Inasmuch as He became partaker of our human nature, we pray that we may be made
partakers of His divine nature. What a beautiful reciprocal
relationship! The Divinity becomes human that the human
may be made divine. "By whom He hath given us most great
and precious promises: that by these you may be made partakers of the divine nature. . . ." [15]

In this sacrament, water is used by way of refreshment, according to the Scriptures, which state: "He hath brought me
up, on the water of refreshment. . . ." [16] And the wine from

[13] *Ibid.*, IIIa, q.74, a.8.
[14] *Ibid.*, ad 2.
[15] II Pet. 1:4.
[16] Ps. 22:3; cf. *Summa theol.*, IIIa, q.74, a.6, ad 2.

the grape is the proper matter of this sacrament, because it was instituted by Christ Himself, when He said: ". . . I will not drink from henceforth of this fruit of the vine. . . ." [17] Moreover "the wine from the grape is more in keeping with the effect of this sacrament which is spiritual, because it is written: 'That wine may cheer the heart of man.' " [18]

Thus Christ sanctified the fruit of the grape, for, by its instrumentality He wishes to bring spiritual joy, the joy of union with Him, to the priest. Christ did not suddenly raise the fruit of the grape to so exalted a mission. He worked His first miracle by giving to man, at the marriage of Cana, abundantly of a superior quality of wine.[19] He compared Himself to the vine: "I am the true vine. . . ." [20] He used the vineyard as the symbol of His Church.[21]

Among all the fruits of the earth the grape was created, from the beginning, to gladden the heart of man. "Wine was created from the beginning to make men joyful, and not to make them drunk. Wine drunken with moderation is the joy of the soul and heart. Sober drinking is health to soul and body." [22]

How excellent was our Lord's choice in selecting the matter for this sacrament! Bread, the substance that gives nourishment to our physical body, was chosen to be changed into the body of Christ for our spiritual food. The wine, which by its nature gives vigor, satisfaction, and joy, was selected to be changed into the sacred blood of our Lord, and thus to become the chalice of salvation to bring heavenly joy to the children of men. At the Eucharistic banquet the joy of Christ enters our heart, invigorates our spiritual life, and takes pos-

[17] Matt. 26:29.
[18] Ps. 103:15; *Summa theol.*, IIIa, q.74, a.5.
[19] John 2:1–11.
[20] John 15:1.
[21] Matt. 20:1–16.
[22] Ecclus. 31:35–37.

session of our being. Christ's joy becomes our joy: ". . . My joy may be in you, and your joy may be filled." [23]

Now, this spiritual joy that fills the heart of the priest who celebrates worthily, is not a special gift or a particular virtue. This sacrament of the Holy Eucharist confers, as St. Thomas teaches, "grace spiritually together with the virtue of charity." [24] In explaining these ideas, as set forth by the Angelic Doctor, we wish to state that "the spiritual joy which comes from God is caused by charity." [25] For "joy is not a virtue distinct from charity, but a certain act or effect which proceeds from charity." [26] Or, to translate this scholastic formula into biblical language: let us say, in the words of St. Paul, "If the charity of God is poured forth in our hearts," [27] then "justice and peace and joy in the Holy Ghost" [28] are given to us.

Let us, who have been ordained to the priesthood, rejoice in the Lord. "The light of Thy countenance, O Lord, is signed upon us; Thou hast given gladness in my heart." [29] Let us find our happiness in the Sacrifice of the holy Mass: ". . . my soul shall rejoice in the Lord; and shall be delighted in His salvation." [30] Every Mass celebrated worthily by the priest is a new cause of jubilation and exaltation to the angels in heaven, and each time the priest dons his vestments for holy Mass, the saints rejoice anew. The omnipotent Majesty of God the Father contemplates every Mass with infinite pleasure and satisfaction, and the kingdom of God celebrates a new triumph

[23] John 15:11.
[24] *Summa theol.*, IIIa, q.79, a.1, ad 2.
[25] *Ibid.*
[26] *Ibid.*, a.4.
[27] Rom. 5:5.
[28] Rom. 14:17.
[29] Ps. 4:7.
[30] Ps. 34:9.

and victory. In view of the fact that we are the ministers of the Sacrifice, let us bless each day allotted to us for the celebration of this great mystery of our faith. The happiness of our soul, the satisfaction of our priesthood, the joy and gladness of our Christian heart must consist in nothing less than the celebration of the Eucharistic Sacrifice, the offering of Mass. May this be the foremost object of our life and priestly vocation!

# CHAPTER 16

## *The Chalice of Salvation*

Offerimus tibi, Domine, calicem salutaris, tuam depre-
cantes clementiam: ut in conspectu divinae majestatis
tuae, pro nostra et totius mundi salute, cum odore suavi-
tatis ascendat. Amen.

FOOD and drink are required to sustain life, and without them
we cannot exist. In a similar way, we need spiritual food and
spiritual drink to maintain our spiritual life. "This sacrament"
[the Holy Eucharist], says St. Thomas, "is ordained for spiritual refreshment, which is conformed to corporal refreshment.
Now there are two things required for corporal refreshment,
namely, food, which is dry sustenance, and drink, which is
liquid sustenance. Therefore, two things concur for the integrity of this sacrament, to wit: spiritual food and spiritual
drink, according to St. John: [1] 'My flesh is meat indeed, and
My blood is drink indeed.'" [2] Accordingly, after the priest
has offered the oblation of bread, made of flour and water
which becomes, in the act of consecration, the bread of life,
he proceeds to offer the chalice which contains wine of the
grape and a few drops of water. The contents become, in virtue
of the words of the transubstantiation, the chalice of salvation.
"I will take the chalice of salvation; and I will call upon
the name of the Lord." [3] "The chalice of benediction, which

[1] John 6:56.
[2] *Summa theol.*, IIIa, q. 73, a. 2.
[3] Ps. 115:13.

87

we bless, is it not the communion of the blood of Christ?" [4]

In considering the chalice, who is not reminded of our Lord's prayer in the garden of Gethsemane: "My Father, if it be possible, let this chalice pass from Me. Nevertheless not as I will, but as Thou wilt"? [5] But this chalice is more than the bitter cup of the Passion; it becomes to us the chalice of salvation. Passion and salvation are related to each other as cause and effect. "Because without faith in the Passion there could never be any salvation, according to St. Paul: 'Whom God hath proposed to be a propitiation, through faith in His blood. . . .' [6] It was necessary accordingly that there should be at all times among men something to show forth our Lord's Passion; the chief sacrament of which . . . under the New Testament is the sacrament of the Eucharist. . . ." [7] The chalice of the Passion, which Jesus accepted from His heavenly Father in the Garden of Gethsemane, has become the chalice of our salvation, which is placed on our altars that whoever may desire it may partake of spiritual refreshment and thereby strengthen himself with divine graces. The chalice of salvation is the cup of graces. "Except you eat the flesh of the Son of man and drink His blood, you shall not have life in you. He that eateth My flesh, and drinketh My blood hath everlasting life. . . ." [8] The Angelic Doctor explains the graces that flow from the cup of salvation, in the following words:

> The effect of this sacrament ought to be considered, first of all and principally, from what is contained in this sacrament, which is Christ who, just as by coming in the

[4] I Cor. 10:16.
[5] Matt. 26:39.
[6] Rom. 3:25.
[7] *Summa theol.*, q.73, a.5.
[8] John 6:54–55.

world, He visibly bestowed the life of grace upon the
world, according to St. John: '. . . grace and truth came
by Jesus Christ,' [9] so also, by coming sacramentally into
man, causes the life of grace, according to St. John:
'. . . he that eateth Me, the same also shall live by
Me.' [10] Hence Cyril says on Luke: 'God's life-giving
Word by uniting Himself with His own flesh, made it
to be productive of life. For it was becoming that He
should be united somehow with bodies through His sacred flesh and precious blood, which we receive in a life-
giving blessing in the bread and wine.' [11]

Secondly, it is considered on the part of what is
represented by this sacrament, which is Christ's Passion. . . . And therefore this sacrament works in man
the effect which Christ's Passion wrought in the world.
Hence, Chrysostom says on the words, '. . . immediately there came out blood and water.': [12] 'Since the
sacred mysteries derive their origin from thence, when
you draw nigh to the awe-inspiring chalice, so approach
as if you were going to drink from Christ's own side.'
Hence our Lord Himself says: 'This is My blood . . .
which shall be shed for many unto remission of sins.' [13]

Thirdly, the effect of this sacrament is considered
from the way in which this sacrament is given; for it is
given by way of food and drink. And therefore this sacrament does for the spiritual life all that material food
does for the bodily life, namely, by sustaining, giving
increase, restoring and giving delight. Accordingly, Ambrose says: 'This is the bread of everlasting life, which
supports the substance of our soul.' [14] And Chrysostom
says: 'When we desire it, He lets us feel Him, and eat
Him, and embrace Him.' [15] And hence our Lord says:

9 John 1:17.
10 John 6:58.
11 Cf. Luke 22:19.
12 John 19:34.
13 Matt. 26:28.
14 *De Sacram*, V.
15 Hom. 46, *in Joan.*

'My flesh is meat indeed: and My blood is drink indeed.' [16]

Fourthly, the effect of this sacrament is considered from the species under which it is given. Hence Augustine says: 'Our Lord betokened His body and blood in things which out of many units are made into some one whole; for out of many grains is one thing made, viz, bread; and many grapes flow into one thing, namely, wine.' [17] And therefore he observes elsewhere: 'O sacrament of piety, O sign of unity, O bond of charity!' [18] And since Christ and His Passion are the cause of grace; and since spiritual refreshment and charity cannot be without grace, it is clear from all that has been set forth that this sacrament bestows grace.[19]

The chalice of salvation is the source of graces. The Angelic Doctor considers this sacrament the source of graces, for, he continues:

This sacrament has of itself the power of bestowing grace; nor does anyone possess grace before receiving this sacrament except from some desire thereof, from his own desire, as in the case of the adult; or from the Church's desire in the case of children. Hence it is due to the efficacy of its power, that even from desire thereof a man procures grace whereby he is enabled to lead the spiritual life. It remains, then, that when the sacrament itself is really received, grace is increased, and the spiritual life perfected; yet in different fashion from the sacrament of confirmation, in which grace is increased and perfected for resisting the outward assaults of Christ's enemies. But by this sacrament grace receives increase, and the spiritual life is perfected, so that man may stand perfect in himself by union with God.[20]

16 John 6:56.
17 Tract. 26, *in Joan.*
18 *Ibid.*
19 *Summa theol.*, IIIa, q.79, a.1.
20 *Ibid.*, ad 1.

"We offer unto Thee, O Lord, the chalice of salvation," the chalice of the bitter Passion of our Redeemer and Savior Jesus Christ, "beseeching Thy clemency that it may ascend before Thy divine Majesty as a sweet odor for our salvation," as the source of the graces for Thy own people and "for that of the whole world." For this is "a most sweet savor in the sight of the Lord, because it is His oblation." [21]

We priests, who celebrate the Mass daily, should have a great appreciation for the Mass as the source of graces. Out of the Mass, which can be compared with a fountain that never ceases to flow, we may draw all the spiritual benefits and encouragements as well as all the divine graces and blessings we need to successfully attain, in spite of occasional reverses, defeats or temporary relapses, the aim and end of our life: eternal salvation. But alas, let us look back to the day of our ordination. How many years have elapsed since we were ordained? Perhaps only a few, perhaps many; nevertheless, during these many years or during these few years, we behold an abundance of graces, a shower of divine inspirations bestowed on us by the dear Lord. Let us be honest and admit that we did not lend an ear to some of these inspirations and that we let some graces wither away. How many? Too many, far too many! What disregard for divine inspirations! We have to confess that this negligence and indifference is our own fault. The good Lord intended to overwhelm us with His blessing, and it is to our shame that we priests, who daily hold in our hands the cup of salvation, did not respond to His inspirations. Are we, who for so many years have lifted up toward heaven the chalice of salvation, progressing in the spiritual life? Stop for a moment and think of this: with the help of God's grace, if we would correct every year only one

21 Exod. 29:25.

of our failings and shortcomings, towards the end of our life we would be almost perfect. Have you not the courage to correct one single fault of yours in a year? Certainly, God's grace is not wanting to you, who every morning hold the cup of salvation in your hands. Well, try it! Take courage! Let your resolution and your determination to perfect yourself in virtue, in spirituality, and in holiness be joined to, and ascend together with, that sweet odor which our Lord Himself offers to His heavenly Father, the sweet odor of your salvation and that of the whole world.

# CHAPTER 17

# *In the Spirit of Humility*

In Spiritu humilitatis, et in animo contrito suscipiamur
a te, Domine: et sic fiat sacrificium nostrum in conspectu
tuo hodie, ut placeat tibi, Domine Deus.

IN THE midst of the part of the Mass called the "Offertory,"
which includes the prayers from the *Offertorium* to the *Secreta,* there is injected, as it were, a prayer that reminds the
priest to perform the Sacrifice in a spirit of humility and with
a contrite heart. Great as the Eucharistic Sacrifice is, the priest
should not glorify himself in his sacerdotal powers. In other
words, he should not exalt himself due to the greatness of the
act he is performing. All vainglory should be banished from
his soul. He should offer up the Sacrifice in a spirit that is
pleasing to God, and this spirit should be one of humility and
contrition. "A sacrifice to God is an afflicted spirit: a contrite
and humbled heart, O God, Thou wilt not despise." [1]

The text of this prayer is an abbreviation of the prayer of
the three young men who, refusing to adore a golden statue
set up by King Nabuchodonosor, were cast into a fiery furnace.
Unhurt by the fury of the flames they praised God in the spirit
of humility: "That we may find Thy mercy," they chanted,
"nevertheless in a contrite heart and humble spirit let us be
accepted. As in holocausts of rams and bullocks, and as in
thousands of fat lambs: so let our sacrifice be made in Thy

[1] Ps. 50:19.

93

sight this day, that it may please Thee: for there is no confusion to them that trust in Thee." [2] Let us hope and pray that we priests of the New Covenant may follow the example of these three young men. This spirit of humility is required during the Eucharistic Sacrifice, when the Lord shows His power and greatness. Admission to the presence of a worldly ruler stimulates the ambition of the nobles, and flatters the pride of the sons of this world; however, serving the Eucharistic King does not permit such worldly feelings, but requires a service in the spirit of self-denial.

When the bloody sacrifice of Calvary had been performed and the lifeless body of the God-man had hung, nailed to the cross, the earth was enshrouded in darkness, and "all the multitude of them that were come together to that sight, and saw the things that were done, returned striking their breasts." [3] Can we priests, who are called upon daily to renew this same Sacrifice, in an unbloody manner, be animated by a spirit other than that of striking our breasts in humility and contrition?

Let us analyze this prayer. There is a twofold comparison set forth in it. First, in order as worthy priests to be acceptable to the divine Majesty, we should have acquired, to a certain degree, the virtue of humility. In other words, our worthiness depends upon our disposition. Our humility is a precondition for being acceptable to God. "In spiritu humilitatis . . . suscipiamur a te, Domine." However, more is required, for, secondly, the perfect performance of the sacrificial action is an action that depends upon the divine pleasure for its fulfillment. "Et fiat sacrificium nostrum in conspectu tuo hodie, ut placeat tibi, Domine Deus." If we offer the Sacrifice of the

[2] Dan. 3:39–40.
[3] Luke 23:48.

holy Mass in a perfect spirit of humility, we invite the good pleasure of God upon our action. First, the right disposition and, secondly, the correct action are required to please the divine Majesty. May every priest say this prayer with a sincere heart.

Humility is a virtue that must be practiced in our daily life, for, without it the recitation of this prayer becomes one of hypocrisy and mockery. Our Lord Jesus Christ Himself was a model and exemplar par excellence of the virtue of humility. During every moment of His entire life, He practiced self-denial and self-abasement in a heroic degree. As every act in His sacred life was directed and focused toward His sacred passion and death, so our Lord humbled Himself in these last moments of His life. This He did in four respects, as St. Thomas tells us, for, the Angelic Doctor says as follows:

> In the first place as to His Passion and death, to which He was not bound; secondly, as to the place, since His body was laid in a sepulcher and His soul in hell; thirdly, as to the shame and mockeries He endured; fourthly, as to His being delivered up to man's power, as He Himself said to Pilate, "Thou shouldst not have any power against Me, unless it were given thee from above." [4]

Following this example of our Lord, we priests preach humility to the laymen, but do we ourselves practice this virtue to the extent that we expect to see it in others? Let the words of our divine Lord sink deeply into our hearts. ". . . Learn of Me, because I am meek and humble of heart. . . ." [5] Is it not significant that, before He instituted the Holy Eucharist and the sacrament of Holy Orders ("Do this in commemora-

[4] John 19:11; Summa theol., IIIa, q.49, a.6.
[5] Matt. 11:29.

tion of Me"), our Lord gave to His apostles an example of humility, when He washed their feet? And is it not equally significant of human weakness that, precisely at this particular time, there arose, as St. Luke tells us, ". . . a strife amongst them, which of them should seem to be the greater." [6] The apostles quarreled about rank and precedence. To this our Lord replied: ". . . he that is the greater among you, let him become as the younger; and he that is the leader, as he that serveth." [7] A word of divine wisdom to be reflected upon by every priest is this: he that is really a great pastor is so because he has become the servant of his people.

Practicing this virtue in his daily life, the priest will be able to say this prayer in the Mass with a sincere heart, and his sacrifice will become pleasing to the Lord.

The practice of humility is not always easy. There are in every human heart tendencies to pride and ambition, which are laudable when kept under control, but become passions that embitter life when left uncontrolled. Every priest has a natural ambition to see himsef advanced in his career, but not every priest has an opportunity to prove his "extraordinary" ability to his superior. The odds are against him; circumstances are unfavorable. He sees others, sometimes less deserving men, preferred, something that may cause disappointment; and a heart not controlled by spiritual motives may become embittered.

Yet the spiritual man will keep before his mind that, in the eyes of God, neither position, rank, nor distinction counts. Only correspondence with the grace of God is of value for eternity, for, whether a man be in a high or low position, all that he has and all that he accomplishes is due directly and

[6] Luke 22:24.
[7] Luke 22:26.

primarily to God's grace. The realization of this truth should be sufficient at all times to keep the spirit humble and the heart contrite. And thus the priest who lives the spirit of this prayer will deserve to have accepted by almighty God, not only the sacrifice of this day, but the sacrifices of his entire priestly life.

# CHAPTER 18

# Veni Sanctificator

Veni, sanctificator omnipotens aeterne Deus: et bene-
dic hoc sacrificium, tuo sancto nomini praeparatum.

The three divine Persons of the Blessed Trinity collaborated
in the work of the Incarnation and the Redemption. God the
Son, the second divine Person, in the course of time became
man and was born of the Blessed Mary ever Virgin. Only the
second Person of the Blessed Trinity became incarnate. Our
Lord Jesus Christ became "the author of [our] sanctification." [1] Yet the mystery of the Incarnation was brought about
by the cooperation of the first and third divine Persons. It
was the eternal will of the first Person, God the Father, that
prompted God the Son to assume human flesh when the time
was fulfilled. God the Father, too, accepted the work of the
Redemption and with complacency looked upon the sacrifice
of Calvary offered by His beloved Son, our Lord Jesus Christ.

In the Incarnation, the work of the Holy Ghost was no less
cooperative. We are told by the archangel Gabriel that the
Holy Ghost would come upon the Blessed Virgin and that the
power of the Most High would overshadow her.[2] The Holy
Scriptures inform us of "how God anointed Him with the Holy
Ghost. . . ." [3] The same Sacred Records speak of the redeem-

[1] *Summa theol.*, Ia, q.43, a.7.
[2] Luke 1:35.
[3] Acts 10:38.

ing power of the "blood of Christ, who by the Holy Ghost offered Himself unspotted unto God. . . ." [4]

In the Mass, which is the Eucharistic continuation of the Incarnation and the unbloody renewal of the Sacrifice of the Cross, the Blessed Trinity collaborates in a similar manner. For, in the Mass, the second Person of the Blessed Trinity, the person who became man, our Lord Jesus Christ, is both priest and victim. As on Calvary, so now here at the altar, He offers up Himself to His heavenly Father.

The liturgy, in the prayers of the Mass, breathes forth this dogmatic teaching. The "suscipe sancte Pater, omnipotens aeterne Deus" and the "Te igitur, clementissime Pater" are prayers that reflect the spirit of the whole Offertory and Canon.

The cooperation of the Holy Ghost is not ignored in the liturgy of the Mass, inasmuch as throughout the whole length of the Mass liturgy, we find the doxology concluding every prayer. "In unitate Spiritus Sancti" echoes through the Mass. Moreover, the "Veni Sanctificator" is a prayer that specifically invokes the assistance of the Holy Ghost. "Come, the Sanctifier, O almighty and eternal God, and bless this sacrifice which is prepared for the glory of Thy holy name." Of great antiquity, this invocation of the Holy Ghost is found in most liturgies of both the East and the West. The words of the priest become effective due to the power of the Holy Ghost. In the liturgy of St. James, first bishop of Jerusalem, we find the following invocation: "May the Spirit of God, by His sweet and glorious presence, sanctify this bread and cause it to become the body of Jesus Christ." St. John Damascene [5] says: "The change of the bread into Christ's body is caused

---

[4] Heb. 9:14.
[5] *De fide orthod.*, IV.

solely by the power of the Holy Ghost." [6] In the same article,
St. Thomas gives the words of St. John Damascene as his own
opinion. [7] The profession of faith as prescribed to the con-
verted Waldensians speaks of the priest as consecrating, not
by his own merits, but effecting the conversion "in verbo . . .
Creatoris et in virtute Spiritus Sancti." [8] In the fourth and
fifth centuries this dogmatic profession found expression in
liturgical art, for, at that age it was customary to preserve
the Sacred Host in a vessel of gold or silver, shaped in the
form of a dove, the symbol of the Holy Ghost.

In the Mass "the power of the Holy Ghost," as both the
Damascene and the Angelic Doctor express it, is the principal
cause of the change of the bread into Christ's body. In the Incarnation, the same Spirit of God, when the time was fulfilled,
overshadowed the Virgin Mary. A certain relationship between the mysteries, the Incarnation and the Transubstantiation, cannot remain unnoticed, for, the cooperation of the
creature, the Blessed Virgin in the Incarnation and the cooperation of the priest in the Mass, may be considered similar.

In the Annunciation, "the angel Gabriel was sent from God
into a city of Galilee, called Nazareth." [9] Every Mass, too, is
a message sent from heaven into the City of God, the Church.

> To a virgin espoused to a man whose name was Jo-
> seph, of the house of David; and the virgin's name was
> Mary. And the angel said to her: Fear not, Mary, for thou
> hast found grace with God. Behold thou shalt conceive
> in thy womb, and shalt bring forth a son; and thou shalt
> call His name Jesus. And Mary said to the angel: How

[6] *Summa theol.*, IIIa, q.78, a.4, ad 1.
[7] *Ibid.*
[8] Denzinger, *Enchiridion*, no. 424, "Professio fidei Durando de Osca et
sociis eius Waldensibus praescripta. Ex ep. 'Eius exemplo' ad archiepisc.
Terraconenseum, 18 Dec. 1208."
[9] Luke 1:26.

shall this be done because I know not man? And the angel answering, said to her: The Holy Ghost shall come upon thee and the power of the Most High shall overshadow thee. And therefore also the Holy which shall be born of thee shall be called the Son of God.[10]

At the Christian altar stands a priest, a man marked among men by reason of his celibacy. This priest is espoused to the house of David, to the Church; and as the Virgin Mary gave her flesh and blood to the Word incarnate, so the priest places the host on the paten, fills the chalice with wine, and with the voice of his mouth pronounces the words of the Consecration. Yet it is the Holy Ghost who gives power to the priest's words. The power of the Most High overshadows the priest, giving divine life and strength, supernatural power and vitality to his human words and bringing about the great work of the transubstantiation. For by the power of the Holy Ghost, the priest's words convert the substance of bread and wine into the body and blood, the humanity and divinity of our Lord Jesus Christ. Mary and the priest have similar missions. Mary was chosen to become the handmaid of the Lord in the work of the Incarnation. The priest is ordained to continue the Incarnation in the celebration of the Holy Mass. Both Mary and the priest are instruments in the hands of the Most High. Both are overshadowed by the Holy Ghost. Mary became the instrument of God at the Annunciation. The priest, overshadowed by the power of the Holy Ghost, is enabled to continue Mary's work when the third Person of the Blessed Trinity is invoked to descend upon him at his ordination to the priesthood. Here, at the Mass, the priest once more calls upon the Holy Ghost, the Sanctifier, the Spirit who is consubstantial with God the Father and God the Son, to come and bless this

[10] Luke 1:27–35.

Sacrifice, to penetrate these material gifts of bread and wine by His divine power, and to change them into the body and blood of Christ.

As the Holy Ghost through the ministry of the priest, who pronounces the words of consecration, brings about the transubstantiation, so the same divine Spirit, whenever the priest administers the sacraments, pours His graces into the hearts of the recipients. Whenever the priest pronounces the words of the form over the matter, it is the Holy Ghost who gives life to the sacramental sign, who animates and vivifies sacramental matter and form, and who confers supernatural graces. As the Holy Ghost, the Sanctifier, is invoked to bless this Sacrifice of the Mass and to change bread and wine into the body and blood of our Lord Jesus Christ, so the same divine Spirit is the Sanctifier of all the sacraments. He and no other is the giver of graces in the sacramentals and blessings. His gifts are "the spirit of wisdom, and of understanding, the spirit of counsel, and of fortitude, the spirit of knowledge, and of godliness," and "the spirit of the fear of the Lord." [11] "But the fruit of the Spirit is charity, joy, peace, patience, benignity, goodness, longanimity. . . ." [12] Our whole supernatural life, all our virtues and good deeds, are animated and perfected by graces that we receive from the Holy Spirit. "It belongs to the Holy Ghost, . . . to be the gift of [our] sanctification, to be the sign of [our] sanctification." [13] Yes, the supernatural life of our soul is the work of the Holy Ghost. It is by the operation of the graces of the divine Spirit that we "may be made partakers of the divine nature. . . ." [14] Without His divine assistance we fall back to the state of mortal sin, but with the

[11] Isa. 11:2–3.
[12] Gal. 5:22–23.
[13] *Summa theol.*, Ia, q. 43, a. 7.
[14] II Pet. 1:4.

help of His graces we become sons of God and messengers of heavenly tidings. His spirit illumines our understanding, strengthens our will, and leads us to the mansions of eternal bliss.

In a more particular way, the priest is indebted to the Holy Spirit since the priest's vocation does not deal in earthly goods or material values, but with graces and gifts that proceed from the Holy Ghost. The priest is the Holy Ghost's agent, His servant and His minister. Whatever we priests perform and achieve in the sacred ministry is not our personal accomplishment. Such accomplishment is the result of the outpouring of the graces and blessings of the Spirit of God.

# CHAPTER 19

## *The Lavabo*

Lavabo inter innocentes manus meas: et circumdabo altare tuum, Domine.

Ut audiam vocem laudis, et enarrem universa mirabilia tua.

Domine, dilexi decorem domus tuae, et locum habitationis gloriae tuae.

Ne perdas cum impiis, Deus, animam meam, et cum viris sanguinum vitam meam:

In quorum manibus iniquitates sunt: dextera eorum repleta est muneribus.

Ego autem in innocentia mea ingressus sum: redime me, et miserere mei.

Pes meus stetit in directo: in ecclesiis benedicam te, Domine.

Gloria Patri.

WHAT seems to be an interruption of the Offertory act and prayers (comprising those from the Creed to the Canon) occurs when the priest, who has been engaged in the Offertory of the Mass, goes to the Epistle side for the "Lavabo." Yet the recitation of the second part of the twenty-fifth psalm cannot be called an interruption of the Offertory. On the contrary, the purpose of the recitation is to emphasize the immaculate purity of the oblation of the New Testament, for the priest remembers the words of the prophet: "Who shall ascend into the mountain of the Lord: or who shall stand in His holy place? The innocent in hands and clean of heart. . . ." [1]

[1] Ps. 23:3–4.

The Sacrifice of the New Testament is more than the shedding of the blood of mere animals or the oblation of the products or riches of the land: it is the sacrifice of the body and blood of Jesus Christ. Hence the greatest possible reverence is required by the priest in offering this great sacrifice. "We are not wont," remarks St. Thomas, "to handle precious objects except the hands be washed; hence it seems indecent for anyone to approach so great a sacrament with hands that are, even literally, unclean." [2] Also, the "Lavabo" has another significance. "The washing of the extremities of the limbs," the Angelic Doctor continues, "denotes cleansing from even the smallest sins." [3] Verily, the sacrifice of the divine Lamb must not be stained by even the slightest impurities of the priest: angelic innocence is required. The "Lavabo" is in accordance with ancient customs, for, the priest of the Old Covenant, before approaching the altar to offer sacrifice or before entering the tabernacle of the Lord, was required under pain of death to wash his hands and feet, as a sign of bodily and spiritual cleanliness. As the hand is the "organ of organs," [4] the symbolic cleansing of the hands suffices in the New Covenant in denoting the purity of the entire man. In this connection, St. Cyril of Jerusalem fittingly remarks: "This betokens that ye should be cleansed from all sins and stains; since, as by the hands are meant our doings, the washing thereof fitly denotes the purity of our actions." [5]

"I will wash my hands among the innocent." The Psalmist suggests that the priest be in innocence or among the perfect, that is, be perfect himself. The washing of hands in innocence is, indeed, required of the priest so that he be in a disposition

[2] *Summa theol.*, IIIa, q. 83, a. 5, ad 1.
[3] *Loc. cit.*
[4] *Ibid.*
[5] James M<sup>c</sup>Swiney, *Translation of the Psalms and Canticles*, p. 85.

to approach worthily the altar of the Lord. For if he should not be free from sin, his "Lavabo" would become the hypocritical action of another Pontius Pilate. From this sin protect Thy priests, O Lord! "And I will compass Thine altar, O Lord." As the priests and participants reclined around the banquet table at the sacred repasts of olden times, so the priests of the Church of Christ will spend their time "at" and "around" the altar of the Lord.

"That I may hear the voice of praise, and tell of all Thy wondrous works." The man who meditates upon the truth, the man who sees the works of this world in the light of religion discovers new values. He sees the wonderful hand of God in all things. To him the world becomes a praise of God; and the Psalmist prays that he may be favored with an intelligent ear in order to hear these voices of praise.

"O Lord, I have loved the beauty of Thy house, and the place where Thy glory dwelleth." With filial confidence the priest lays open his heart. He feels at home in the Father's house, appreciates the beauty of the sanctuary, and is happy to be near the tabernacle of the Lord. Many a dark hour encompasses the life of a priest, many a temptation aims to lure him away from the place assigned to him by his sacred calling, but the good priest is always happy in his vocation, at home in the priesthood and thankful to the Lord for his ordination. He never feels sorry that he has become a priest; he is happy that he has never chosen any other profession. "I give Him thanks who hath strengthened me, even to Christ Jesus our Lord, for that He hath counted me faithful, putting me in the ministry. . . ." [6]

The priest who really loves the beauty of the house of God takes a personal interest in the decorations of the church and

[6] I Tim. 1:12.

altar. To leave the adornment of the altar or the care of the altar linen entirely in the hands of the sacristan, the priest's housekeeper, some pious ladies, or the altar society, without the least supervision, would be neglect on the part of the pastor. Disgust is experienced when one notices carelessness with regard to articles that pertain to the altar, that is, books, altar cards, altar linen, candles, wine and water cruets, finger towels, and so forth. The excuse that there are no religious sisters to take care of the altar would be an acknowledgment of a person's loss of zeal for the glory of the house of God. There are two things that make up the beauty of the altar: the liturgical exactness and a certain personal touch in the arrangement of the decorations. Where the pastor observes the rubrics and delights in displaying his genius and good taste in decorating the altar, there "the Lord . . . is clothed with beauty," [7] and there "holiness becometh Thy house, O Lord. . . ." [8] Moreover, the eyes of both priest and laymen find rest and delight, and their souls find inspiration and devotion.

While the priest is still reflecting on the beauty and glory of the place where the Lord dwelleth, a thought of the hostile world outside the temple comes to his mind and, in the fear that enters his soul, he cries out to the Lord: "Take not away my soul, O God, with the wicked, nor my life with men of blood. In whose hands are iniquities: their right hand is filled with gifts." Let me not be involved in the fate awaiting the evil ones. Save me, O God, that I may not die the sudden and bitter death of the godless, of men whose hearts are filled with wicked thoughts and iniquities. Protect me against the man who works deeds of injustice and who is filled with corruption

[7] Ps. 92:1.
[8] Ps. 92:5.

and bribery. "But as for me," dear Lord, I have despised the riches of this world and the ways of the wicked. "I have walked in my innocence: redeem me and have mercy on me." I have confidence in Thy justice, O God. Extend Thy protecting arm over me and save me from my enemies. I have walked the way of the Lord: "My foot hath stood in the direct way." I will continue in my work as a priest in the meetings of Thy people, "in the churches I will bless Thee, O Lord. Glory be."

# CHAPTER 20

## *The Prayer of Intercession*

Suscipe, sancta Trinitas, hanc oblationem, quam tibi offerimus ob memoriam passionis, resurrectionis, et ascensionis Jesu Christi Domini nostri: et in honorem beatae Mariae semper Virginis, et beati Joannis Baptistae, et sanctorum Apostolorum Petri et Pauli, et istorum, et omnium Sanctorum: ut illis proficiat ad honorem, nobis autem ad salutem: et illi pro nobis intercedere dignentur in caelis, quorum memoriam agimus in terris, Per eumdem Christum Dominum nostrum. Amen.

ON ACCOUNT of the limitations of the human language, we cannot express in a single sentence or in one short prayer all the mysteries and truths that are contained in the Eucharistic Sacrifice. We have to proceed step by step, and only gradually are we able to unfold the beauty of the Sacrifice of the New Testament. The truth of this is verified in the oblation prayers of the Mass. The first of the oblation prayers is the "Suscipe sancte Pater." This prayer is addressed to God the Father, the first Person of the Blessed Trinity. In the prayer, "Veni Sanctificator," the third Person of the Blessed Trinity is invoked to "bless this sacrifice which is prepared to the glory of Thy holy name." In order not to overlook an important fact, let us add that the Eucharistic Sacrifice is, in a special manner, the work of the second Person of the Holy Trinity. Now, in this present prayer, "Suscipe sancta Trinitas," the oneness of God is set forth, for this prayer is addressed to the Blessed Trinity. The

Eucharistic Sacrifice is offered up to the honor, glory, and praise of the triune God, of the Blessed Trinity.

The Holy Trinity is petitioned to accept this oblation "in memory of the passion, resurrection, and ascension of our Lord Jesus Christ." The Eucharistic Sacrifice is celebrated in this intention, namely, in memory of the passion and death of our Lord Jesus Christ. But this sacrifice is not the commemoration of a dead and lifeless body, but the signification of the glorious Christ, who overcame death, who arose from the dead, and who ascended into heaven.

While we offer the Eucharistic gifts to the triune God in memory of our Lord Jesus Christ, we unite our prayers with those of the saints and we offer this oblation "in honor of the Blessed Mary ever Virgin, of blessed John the Baptist, of the holy apostles Peter and Paul, of these and of all the saints; that it may be to their honor and to our salvation: and may they vouchsafe to intercede for us in heaven, whose memory we celebrate here on earth."

Why do we commemorate the saints during the celebration of the Holy Mass? By its own virtue, the Eucharistic Sacrifice is certainly self-sufficient. Since the Eucharistic Sacrifice is the sacrifice of the body and blood of our Lord, it is of infinite value and does not require any additional help or merits. From the beginning of the early Church, however, the custom has been to mention the saints during the celebration of the Mass. The reasons for that practice are manifold. Where honor and respect are shown to God's chosen friends, homage is paid to almighty God at the same time. "Devotion," remarks St. Thomas, "to God's holy ones, dead or living, does not terminate in them, but passes on to God, so far as we honor God in His servants." [1]

[1] *Summa theol.*, IIa IIae, q.82, a.2, ad 3.

In remembering the saints, tribute is paid to almighty God. For, the miracles and wonderful deeds of the saints, their humiliations, sacrifices, prayers, acts of penance, their triumphs, and their glory are hymns of praise to the holy name of God. Should we not pray that the knowledge, the heroism, and the virtuous attainments of the saints be recognized by all men? May we not hope that their veneration will spread, and that the kingdom of God on earth will be extended and perfected?

In the presence of a sacrifice so holy, so august, and so sublime as that of the Sacrifice of the body and blood of our Lord Jesus Christ, man, poor, humble man, becomes conscious of his own weakness and spiritual unworthiness. It is natural for man to seek help and to look for support in his distress by imploring God's best friends; and his best friends are the saints. Man beseeches them to be his advocates and to intercede for him before the throne of God.

Do the saints know that we pray to them, and how do our prayers become known to the saints, since "the dead, if we consider their natural condition, do not know what takes place in the world, especially the interior movements of the heart?" [2]

To these two questions, the Angelic Doctor quotes the answer of St. Jerome who said: "If the apostles and martyrs, while yet in the body and having to be solicitous for themselves, pray for others, how much the more now that they have the crown of victory and triumph." [3] For St. Thomas says: "Whatever it is fitting the blessed should know about what happens to us, even as regards the interior movements of the heart, is made known to them in the Word: and it is most becoming to their exalted position that they should know the

[2] *Ibid.*, q. 83, a. 4, ad 2.
[3] Quoted from St. Jerome by St. Thomas, *Summa theol.* IIa IIae, q. 83, a. 11.

petitions we make to them by word or thought; and consequently the petitions which we raise to them are known to them through divine manifestation." [4]

This is the teaching of St. Thomas. This has been the practice of the Church throughout the ages. How happy we are in the realization that we are not left to ourselves in this struggle of life! Before the throne of the Blessed Trinity we have powerful friends and advocates: there our Blessed Mother intercedes for us; the greatest among the prophets of old, St. John the Baptist, takes our part; the princes of the apostles, Sts. Peter and Paul, lead the endless procession of saints and blessed who ever stand ready to join our petitions. And there our guardian angel, as well as our own patron saint and the whole choir of favorite saints, lend a willing ear and intercede for us in the concerns we entrust to their mediation. They certainly will not fail us while we assist at Mass and ask for their prayers.

[4] *Summa theol.*, IIa IIae, q.83, a.4, ad 2.

# CHAPTER 21

# *The* Orate Fratres

Orate, fratres: ut meum ac vestrum sacrificium acceptabile fiat apud Deum Patrem omnipotentem.

Suscipiat Dominus sacrificium de manibus tuis ad laudem et gloriam nominis sui, ad utilitatem quoque nostram, totiusque Ecclesiae suae sanctae. Amen.

Secreta.

Per omnia saecula saeculorum. Amen.

AFTER invoking the help of the saints in heaven, the priest turns from the altar and faces the people. He implores the faithful to pray: "Orate, fratres."

The priest addresses his brethren; the whole congregation; all the faithful without distinction; men and women, young and old. They are all the members of his family, they are all united, forming the kingdom of God on earth; constituting the mystical body of Christ. ". . . All you are brethren . . . for one is your Father, who is in heaven." [1] The apostles, when addressing the Christians, used this expression, and the faithful have ever been honored by this title. For we all should be "brethren," united and one in our Lord Jesus Christ.

"Brethren, pray that my and your sacrifice may become acceptable to God the Father almighty." The people join the priest in prayers. Is not this sacrifice offered by Christ, who is priest and victim, in itself acceptable to God? Can the sacrifice

[1] Matt. 23:8, 9.

of Christ be improved or perfected by the prayers of men?

The value and perfection of a sacrifice are determined by, (1) the sanctity of the priest, (2) the value of the sacrificial gift, and (3) the perfection of the sacrificial action.

Let us take up this question and investigate each one of these three points. First, the sanctity of the priest. There can be no doubt that Christ possessed infinite sanctity and that the holiness of His priesthood cannot be increased or perfected by the prayers and good works of the faithful. In place of Christ, the invisible priest, His minister on earth performs the sacred function. Whatever the priest does, in the name and by order of Christ, has the value of the One who commissioned the priest. Yet the priest, though representing, in his official capacity, Christ at the altar, has not lost his human personality. As an individual the priest is capable of a greater or lesser personal sanctity. Does the personal sanctity of the celebrant give a greater value to the Eucharistic Sacrifice? Or does the lack of devotion decrease or lessen the worth of holy Mass? This is the problem that we wish to investigate now. May the Angelic Doctor be our guide.

In answer to the question, whether the Mass of a sinful priest is of less worth than the Mass of a good priest, St. Thomas answers as follows: "There are two things to be considered in the Mass: namely, the sacrament itself, which is the chief thing; and the prayers which are offered up in the Mass for the quick and the dead. So far as the Mass itself is concerned, the Mass of a wicked priest is not of less value than that of a good priest, because the same sacrifice is offered by both.

"Again, the prayer put up in the Mass can be considered in two respects: first of all, in as far as it has its efficacy from the devotion of the priest interceding, and in this respect there

is no doubt but that the Mass of the better priest is more fruitful. In another respect, inasmuch as the prayer is said by the
priest in the Mass in the place of the entire Church, of which
the priest is the minister; and this ministry remains even
in sinful men. . . . Hence, in this respect the prayer even of
the sinful priest is fruitful, not only that which he utters in
the Mass, but likewise all those he recites in the ecclesiastical
offices, wherein he takes the place of the Church. On the other
hand, his private prayers are not fruitful, according to Proverbs: [2] 'He that turneth away his ears from hearing the law,
his prayers shall be an abomination.' " [3]

Christ, in His infinite charity, has placed His sacred body
and blood in the hands of the Church so that His mystical
body, the Church, may have a worthy gift to offer to God the
Father. Hence, the first Person of the Blessed Trinity can forever look upon the bride of Christ and upon the Eucharistic
Sacrifice, offered by her, with infinite pleasure and satisfaction. Even if an unworthy priest should happen to stand at
the altar, the Sacrifice of the holy Mass itself will be pleasing
to God the Father as long as the priest performs the sacred
function correctly and in the name and by the authority of
the Church. However, the private prayers of an unfortunate
priest are an abomination to the Lord. Nevertheless in his
official capacity as priest and representative of the Church,
the powers and functions of such a priest remain unimpaired.

Secondly, the sacrificial gifts, too, must be considered. The
body and blood of Christ are of infinite value. There are no objects more holy in the entire world than the Eucharistic
species of bread and wine, under the appearance of which
our Lord offers Himself on the altar of the Catholic Church.

[2] Prov. 28:9.
[3] *Summa theol.*, IIIa, q. 82, a. 6.

The infinite value of Christ's body and blood cannot be increased or decreased by values that man has to offer. Yet the faithful and the priest may join their good works and pious prayers to the Eucharistic gift; may offer them in conjunction with the Sacrifice of the holy Mass. Here again God the Father will be better pleased by the Eucharistic Sacrifice, offered to His omnipotence, by a priest and by an attending congregation united in adding their own good works and pious prayers. Do we human beings not like to receive our pay check in a neat, clean envelope? Do we not appreciate more the gifts that come to us handsomely decorated and properly packed? Certainly the piety of the priest contributes, in no small degree, toward the pleasure God almighty will show when bestowing His gifts and graces for the sake of the Eucharistic Sacrifice. In like manner, the piety of the laity, attending Mass devotedly, will be a factor. Where people unite in piously assisting at Mass, the benevolent eye of a merciful God will not be wanting. Graces and spiritual benefits will flow with greater abundance from an altar surrounded by a pious and holy congregation. This effect the Prince of the apostles, St. Peter, had in mind when he wrote and exhorted all the Christians to be "a holy priesthood, to offer up spiritual sacrifices, acceptable to God by Jesus Christ." [4]

Thirdly, in holy Mass the sacrificial action takes place at the moment of the double Consecration, when the body and blood of our Lord, Jesus Christ, under the appearances of bread and wine, is mystically slain or immolated. Hence the dual Consecration constitutes the very essence of the sacrifice. Without a double Consecration no sacrifice would be performed. It is true that bread and wine are required to be present at the altar, but merely the oblation of these two would

[4] I Pet. 2:5.

not bring about a sacrifice. Only when the body and blood of our Lord is placed in a state of sacrifice, brought about by the dual Consecration of the sacred species, is the sacrifice perfected. The body and blood of Christ becomes mystically immolated; the sacrifice of our Lord on the cross is renewed; the memorial of Christ's sacred passion and death is celebrated. "Whenever the commemoration of this sacrifice is celebrated, the work of our redemption is enacted." [5] The Communion of the celebrant, in like manner, is required to bring the Eucharistic Sacrifice to an end, yet the consuming of the sacred species is not the constituting of the sacrifice. The sacrifice was actually and really constituted at the moment of the dual consecration when Christ's body and blood were mystically immolated, or sacrificed by the eternal high priest, Jesus Christ Himself.

These, as we have seen, are the essentials of the Eucharistic Sacrifice: (1) the sacrificial gift of the body and blood of our Lord, Jesus Christ (2) mystically slain or immolated in the sacrificial action of the dual Consecration (3) by the priest representing the eternal high priest Himself. But these essentials are not enacted by themselves, bare and plain, but are surrounded by the liturgy of the Church. The liturgy, that is, the prayers and ceremonies making up the Mass rite may be compared to the flowers, decorations, and adornments surrounding a picture or statue of a saint or a prominent citizen. The picture or statue is not, in itself, constituted by the decorations. The statue remains the same whether placed atop a beautiful pedestal or placed in the midst of miserable surroundings. But the beauty of the statue or picture is certainly enhanced by the background and surroundings, including

[5] Secret of the Ninth Sunday after Pentecost. Quoted by St. Thomas, in his *Summa theol.*, IIIa, q. 83, a. 1.

the position of the decorations and adornments. So it is with the liturgy of the Mass, surrounding the essentials of the Eucharistic Sacrifice. When we consider the prayers and ceremonies of the Mass, it is certain that the sanctity and devotion of both priests and people play a prominent part. For, the Mass liturgy depends greatly on the exactness with which the prayers are said and with which the ceremonies are performed, and on the spirit of piety animating the celebrant. And here the priest is perfectly correct in asking the laity to increase its devotion and to join its prayers with those he is sending to heaven. Now we can understand, too, the prayer of the priest: that his sacrifice and theirs "be acceptable to God the Father almighty": that the infinite sacrifice of Jesus Christ, by its very nature always acceptable to God the Father, may be adorned and rendered more pleasing, though in a limited way, by the devotion of the priest and the piety of the faithful.

In response to the prayer of the priest, the acolyte, representing the congregation, replies in the same spirit when he says: "May the Lord receive this sacrifice out of your hands, to the praise and glory of His name, to our usefulness and to that of all His holy Church." Yes, the praise and glory of the holy name of God is the primary object of every Mass. The Sacrifice of the divine Lamb is, first, an act of worship and adoration of the Divinity. Let us pray that we human beings, too, may derive some benefit from this Sacrifice, and that it may be a spiritual benefit to us who are now assisting in the celebration of Mass. May it also be a source of spiritual refreshment and graces to all Catholic people.

According to the time and the occasion, the priest silently says the "Secret," and presents to God a prayer that sets forth the special purpose for which the Mass is celebrated. After completing this prayer, the priest ends the "Secret" with the words of the doxology: "Per omnia saecula saeculorum. Amen," and begins to say or sing the "Preface," the great song of thanksgiving.

# CHAPTER 22

# *The Preface*

P. Dominus vobiscum.
S. Et cum spiritu tuo.
P. Sursum corda.
S. Habemus ad Dominum.
P. Gratias agamus Domino Deo nostro.
S. Dignum et justum est.
P. Vere dignum et justum est, aequum et salutare, nos tibi semper, et ubique gratias agere: Domine sancte, Pater omnipotens, aeterne Deus: per Christum Dominum nostrum. Per quem majestatem tuam laudant Angeli, adorant Dominationes, tremunt Potestates. Caeli caelorumque Virtutes, ac beata Seraphim, socia exsultatione concelebrant. Cum quibus et nostras voces ut admitti jubeas, deprecamur, supplici confessione dicentes.

THE Mass is the praise of God. Jesus Christ offers up Himself to the honor and glory of His heavenly Father. The Church, by the Sacrifice of the Mass, renders to the Almighty the praise and adoration that the Christian community owes to God. It is difficult to imagine that this fundamental idea would not find expression in the liturgy. Correspondingly, we find references to the praise of God throughout the length of the sacred function. Thus, pointing to a few instances, in the Commemoration for the Living, the Eucharistic Sacrifice is called "the sacrifice of praise." The great doxology states: that through, with, and in Christ, all honor and glory is given to God the

120

Father almighty in unity with the Holy Ghost. Here, in the great doxology, Christ gives praise to the first and third Persons in the Godhead; in the Gloria and in the Preface the Church chants a song of jubilation to the triune God. The distinction between the Gloria and the Preface is this: the latter changes according to the feasts and seasons; the former is always the same. Again, the Gloria is Trinitarian; the Preface is addressed to God the Father.

Why, we may ask, should this prayer of praise be said in a loud voice (*clara voce—Missal*) in a Low Mass, or be sung in a High Mass? Is not the praise that comes from the heart and offered to God in a silent prayer sufficient to honor God? We may detect a reason for this in a reflection of St. Thomas that may be appropriately applied to the Preface:

> We employ words in speaking to God not indeed to make known our thoughts to Him who is the searcher of hearts, but that we may bring ourselves and our hearts to reverence Him. Consequently we need to praise God with our lips, not indeed for His sake, but for our own sake since by praising Him our devotion is aroused towards Him, according to the psalmist who says: "The sacrifice of praise shall glorify Me, and there is the way by which I will show him the salvation of God." [1] And for as much as man, by praising God, ascends in his affections to God, by so much is he withdrawn from things opposed to God, according to Isaias: "For My praise I will bridle thee lest thou shouldst perish." [2] The praise of the lips is also profitable to others by inciting their affec‧ tions toward God; wherefore it is written: "His praise shall be always in my mouth," and farther on: "Let the meek hear and rejoice. O magnify the Lord with me." [3]

1 Ps. 49:23.
2 Isa. 48:9.
3 Ps. 33:1–4; *Summa theol.*, IIa IIae, q.91, a.1.

This thought shows us why song and music are employed at times; for song and music are, as we have seen above, the best means to arouse man's devotion toward God and to render to the Almighty the praise and adoration of man's body and soul.[4]

"Sursum corda." "Let us lift up our hearts with our hands to the Lord in the heavens." [5] "I will praise Thee, O Lord, my God, with my whole heart, and I will glorify Thy name forever." [6] "Habemus ad Dominum." "My soul doth magnify the Lord." [7] "Praise the Lord, O my soul, in my life I will praise the Lord: I will sing to my God as long as I shall be." [8] ". . . My mouth shall praise Thee with joyful lips." [9]

"Gratias agamus Domino Deo nostro." "Dignum et justum est." "Offer to God the sacrifice of praise," [10] exhorts the Psalmist. "It is good to give praise to the Lord and to sing to Thy name, O most High." [11] "O praise the Lord all ye nations: praise Him all ye people." [12] "What shall I render to the Lord for all the things that He hath rendered to me?" [13]

To give thanks to God is a holy obligation of humanity, for, the dignity (*dignum*) of man requires that he acknowledge goods and benefits received from the merciful hand of his heavenly Father. It is just (*justum*) to render thanks to the Almighty, because the virtue of justice prompts man to gratitude. Moreover, it is becoming and proper (*aequum*) to return thanks for gifts and graces received. Finally, it is salutary

[4] *Ibid.*, a.2.
[5] Lam. 3:41
[6] Ps. 85:12.
[7] Luke 1:46.
[8] Ps. 145:2.
[9] Ps. 62:6.
[10] Ps. 49:14.
[11] Ps. 91:2.
[12] Ps. 116:1.
[13] Ps. 115:12.

(*salutare*) to us, for, a gift acknowledged stimulates the donor to still greater benevolence. Hence the priest is justified in singing: "It is truly meet and just, right, and wholesome, that we should always, and everywhere give thanks to Thee, O holy Lord, Father almighty, eternal God, through Christ our Lord." "In all things give thanks; for this is the will of God in Christ Jesus. . . ." [14] "Giving thanks always for all things, in the name of our Lord, Jesus Christ, to God and the Father. . . ." [15]

Now that the priest, in the name of the Church, has given thanks to God for all the good things in general, he specifies, according to the ecclesiastical times and seasons, some particular blessings the Church is indebted for, since the Church owes special thanks to God, because "by the mystery of the Word made flesh a new ray of Thy glory has appeared to the eyes of our souls" (Nativity); because "the salvation of mankind [was] be wrought on the Cross" (Passion); because "Christ our Passover was sacrificed for us" (Easter). In this, or similar ways, the foremost seasons or feasts of the liturgical year are commemorated in the spirit of gratitude and praise.

The Church exults in the glorious deeds of our Lord. Jubilant and glorifying God, she forgets, as it were, her earthly bondage. Filled with joy, the heavens open. Praising the Lord, she calls upon the powers invisible to aid her in magnifying the name of God. "Through whom the angels praise Thy majesty, the dominations adore Thee; the heavens and the powers of heavens, together with the blessed Seraphim, in united joy, announce Thy praise. With these we ask you to join our voices that we may profess while saying as follows": "Bless the Lord, all ye His angels: you that are mighty in

[14] I Thess. 5:18.
[15] Eph. 5:20.

strength, and execute His words, hearkening to the voice of His orders." [16] "Praise ye the Lord from the heavens: praise ye Him in the high places. Praise ye Him, all His angels: praise ye Him, all His hosts." [17]

What a dignity to men to lift up their hearts to God! What an honor for the priest to join the choir of the angelic spirits! What a noble task of life to forget our little selves and to think of the glory and praise of the Almighty! And where is there a place better suited, or a time more eminently fitted for this act, than here in the Mass? When the Preface is said or sung, let us raise our minds and hearts to the heights of the celestial courts. We are sure that the faint sounds of the priest's voice, when reaching the ceiling of heaven, will be echoed a thousand times, and will be magnified and perfected by the celestial acoustics. Angels will rejoice, and the heavenly Father will be pleased, for, the song that the priest intones is not of his own making, but is the song of the divine Lamb.

"And I beheld, and lo a Lamb stood upon Mount Sion, and with him an hundred forty-four thousand, having his name, and the name of his Father, written on their foreheads. And I heard a voice from heaven, as the noise of many waters, and as the voice of great thunder; and the voice which I heard was as the voice of harpers harping on their harps. And they sung as it were a new canticle, before the throne. . . ." [18] "And singing the canticle of Moses, the servant of God, and the canticle of the Lamb, saying: Great and wonderful are Thy works, O Lord God Almighty; just and true are Thy ways, O King of ages." [19]

[16] Ps. 102:20–21.
[17] Ps. 148:1–2.
[18] Apoc. 14:1–3.
[19] Apoc. 15:3.

# CHAPTER 23

# *The Trisagium*

Sanctus, Sanctus, Sanctus, Dominus Deus Sabaoth.
Pleni sunt coeli et terra gloria tua.
Hosanna in excelsis.
Benedictus qui venit in nomine Domini.
Hosanna in excelsis.

THE Preface has been said in a loud voice or solemnly sung by the priest. The celebrant can have no greater faculty at his disposal than that of the human voice. Yet, the words that follow the Preface are so profound and holy of meaning, that they can be grasped only in silent prayer and meditation. Joining the choir of the angels in heaven and taking part spiritually in the triumphant procession of our Savior, the priest prays the words of the "Trisagium." St. Thomas points out the two-fold aspect of this prayer, when he says: "The priest and the people devoutly praise Christ's Godhead, saying with the angels: Holy, Holy, Holy; and His humanity, saying with the children: Blessed is He that comes." [1]

The "Sanctus" of the Holy Mass is evidently taken from the prophet Isaias, who, in a vision, heard the seraphim chanting one to another and saying: "Holy, Holy, Holy, the Lord God of hosts, all the earth is full of His glory." [2] St. John, when writing his revelations, reports to us words of a similar nature:

[1] *Summa theol.*, IIIa, q. 83, a. 4.
[2] Isa. 6:3.

"And the four living creatures had each of them six wings.
. . . And they rested not day and night, saying: Holy, holy,
holy, Lord God Almighty, who was, and who is, and who is
to come." [3]

God is called "holy." What is in the name? Because God
does not belong to any class of beings or is not to be dis-
tinguished from any other being of its own kind, He is, strictly
speaking, without a name. "The reason why God has no name,"
St. Thomas explains, "or is said to be above being named, is
because His essence is above all that we understand about
God and signify in word." [4] For "we can give a name to anything in as far as we can understand it. In this life we cannot
see the essence of God; but we know God from creatures as
their principle, and also by way of excellence and remotion.
In this way, therefore, He can be named by us from creatures,
yet not so that the name which signifies Him expresses the
divine essence in itself." [5] If we proceed along these lines,
and apply certain marks or qualities of creatures to God, it is
to be understood that they define the Divinity only in an
imperfect, inadequate, analogical way. The New Testament
in naming the Divinity, in most instances adopted the usage
of speech found in the Old Testament. In the Old Covenant
there were seven holy names given to God. He was called:
"the Powerful," "the Highest," "the Holy," "the Jehovah," or
"the Being" (I am who am), "the Strong One," "the Adorable,"
and "the Lord." Most of these names refer to the might or
foremost position of God, the qualifications that impressed the
minds of the Israelites. But, by calling God "the Holy One,"
the ethical goodness of the Divinity was expressed.

The Holy Scriptures speak frequently of the holiness of

[3] Apoc. 4:8.
[4] *Op. cit.*, Ia, q. 13, a. 1, ad 1.
[5] *Ibid.*, a. 1.

God. The last book of Moses, Deuteronomy, when invoking the name of the Lord, says this: "God is faithful and without any iniquity, He is just and right." [6] The psalms praise the Divinity in the following words: "Thou hast loved justice, and hated iniquity." [7] And "The Lord is just in all His ways: and holy in all His works." [8] In the first book of Kings the inspired writer expresses the same idea in similar words: "There is none holy as the Lord is. . . ." [9] St. Luke states as follows: "None is good, but God alone." [10]

Let us ask: what is sanctity? When do we ascribe sanctity to somebody? When do we say that somebody is holy? Let us analyze the term "sanctity," or "holiness."

The thought first occurring to most people is that a person who is holy is free from sin. Sanctity is considered simply as the lack of sin or as the absence of any imperfection. We think of a holy person as him who in no way turns from the will of God or a person who is in full conformity with the divine will. To the saint, disobedience to the laws of God is unknown.

This popular idea is, however, only a negative consideration. The idea of sanctity, in its positive aspect, involves goodness and perfection. In the human being, goodness does not rest in the perfection of the individual, for the goodness of man is derived from the union of the creature with God. The union of a saint with his Lord and God arises from faithful adherence of the holy person to the will of the Creator, and this faithfulness is achieved by the strict fulfillment of the laws of God.

[6] Deut. 32:4.
[7] Ps. 44:8.
[8] Ps. 144:17.
[9] I Kings 2:2.
[10] Luke 18:19.

Besides goodness and perfection, a second item enters the idea of sanctity. Holiness consists in more than an occasional conformity with the will of God. Sanctity presupposes stability or firmness, a state in which a person is permanently good and perfect, a state in which a person lives a life in perfect conformity with the will of God.

These requirements, then, are the two pillars on which sanctity rests: first, goodness and perfection, and, secondly, stability or firmness. This idea conforms exactly with the idea of the Angelic Doctor, for he says as follows: "The word 'sanctity' seems to have two significations. In one way it denotes purity. . . . In another way it denotes firmness." [11] The great teacher explains that

> Purity is necessary in order that the mind be applied to God, since the human mind is soiled by contact with inferior things, even as all things depreciate by admixture with baser things, for instance, silver being mixed with lead. Now, in order for the mind to be united to the Supreme Being it must be withdrawn from inferior things: and hence it is that without purity, the mind cannot be applied to God. Wherefore it is written: "Follow peace with all men, and holiness: without which no man shall see God." [12] Again, firmness is required for the mind to be applied to God, for it is applied to Him as its first beginning and last end and such things must needs be most immovable. Hence the Apostle said: "I am sure that neither death, nor life . . . shall be able to separate us from the love of God. . . ." [13]

So far we have studied the philosophical concept of sanctity as applied to the human being. Our next and final step will be

11 *Op. cit.*, IIa IIae, q. 81, a. 8.
12 Heb. 12:14.
13 Rom. 8:38–39; *Summa theol.*, *loc. cit.*

to investigate the idea of sanctity in the Divine Being. Let us proceed along the same lines.

We have seen that the first pillar on which sanctity rests is goodness and perfection. In the human being, unqualified goodness is not found in mere existence, or in activity, be it ever so noble, exercised on himself or on other creatures. The unqualified goodness of the human being is derived from the activity that makes up his union with God.

In God Himself, however, it is impossible that goodness and perfection be relative in character. It is impossible that the goodness that makes God good should be derived in any way from an object or thing external to the Divine Being. For, in God goodness and being are really the same. These attributes differ only in the mind of men. When we speak of the goodness of God, we think of the Divine Being as the ultimate end of our desires. And in God His goodness belongs essentially to His Divine Being.

God is, furthermore, good in an immanent way. He is supremely good because there are no limitations in the Divine Being. Since the being and goodness of God are really the same, it follows that His goodness is as unchangeable as His Divine Being is immutable. The goodness of God is ever stable and firm, never subject to any increase or decrease. The goodness of God is infinite. ". . . I am the Lord, and I change not," [14] exclaimed the prophet Malachias.

Since the goodness of God is of a permanent nature, God is truly and essentially holy. Hence the sanctity of God rests philosophically, as we have seen, on the same pillars as does the sanctity of men: goodness and stability. The sanctity of God is supreme: sanctity is essential to the Divine Being.

Such is the beauty of Christian philosophy. But this was

[14] Mal. 3:6.

not the point of view of a pagan world. The deities of paganism are stained with imperfections and sin. To the Christian mind, however, it is not difficult to see that God not only does not commit any sin (*impeccantia*) but cannot commit any sin (*impeccabilitas*).

The sanctity of God is a profound mystery of our holy faith. Fear and awe seize man: ". . . Holy and terrible is His name. . . ." [15] When the name of Jehovah was solemnly pronounced once a year by the high priest, every Israelite who stood in the Temple grounds fell on his knees in an act of worship and adoration. Could it be different in the New Covenant? Surely the profound mystery of God's sanctity or God's love calls forth the deepest respect and reverence of both priest and people. The priest bends down and the laity falls on its knees when the holiness of God is adored at the end of the "Preface": "Sanctus, Sanctus, Sanctus, Dominus Deus Sabaoth," the almighty Majesty of the celestial armies, the Lord God of heaven and earth, "Pleni sunt caeli et terra gloria tua." "Hosanna in excelsis."

"Hosanna" has become to us an exclamation of jubilation. Yet, originally it was a cry for help, a prayer to be saved: "O Lord, save me; O Lord, give good success." [16] On each of the first six days of the feast of Tabernacles, this verse of King David was sung while priests and people passed in solemn procession around the altar of holocausts. On the seventh day, also called "the day of the great Hosanna," the altar was surrounded seven times while green palm branches with myrtles attached were held in the hand, and this same verse was chanted.[17]

"Benedictus qui venit in nomine Domini." This is the

[15] Ps. 110:9.
[16] Ps. 117:25.
[17] Cf. J. McSwiney, *Psalms and Canticles*, p. 502.

twenty-sixth verse of the one hundred seventeenth psalm; the verse that follows the "Hosanna." The sense of this twenty-sixth verse is: Blessed in the name of Jehovah is he that cometh. The words of this verse remind us of the way the Lord God wished the priests to bless the people of Israel. "And the Lord spoke to Moses, saying: Say to Aaron and his sons: Thus shall you bless the children of Israel, and you shall say to them: The Lord bless thee, and keep thee. The Lord show His face to thee, and have mercy on thee. The Lord turn His countenance to thee, and give thee peace." [18]

This or a similar prayer was the formula pronounced by the priest when blessing the worshipers in the Temple of Jerusalem. From the Midrash, we learn that the twenty-sixth verse of the one hundred seventeenth psalm, "Blessed is he that cometh in the name of the Lord," was the customary welcome by which the people of Jerusalem greeted the pilgrims for the feast, upon their arrival in the Holy City. With the same chant, Christ, upon His solemn entry into the City of Jerusalem, when people escorted Him with palm branches in their hands, was welcomed and greeted as the promised Messias. The greetings our Savior received were jubilant and brilliant. It was a triumphant procession. The people were animated by a spirit of gladness and joyfulness. They were happy to have in the midst of them the long expected Messias. They wished to pay homage and honor to their Messianic king.

Yet this entrance into the Holy City was a humble one. The men and women who marched in the procession were mostly poor people, the country people of Galilee. The upper classes of the capital city, the priests, the Pharisees, the Sadducees, and the scribes, were all conspicuous by their absence.

[18] Num. 6:22–26.

It was a religious procession. Though there may have been in the procession certain people who entertained political hopes and who were moved by worldly aspirations, the procession had no political coloring. No slaves, prisoners, or war trophies were among them. No worldly victories were celebrated. A religious character pervaded the procession. Religious songs were sung, and a religious spirit prevailed.

The Church also puts the same verse into the mouth of the celebrant, when he chants the praise of the Eucharistic King in the Sacrifice of the Holy Mass. Thus the same chant has echoed and vibrated through the ages of history. With the words intoned by the royal singer, King David, the Messianic King was hailed and proclaimed by the people at Jerusalem. With the same words of praise and jubilation, the King of our hearts, reigning throughout all ages, is heralded, adored, and worshiped in every Holy Mass celebrated within the wide halls of the Catholic Church.

# CHAPTER 24

# The Beginning of the Canon

Te igitur, clementissime Pater, per Jesum Christum
Filium tuum Dominum nostrum, supplices rogamus ac
petimus, uti accepta habeas et benedicas haec ✠ dona,
haec ✠ munera, haec ✠ sancta sacrificia illibata, in
primis, quae tibi offerimus pro Ecclesia tua sancta catho-
lica: quam pacificare, custodire, adunare, et regere digneris toto orbe terrarum, una cum famulo tuo Papa nostro
N., et Antistite nostro N., et omnibus orthodoxis, atque
catholicae et apostolicae fidei cultoribus.

AFTER the priest has finished the triumphant song of the
Preface and glorified God in the Sanctus, he enters into the
silent prayers of the Canon. His first thought is to ask God "the
most merciful Father" to "accept" and "bless" the Sacrifice of
the Mass. The exchange of gifts is a sign of friendship, and
friendship is the love of one person for another, persons on
equal bases. Hence, we may send gifts without reservation
to a person of equal rank, but in order for us to send gifts to
a person higher in rank or social position than our own, we
must secure that person's permission and acceptance. Accordingly, one may not send a present or dedicate a book or
a poem to a prince or ruler of a country, or to a dignitary of
high rank in the Church, unless that person's permission has
first been obtained, and until that person has expressed his
willingness and pleasure in accepting the gift or the dedication. On the basis of this general rule, it would be most disre-

spectful to the majesty of God to offer up the Eucharistic gifts unless the priest had first begged the Almighty to accept them and to bestow upon them His blessings.

We may now ask: What are these gifts we are to offer to almighty God? A wafer of wheat bread and a small quantity of wine in a chalice. Insignificant as these gifts are, they are removed from the use of men and elected to become the most precious objects on earth; they are to be consecrated, thereby becoming the body and blood of our Lord Jesus Christ. By anticipation they are precious and holy even before the act of consecration. They are called "gifts," "presents," "holy, unspotted Sacrifices." These three names designate but one object: the host and chalice containing wine. They are "gifts" and "presents," for they are religious offerings separated from profane use, to be dedicated and presented to God. They are "holy, unspotted sacrifices": "holy," because they are given over to the service of God; "unspotted," because no stain or any imperfection may decrease their value. In the Old Covenant, God had prescribed that the paschal lamb to be eaten by the people, preparatory to their departure from Egypt, should be a lamb without blemish.[1] It was ever to be this way. The paschal lamb was always selected with special care in order to be sure it had no defects. And this is the way it was, too, at Calvary. St. Peter writes in his first Epistle, [You were redeemed] "with the precious blood of Christ, as of a lamb unspotted and undefiled. . . ."[2] Without blemish and without spot are our Lord's body and blood, which we are offering up to almighty God in the Sacrifice of the Holy Mass. Here the Angelic Doctor calls attention to the comparison with the sacrifice of the paschal lamb and to the mystical union existing

[1] Exod. 12:5.
[2] I Pet. 1:19.

between the Passion of Christ and the Sacrifice of the Holy Mass. He says:

> The priest, in celebrating the Mass, makes use of the sign of the cross to signify Christ's Passion which was ended upon the cross. . . . There was Christ's betrayal, which was the work of God, of Judas, and of the Jews; and this is signified by the triple sign of the cross at the words, these gifts, these presents, these holy, unspotted sacrifices.[3]

This holy, unspotted Sacrifice we offer up "in the first place" for our holy Mother Church. The Sacrifice of the Mass is not a private performance of a priest, but the official act of the Church and it is offered up for her welfare. The "merciful Father" is asked "through Jesus Christ" to grant peace, protection, unity, and the blessings of a good government to His Church. We who are priests of this country and sons of this age scarcely know how to appreciate the unity and the happiness and inward peace that the Church at present enjoys. We give almost no thought to the blessings wrought by an impartial and well regulated ecclesiastical administration. And how painful it must have been for a good priest in other times when discord rent asunder the flock of Christ; when heresy divided the minds of Christendom; when schism disrupted the faithful; when quarrels and strife among leaders did harm to the body of Christ; or when mismanagement in the administration or the vices of priests gave rise to scandal in a Christian world. Let us hope and pray that such terrible times may never return. But, while we enjoy the blessings of peace and unity, fellow priests in other countries, in Russia and the Russian satellite states, are persecuted. While we are protected by civil authorities, our fellow members of the same

---

[3] *Summa theol.*, IIIa, q. 83, a. 5, ad 3.

Church are in danger each day of losing their property and their lives for those same acts of profession of faith that we perform daily. And while we go along unmolested and respected by our fellow men, other priests, who serve the same Lord and who stand at the same altar, have to fulfill their daily obligations at the risk of their lives, and are hunted down like beasts or insulted at every move they make. Let us pray for them that they may withstand the assaults of the enemy and may, by their patience, sufferings, and sacrifices, win a victory for Christ and His Church. It is unthinkable to pray for the Church without praying for, as St. Thomas remarks, "those set in high places," [4] that is, for the Pope and the Bishop. The Christian world certainly has not forgotten the exhortation of St. Paul, who wrote in his Epistle to Timothy: "I desire therefore, first of all, that supplications, prayers, intercessions and thanksgivings be made for all men: for kings, and for all that are in high stations: that we may lead a quiet and a peaceable life in all piety and chastity." [5] During the last few centuries, the Church has been singularly blessed because it has been ruled by men of exceptional merits, of high personal integrity, possessing apostolic zeal and a remarkable amount of prudence and wisdom. Consider the responsibility of the Pope. A single word of his may have the most far-reaching results. A simple interest shown by him in this or that problem, in this or that mission, may result in estranging thousands of souls or winning as many to the flock of Christ. Let us pray for our Holy Father and for all the concerns that burden his paternal heart.

Let us pray, too, for the Bishop, under whose direction we labor. His responsibility is great; his trials and worries are

[4] *Ibid.*, q.83, a.4.
[5] I Tim. 2:1–2.

many. As sons and priests of his diocese, let us lighten his burden by our faithful support, and by our prayers for his welfare and that of his diocese.

Not to be forgotten are our own brethren in the faith, "all orthodox believers and promoters of the Catholic and Apostolic faith." We pray for all of them when celebrating Mass.

# CHAPTER 25

# The Commemoration of the Living

Memento, Domine, famulorum famularumque tuarum, N. et N. et omnium circumstantium, quorum tibi fides cognita est, et nota devotio; pro quibus tibi offerimus, vel qui tibi offerunt hoc sacrificium laudis, pro se, suisque omnibus, pro redemptione animarum suarum, pro spe salutis et incolumitatis suae: tibique reddunt vota sua, aeterno Deo, vivo et vero.

IN THE preceding prayer of the "Te igitur," the priest petitions heaven for the welfare of the Church. For, the Sacrifice of the Mass is offered up to almighty God "in the first place," the text reads, for the benefit of the Church (*fructus generalis*). This is the intention of Christ; an intention absolutely independent of the will of the priest. But now, in the "Memento," the Church concedes to the priest the right to say the Mass for whomever he chooses.

At the "Remember O Lord, Thy servants and handmaids, N. and N.," the priest may stop for a moment to place his own intentions on the altar. He ought, however, to take care not to prolong unduly or to cut short his reflections. At this particular place, a short recollection is advisable, but it is not obligatory. If the priest forms his intention when he prepares for Mass, or when he signs his Mass-stipend book, or even before the consecration of the chalice, he does all that is required in order to apply the fruits of the Mass. But irrespective of the time when the intention is formed by the priest, the wording of the prayer "Remember, O Lord, Thy servants and handmaids, N. and N." seems to indicate that it is here the petition to almighty God is made that the Eucharistic Sacrifice be accepted for certain benefits or for the benefits of certain souls.

Now there are two intentions that the priest may have: first, the intention to say the Mass for the benefit of the donor, and secondly, his own personal intention. Let us speak of the first intention and the *fructus* resulting from the stipend.

Whenever a priest accepts a stipend and says the Mass for the intention of the giver, the giver becomes the recipient of the *fructus ministerialis* or *medius*. (Some authors call the benefits *fructus specialis.*) And, certainly, there is no more profitable way to implore the help of heaven than the one in which the Lamb of God offers Himself on the altar, and pleads for the concerns of some particular soul. For this very reason, Catholics have always been most willing to offer a stipend to the priest, for they well know that by doing so they receive special benefits from the Mass and draw the blessings of heaven down upon themselves. And a pastor ought to be on the watch lest perhaps the persons committed to his charge, when they attach great importance to various forms of devotion, should lose sight of the most abundant source of all spiritual benefits and graces: the holy Sacrifice of the Mass.

Since he has accepted a stipend, the obligation on the part of the priest is grave, for he is bound in justice to offer up the Mass for the intention of the giver. It is to their credit that priests are careful with keeping an account of the stipends "received" and "said." But, though no willful omission will occur, mistakes may happen even for the most careful priest.

Of all the Masses a priest says during the year, a stipend may have been forgotten, not accounted for, or misplaced. For this reason, many a good priest is accustomed to say a Mass occasionally without accepting a stipend in order to compensate for a possibly forgotten obligation and thus to direct the *fructus ministerialis* to the souls that otherwise would have been deprived of this fruit. Such a practice is praiseworthy and should be encouraged.

Besides this first intention, to which the priest is bound by justice due to the accepted Mass stipend, he is at liberty to place his own concerns on the altar of the Lord. He may pray for some particular blessings, for, it is hardly conceivable that the priest, who has the closest and most prominent part in the celebration of the Mass, should derive no spiritual benefits. Though the priest, who is in the state of sanctifying grace, offers up the Sacrifice of the holy Mass attentively, and performs his sacerdotal duties, receives the *fructus specialissimi vel individuales* (*personales*), which in themselves are great, he may nevertheless augment these *fructus personales* by his personal devotion and piety. In disposing of such treasures, the priest may ask God to apply these *fructus personales* according to the former's wishes. For this reason, it is good for the priest to insert a second intention. And this is the moment when the priest may do much good. How often during the day, or during the week, is he asked by people: "Father, please remember me in Mass." By including a second intention in his "Memento" in favor of all those who recommended themselves and their concerns to him, the priest is able to dispense many spiritual benefits to his people.

It is natural that "all here present whose faith and devotion are known to Thee" will share in the fruits of the Mass (*fructus specialis*). And while we priests urge the faithful to attend

Mass, we ourselves ought to give the people an example and welcome every opportunity we have to attend a second Mass. The ever-busy pastor should never be too busy to attend another Mass. Nor does a priest embarrass a fellow priest by being present at his Mass. It certainly would be wrong to assume that the task of the clergy is to celebrate Mass and that the duty of the people is merely to attend. No priest is busier than the Pope, and there is no priest that represents the clergy more fully than the Pope. His august presence, more than that of anyone else, is certainly bound to make a celebrating priest nervous, yet, as an example to the whole clergy, the Holy Father every day attends Holy Mass, as a thanksgiving, after he has finished his own Mass.

And, when celebrating in some convent, are not we priests edified to see a large number of sisters willingly and gladly attending a second and third Holy Mass, and afterwards thanking the priest for coming to their chapel and drawing down the blessings of heaven upon their community?

Spiritual fruits are gained by those who join themselves in the sacrifice and "who offer up to Thee this Sacrifice of praise for themselves and all pertaining to them." As the words clearly indicate, the Church wishes that we include in our prayers our own family, relatives, and friends, "suisque omnibus," for, the Holy Mass is offered up "for the redemption of souls, for the hope of salvation and safety." For all those "who pay their vows unto Thee." In sum, may all those who worship "Thee the eternal God, living and true" derive great spiritual benefits from the Holy Mass.

In summarizing this chapter, we shall do well to quote the words of the Angelic Doctor, who answers in the following way the question whether this sacrament benefits others besides the recipients: "This sacrament benefits recipients by way both of sacrament and of sacrifice, because it is offered for all who partake of it. For it is said in the Canon of the Mass: May as many of us as, by participation at this altar, shall receive the most sacred body and blood of Thy Son, be filled with all heavenly benediction and grace." [1]

> But to others who do not receive it, it is beneficial by way of sacrifice, inasmuch as it is offered for their salvation. Hence it is said in the Canon of the Mass: Be mindful, O Lord, of Thy servants, men and women . . . for whom we offer, or who offer up to Thee, this sacrifice of praise for themselves and for all their own, for the redemption of their souls, for the hope of their safety and salvation. And our Lord expressed both by saying: "Which for you, i.e., who receive it, and for many, i.e., others, shall be shed unto remission of sins." [2]

Let us recall here the beautiful prayer that the priest is admonished to say as a preparation for Holy Mass, and that summarizes the various intentions in the following words:

> I wish to celebrate this Holy Mass and take the body and blood of our Lord Jesus Christ as prescribed by the ritual of the holy Roman Catholic Church. I wish to do it as a praise to almighty God and to the heavenly courts. May it be to my benefit and to that of the whole Catholic Church. I include also all those who recommended themselves to my prayers or who wished to be remembered in general or for one particular reason. My intention is to celebrate this Holy Mass for the welfare of the holy Roman Church. Amen.

[1] From the third prayer after the Consecration: "Supplices te rogamus."
[2] Luke 22:20, Matt. 26:28; *Summa theol.*, IIIa, q.79, a.7.

# CHAPTER 26

# *In Communion with the Saints*

Communicantes, et memoriam venerantes, in primis gloriosae semper Virginis Mariae, Genitricis Dei et Domini nostri Jesu Christi: sed et beatorum Apostolorum ac Martyrum tuorum, Petri et Pauli, Andreae, Jacobi, Joannis, Thomae, Jacobi, Philippi, Bartholomaei, Matthaei, Simonis et Thaddaei, Lini, Cleti, Clementis, Xysti, Cornelii, Cypriani, Laurentii, Chrysogoni, Joannis et Pauli, Cosmae et Damiani: et omnium Sanctorum tuorum; quorum meritis precibusque concedas, ut in omnibus protectionis tuae muniamur auxilio. Per eumdem Christum Dominum nostrum. Amen.

IN THE first prayer of the Canon, the "Te igitur," the priest thinks of the Church; in the second, the "Memento," he remembers some special intentions. Now, in the prayer "Communicantes" the radius is expanded, for, the Church here on earth belongs to a threefold community, which in its entirety forms the kingdom of God. The Church militant, the Church triumphant, and the Church suffering constitute the one "communion of saints." We are all fellow citizens, children, of the one and undivided house of the heavenly Father, whether we are pilgrims still combating evil on earth; or souls making atonement for our sins in the place of purification; or saints celebrating the final achievement amid the glories of heaven. There exists among these children a reciprocal exchange of prayers and graces, good deeds, and merits, which

143

help us here on earth in our struggle to reach our final destination, and which help in freeing the souls in purgatory as well
as augmenting the glories of the saints in heaven. Since these
three parts of the Church are united, they all converge at the
altar to be present when the Lamb of God is slain and offered
up to almighty God. And here, at the altar, the saints of heaven
intercede for the children of the Church militant, when they
petition God to grant us victory over sin and death and at the
same time they join us in praying that our brethren in purgatory be freed from their purifying pains. Here, in the prayer
"Communicantes," the priest becomes conscious that he is
not an isolated wanderer in this valley of tears, but that he
himself belongs to and is a fully constituted member of that
great communion of saints with its advocates in heaven,
who intercede for him.

Loneliness is one of the great trials of life, and isolation is
destructive to the human being. But the priest at the altar can
feel neither lonely nor isolated, for he belongs to the body
of Christ and to the communion of saints. What a great consolation this knowledge should be to the priest in the most
isolated parish, and what a great assurance the communion
of saints should instill in the loneliest and most deserted soul
among the clergy!

Let us not forget there exists, apart from our spiritual relationship with the saints in heaven and the poor souls in purgatory, a very intimate spiritual bond that unites all Christians.
We Catholics, redeemed by the blood of our Lord Jesus
Christ, are the sons and daughters of one heavenly Father. We
form one Christian family and constitute, to use the very
words of the great Apostle St. Paul, "one body" of which
Christ is the head. We are of the mystical body of Christ.

". . . We being many, are one body in Christ,"[1] says St. Paul. "Now you are the body of Christ, and members of member,"[2] the same Apostle writes to the Corinthians. We become one in the Eucharistic Sacrifice: "And the bread, which we break, is it not the partaking of the body of the Lord? For we, being many, are one bread, one body, all that partake of one bread."[3]

From this sentence in the first Epistle to the Corinthians, St. Thomas draws the conclusion: ". . . it is clear that the Eucharist is the sacrament of the Church's unity,"[4] and ". . . that the reality of the sacrament is the unity of the mystical body."[5] Since we are members of the mystical body of Christ, we are united with Christ, and in Christ the union of the faithful is effected. The Council of Trent, in its thirteenth session, declared that we the faithful, one in the body of Christ, should become united by the close bonds of faith, hope, and charity, even to the point where among ourselves we could speak the same mind, and know not any divisions.[6] That is exactly what St. Paul had in mind when he wrote to the Corinthians: "There might be no schism in the body, but the members might be mutually careful one for another. And if one member suffers anything, all the members suffer with it; or if one member glory, all the members rejoice with it."[7] How beautiful life would be if all would hearken to these words of St. Paul! Yet how disturbing it is to see disharmony

---

[1] Rom. 12:5.
[2] I Cor. 12:27.
[3] I Cor. 10:16–17.
[4] *Summa theol,* IIIa, q.73, a.2.
[5] *Ibid.,* a.3.
[6] Denz., no. 756, "Council of Trent," session 13, cap. 2; see also Rev. John J. Burke, *The Doctrine of the Mystical Body of Christ,* p. 120.
[7] I Cor. 12:25.

and uncharitableness prevailing in a community that by right should be called the communion of saints, for, the expression, the "Communion of Saints," as the Apostle to the Gentiles has shown repeatedly, may be applied in its strictest sense to the living members of the Christian Church! We point out, in all charity, one aspect in the life of the Catholic clergy that has a bearing on this doctrine: except for a few priests here and there, the Catholic priesthood is composed of men who are good and who are filled with apostolic zeal. All priests, with very few exceptions, go to the sacrament of penance regularly, and offer their daily Mass with piety. And yet, while all of them strive earnestly for sanctity, probably there is no society on earth that is composed of more heterogeneous elements than the Catholic clergy, for, priests are men of different types. There exists no other body of men that varies as much in character, degree of learning, social standing, nationality, racial characteristics, and a hundred and one idiosyncrasies. Therefore, let us see to it that these varieties in the make-up of the clergy will not cause, on the one hand, the formation of separate groups within a diocese, or a religious order, or society; and, on the other hand, the exclusion of certain groups or individuals from the rest of the community. The members of the clergy of a diocese, or the members in a religious community, should not band more or less together in groups, or associate more frequently with one group than another, since this conduct causes harm to the persons who are excluded. This spirit of keeping ourselves apart from the rest or excluding others from our society, even if this exclusion does not go to the length of ostracism, militates gravely against the spirit of charity and offends the dogma of the communion of saints. Let us eliminate these defects, even if they are only minor shortcomings, for we wish to belong to the communion of saints. We pray daily the "Communicantes"; therefore, let us priests be charitable toward one another: this is the greatest example we can give to the laity and to non-Catholics.

"In communion with and honoring the memory, especially of the glorious ever Virgin Mary, Mother of God and our Lord Jesus Christ," certainly needs no words of explanation for us to see that our heavenly Mother is especially mentioned and set forth in the Canon of the Mass. We are glad and rejoice in recalling her blessed memory. She, who bore in her womb the incarnate Word, will always be pleased to be near us priests when we hold in our hands, at the Consecration, the body and blood of her divine Son. We also call to memory the names of "Thy blessed Apostles and Martyrs, Peter and Paul, Andrew, James, John, Thomas, James, Philip, Bartholomew, Matthew, Simon and Thaddeus." They were the first ones privileged to say Mass and they have taught us to perform the mysteries of our religion according to the mind and will of our blessed Lord and Savior.

Next to the blessed members of the Apostolic College, we recall the memory of some of the most outstanding figures of the early Roman Church. The names of five popes are given: "Linus," the successor to St. Peter in the See of Rome; "Cletus, Clement, Xystus and Cornelius." After these, "St. Cyprian," the saintly bishop and martyr of Carthage, and "St. Lawrence," held high in the esteem of the Roman Church, are chosen as representatives. And, finally, five martyred laymen are accorded the honor of being remembered in the Canon: "Sts. Chrysogonus, John and Paul, Cosmas and Damian." They are but a few of the great number of saints. Nay, all saints are invited to be present at the celebration of this Eucharistic Sacrifice: "All Thy saints; by whose merits and prayers grant that we may in all things be made secure by the aid of Thy protection. Through the same Christ our Lord. Amen."

Before bringing this present chapter to a close, let us remind ourselves that we should not pray to God alone.

> For we pray to the saints, whether angels or men, not that God may through them know our petitions, but that our prayers may be effective through their prayers and merits. Hence it is written that ". . . the smoke of the incense of the prayers of the saints ascended up before God." [8] This is also clear from the very style employed by the Church in praying, since we beseech the Blessed Trinity to have mercy on us while we ask any of the saints to pray for us.[9]

St. Thomas, furthermore, states as follows:

> According to Dionysius,[10] the order established by God among things is that the last should be led to God by those that are midway between. Wherefore, since the saints who are in heaven are nearest to God, the order of the Divine law requires that we who while we remain in the body are pilgrims from the Lord, should be brought back to God by the saints, who are between us and Him; and this happens when the Divine goodness pours forth its effect into us through them. And since our return to God should correspond to the outflow of His boons upon us, just as the Divine favors reach us by means of the saints' intercession, so should we, by their means, be brought back to God that we may receive His favors again. Hence it is that we make them our intercessors with God, and our mediators, as it were, when we ask them to pray for us.[11]

[8] Apoc. 8:4.
[9] *Summa theol.*, IIa IIae, q.83, a.4.
[10] *Eccl. Hier.*, V.
[11] *Summa theol.*, Suppl., q.72, a.2.

It is difficult to think that a doctrine as thoroughly Catholic as this one of the prayers of the saints could be amiss in the Holy Sacrifice of the Holy Mass, a sacrifice that is the embodiment of all that is Christian and Catholic. Verily, the Catholic doctrine of the intercession of the saints takes on life and spirit in the prayer "Communicantes": "All Thy saints, by whose merits and prayers grant that we may in all things be made secure by the aid of Thy protection. Through the same Christ our Lord. Amen."

# CHAPTER 27

# *The Last Warning*

Hanc igitur oblationem servitutis nostrae, sed et cunctae familiae tuae, quaesumus, Domine, ut placatus accipias; diesque nostros in tua pace disponas, atque ab aeterna damnatione nos eripi, et in electorum tuorum jubeas grege numerari. Per Christum Dominum nostrum. Amen.

THE prayers of the Canon are not, as they may seem, independent prayers, each one separated from the others. All prayers of the Canon are related to each other; are connected with one another, and form one organic whole. In this prayer, "Hanc igitur," the spirit and thought of the preceding prayers are continued. The second Latin word, "igitur" (therefore), forms the link between this and the preceding prayer.

"This oblation, therefore, of our service, and that of Thy whole family, we beseech Thee, O Lord, graciously to accept."

"This oblation of our service." What is an oblation, and what is meant by "our service"? Let us first investigate the idea, or conception, of an oblation. In order to clarify our notions, it will be useful to distinguish between an oblation and a sacrifice. Therefore, let us follow the terminology of St. Thomas in making this distinction:

"A sacrifice, properly speaking, requires that something be done to the thing which is offered to God, for in-

150

stance, animals were slain and burnt; the bread is broken, eaten, blessed: The very word signifies this since sacrifice is so called because a man does something sacred (*facit sacrum*). On the other hand an oblation is properly the offering of something to God even if nothing be done thereto, thus we speak of offering money or bread at the altar, and yet nothing is done to them. Hence every sacrifice is an oblation, but not conversely." [1]

At this particular moment, while the "Hanc igitur" is said, there is present on the altar the oblation of bread and wine which, a few seconds later at the moment of the Consecration, will become a true and real sacrifice: the bread and wine being changed into the body and blood of our Lord Jesus Christ. However, at present, we are correct in speaking of the oblation, and this offering of bread and wine is the oblation of our service.

Why of "our service"? Work may be defined as the employment of human activities in the production of something. Work is done for a person's own benefit or in order to acquire money in payment for services rendered of equal value. But work becomes a service when it is dependent on another's overlordship. Since the overlordship of all creatures is the prerogative of God alone, it is evident that man owes service to the Creator and overlord of all. [2] The Christian world renders to God this service by offering the Sacrifice of the Holy Mass. Hence the Mass is substantially a certain service that is due the Divinity. It is not at the caprice or good will of man, but in the relation of man as a servant and dependent on the divine Creator, that the Christian world performs the Eucharistic service. Recognizing the overlordship of God and man's servitude to the Divinity, the pagan nations of old per-

---

[1] *Summa theol.*, IIa IIae, q.85, a.3, ad 3; q.86, a.1.
[2] Cf. *Ibid.*, q.81, a.1, ad 3.

formed numerous rites and offered various sacrifices. In the
Old Law, God Himself ordered the divine religious service
and legislated the laws regarding the sacrifices that were to
be performed by Israel. In the New Law, the kingdom of
God on earth, the Christian Church, renders this service of
dependency on the overlordship of God by the oblation and
Sacrifice of the Holy Mass.[3] Hence the expression in the
Canon, "the oblation of our service," has a profound meaning
in reminding us human beings of the duty we owe to almighty
God as His subjects and servants. The priest does not stand
alone at the altar in his wretchedness and personal spiritual
poverty and misery, but in communion with all the saints, who
enrich and support him by their prayers and merits. Filled
with new confidence, the priest ventures to petition the Lord
"graciously to accept" this oblation. He storms heaven to
receive and accept the sacrificial gifts he is offering, and begs
God to accept this bread and wine which is destined to become presently the very body and blood of our Lord Jesus
Christ.

This oblation is called that "of our service and that of Thy
whole family." The priest at the altar, that is, the priest in
his official capacity as the minister of the Church, offers up this
sacrifice, and thus the Mass becomes the oblation of his
"service." But the purpose and the benefit of this sacrifice are
not confined to the priesthood. It is the oblation of "Thy whole
family." The communion of saints, referred to in the preceding prayer, is here characteristically designated as "whole
family."

As the minutes quickly pass, becoming more precious in
view of the approaching Consecration, it is as if the priest
whispered from the bottom of his heart a last petition into the

[3] Cf. Ibid., q. 85, a. 4.

ear of a loving God: "Lord, save me." [4] Accept this sacrifice for our salvation. This salvation is composed of three benevolent acts of the good God: first, His pleasure "to dispose our days in Thy peace"; secondly, "to command us to be delivered from eternal damnation"; and thirdly, "to be numbered in the flock of Thine elect."

The priest prays, first, for peace. Not the unstable peace of the world, but the peace of God; the peace of a good conscience; the peace that comes from charity; the peace that is free from sin and evil. Peace, certainly, is the greatest blessing man may enjoy here below.

While the prayer for peace in this life with all the blessings that accompany it and the prayer for our future glory in heaven, are perfectly self-evident, the sudden reminder of eternal damnation may seem a surprise, here, in the midst of the most elevating prayers and at this particular moment, when every priest should certainly be in the state of sanctifying grace. This prayer refers to the priest, personally, as well as to the Church. The priest, as every other member of the kingdom of God on earth, is a mortal being and, consequently, exposed to the dangers of sin and the perils of eternal damnation. Though standing in the sanctuary of the Lord, the priest is not immune against the attacks of Satan.

If we note the position of this prayer, "Hanc igitur," in the Canon of the Mass, and recall an incident in the life of our Lord that occurred after He had instituted the Holy Eucharist, and previous to His death on the cross, we may conceive the full meaning of these words. Since the Preface, which has been said with a loud voice or sung by the priest, has come to an end, a most solemn silence reigns in the sanctuary. The priest while saying the prayers of the Canon entered into the most

[4] Matt. 14:30.

sacred moments of the Mass. The sacrificial gifts lay in readiness on the altar. Only a few seconds more and the Consecration will take place, recalling the death of our Lord on the Cross. During His earthly mission, when our Lord had entered into the most solemn hours of His life, had instituted the Holy Eucharist, and was about to lay down His life as a bloody sacrifice for the redemption of the world, at the altar of the cross, a most unhappy priest and apostle left the upper chamber to betray his Lord and Master. It is by these words, "to command us to be delivered from eternal damnation," that we are exhorted not to follow the way of the traitor. This warning is by no means unnecessary, for every sin of the priest is an unfaithful act, an act of betrayal against the dear Lord, to whom the priest is bound in conscience, and as his most particular life task, to serve. And while the laity, in many instances, can be partly or wholly exculpated on the ground of lacking real understanding or knowledge, the priest can never claim such excuse.

The high office of the priest is no safeguard against personal falls, or sin and all its unhappy consequences. Of this St. Paul is fully convinced, for he tells us in words that cannot be misunderstood: "But I chastise my body, and bring it into subjection: lest perhaps, when I have preached to others, I myself should become a castaway." [5] A concept that possesses a negative side, also possesses a positive side. After the priest has prayed to be delivered from eternal damnation, he begs almighty God "to be numbered in the flock of Thine elect." It is the desire and aim of every good Christian to be counted among God's chosen friends in eternity. What a wonderful thing it will be to belong to a society composed exclusively of the most noble souls! What an experience to live and walk

[5] I Cor. 9:27.

in the very sight of an all-holy God! How grand to be forever, and to remain forever, in the state of sanctifying grace, and to associate only with holy souls, innocent souls, souls knowing no sin or evil, souls filled with charity, goodness, kindness, and love! What happiness to be surrounded by virtue, heroism, and nobility! No words of man are capable of describing what it must be like to live forever in pleasure, peace, happiness, and everlasting security. How delightful will be the company of the angels and saints! How wonderful will be the enjoyment of the friendship of all the great and noble souls! Who, here below, has an approximate idea of heaven's bliss? Who can imagine the happiness in store for those who are the object of delight, pleasure, and love of the Blessed Trinity? And this joy and delight will last forever, throughout eternity. "Be glad and rejoice for your reward is very great in heaven." [6]
". . . Eye hath not seen, nor ear heard, neither hath it entered into the heart of man, what things God hath prepared for them that love Him." [7]

[6] Matt. 5:12.
[7] I Cor. 2:9.

# CHAPTER 28

# *The Definition of the Sacrifice*

Quam oblationem, tu Deus, in omnibus quaesumus, benedictam ✠ adscriptam ✠ ratam ✠ rationabilem, acceptabilemque facere digneris: ut nobis Corpus ✠ et Sanguis ✠ fiat dilectissimi Filii tui Domini nostri Jesu Christi.

THE prayer, "Quam oblationem," contains several words not easily comprehended and difficult to interpret, yet the general meaning of this prayer is easy to understand. But before we proceed to explain it, let us observe its peculiar position within the framework of the Canon.

Since entering into the sacred silence of the Canon, the priest has placed on the paten the prayers for the Church and the commemoration of the living. He has fortified himself with the thought that he does not stand alone at the altar, but is surrounded by the blessed and saints of heaven, who come to his spiritual aid and support him by their prayers of intercession. And, finally, the priest has prayed for the blessings of peace, for his escape from eternal perdition, and for his final salvation.

But, now, the awful moment is at hand. The Consecration is to take place. In a second or two, the priest is to pronounce the very words that will effect the change of the bread and wine into the body and blood of our Lord Jesus Christ. In an instant, the Eucharistic Christ will be in the hands of the priest: "For thus saith the Lord of hosts: Yet one little while, and I will move the heaven and the earth. . . . And the desired of all nations shall come: and I will fill this house with glory. . . ." [1] But since he still prays over the material gifts that lie in readiness on the altar awaiting the moment of the transubstantiation, the priest, in order to exclude all errors or misconceptions, formulates for the last time the essentials of the Eucharistic Sacrifice: This oblation is to become the body and blood of Thy most beloved Son, our Lord Jesus Christ.

To effect this sacrament "we beseech Thee," O God. Why, one may object, should we beseech God for something which we know He will do? Is it not certain that the divine power will never fail in effecting this sacrament? "Therefore it is to no purpose, we may object, that the priest asks for the perfecting of this sacrament, saying: Which oblation do Thou, O God, in all, . . ." [2] To the above objection, the Doctor of the schools replies most accurately: "The efficacy of the sacramental words can be hindered by the priest's intention. Nor is there anything unbecoming in our asking of God for what we know He will do, just as Christ [3] asked for His glorification." [4]

To whom is this prayer addressed? Is it addressed to the good and holy God? No, the words read otherwise. Is this prayer addressed to "clementissime Pater," or to the "Deus omnipotens"? No, such attributes are purposely omitted. No qualities of God are referred to, nor is even the word "Domine" used, an expression which brings out the benevolence of the Omnipotent. No, the prayer is directed to "God." The word

[1] Agg. 2:7, 8.
[2] *Summa theol.*, IIIa, q.83, a.4, obj. 7.
[3] John 17:1, 5.
[4] *Ibid.*, a.4, ad 7.

"Deus" stands alone here, without any qualification, in perfect solemnity; an unaided, complete concept, "God": "the being," "the *ens per se*," "the He who is." Let us observe that this is the only place in the whole Canon where the word "Deus" is used without qualification, a fact that plainly indicates the exclusiveness of its use.

The work of the transubstantiation is brought about not by merely human agencies: it is the work of "Divine power." [5] "It is effected by God's infinite power." [6] "In this sacrament the consecration of the matter consists in a miraculous change of the substance, which can only be done by God; hence the minister in performing this sacrament has no other part save the pronouncing of the words." [7] And a little farther on, St. Thomas says again, "The minister does nothing in perfecting this sacrament, except to pronounce the words of Christ." [8] "It is Christ's words that perfect this sacrament." [9] "For when the time comes for perfecting the sacrament, the priest uses no longer his own words, but the words of Christ." [10]

"There is in the words of the form of this sacrament a created power which causes the change to be wrought in it: instrumental, however, as in the other sacraments. For, since these words are uttered in the person of Christ, it is from His command that they receive their instrumental power from Him." [11]

St. Thomas explains what he means by "sacramental power," when he says: "No creature can work miracles as the

[5] *Ibid.*, q.75, a.4.
[6] *Ibid.*, a.7.
[7] *Ibid.*, q.78, a.1.
[8] *Loc. cit.*
[9] *Loc. cit.*
[10] *Loc. cit.*
[11] *Ibid.*, a.4.

chief agent; yet it can do so instrumentally, just as the touch of Christ's hand healed the leper. And in this fashion Christ's words change the bread into His body." [12] Such then is the power of a priest that he may direct the power of almighty God. Each time a priest offers Mass, he himself is the instrumental cause through which God, the principal agent, exercises His infinite power in changing the bread into the body of Christ. At the priest's command, the power of God operates. Would that we priests fully realized the extent to which the good God has, in this wonderful sacrament, entrusted to us His own divine power!

The oblation of bread and wine are lying in readiness on the altar, and God is asked to "vouchsafe," that is, to "grant condescendingly" "to make them in all things blessed ✠, approved ✠, ratified ✠, reasonable and acceptable."

Some of these epithets recall to our minds two quotations from Holy Scripture, quotations that will enable us to understand more comprehensively the meaning of these epithets. For, does not St. Paul in the first Epistle to the Corinthians use a similar expression when he says: "The chalice of benediction, which we bless, is it not the communion of the blood of Christ?" [13] And to the Romans he writes: "I beseech you therefore, brethren, by the mercy of God, that you present your bodies a living sacrifice, holy, pleasing unto God, your reasonable service." [14] If our service is a "reasonable service," then how much more of a "reasonable service" is the one in which Christ is offered up to His heavenly Father! This consecration is to be accomplished for our benefit, for we pray that this oblation "may become for us the body and blood of

[12] *Ibid.*, ad 2.
[13] I Cor. 10:16.
[14] Rom. 12:1.

Thy most beloved Son, our Lord Jesus Christ." "For us!" Indeed, Isaias prophesied the future Redeemer to be born for our benefit. "For a child is born to us, and a son is given to us. . . ." [15] St. Luke gives us the words of the angel who appeared to the shepherds announcing the mystery of the Incarnation: "This day is born to you a Savior, who is Christ the Lord. . . ." [16] Hence, St. Thomas is right when he says in the *Pange lingua:* "Nobis datus, nobis natus." And it is from this same point of view that the Angelic Doctor views and interprets the whole prayer "Quam oblationem." The Consecration, which is to take place in a moment, is to be for our benefit. For, he says:

> The priest does not seem to pray there for the Consecration to be fulfilled, but that it may be fruitful in our regard; hence he says expressively: That it may become "to us" the body and the blood. Again, the words preceding these have that meaning, when he says: Vouchsafe to make this oblation blessed, i.e., according to Augustine,[17] ". . . that we may receive a blessing, namely through grace"; "enrolled," i.e., that we may be enrolled in heaven; "ratified," i.e., that we may be incorporated in Christ; "reasonable," i.e., that we may be stripped of our animal sense; "acceptable," i.e., that we who in ourselves are displeasing may, by its means, be made acceptable to His only Son.[18]

The Incarnation was accomplished for our benefit. The Redemption was wrought for our salvation. And the Sacrifice of the Mass is offered up "for us," and all of this the good God has done, and is still doing, for our welfare. While daily celebrating the Holy Mass, we priests must take care lest

[15] Isa. 9:6.
[16] Luke 2:11.
[17] Paschasius, *De Corp. et Sang. Dom.*, chap. 12.
[18] *Summa theol.*, IIIa, q. 83, a. 4, ad 7.

we grow accustomed to the privileges and benefits of the Lord, and accept them as a matter of course. Let us thank our Lord for what He is doing for us in giving us daily His sacred Body and Blood.

# CHAPTER 29

# *The Prayer before the Consecration*

Qui pridie quam pateretur, accepit panem in sanctas
ac venerabiles manus suas, et elevatis oculis in caelum,
ad te Deum Patrem suum omnipotentem: tibi gratias
agens, bene ✠ dixit, fregit, deditque discipulis suis, di-
cens: Accipite, et manducate ex hoc omnes.

No SOUND comes from the choir. The organ becomes silent
in order that the voices from heaven may be heard. The congregation is now on its knees. And the priest bends over
the altar to re-enact what belongs entirely to the domain of
faith. The great mystery of our holy religion, the Eucharistic
Sacrifice, is being performed.

Christ Himself is calling on the priest to pronounce His own
words that change bread and wine into His body and blood,
for ". . . these words are uttered in the person of Christ." [1]

"Quasi ex persona ipsius Christi loquentis." [2] "As if Christ
were speaking in person," the priest re-enacts the sacred pro-
ceedings that took place in the upper chamber at Jerusalem.
He recalls the hallowed events that took place previous to
Christ's bitter Passion, for, when our Lord was about to ascend
the altar of Calvary, He gave to His apostles His last and everlasting will. "Last words," says the Angelic Doctor, "chiefly

[1] *Summa theol.*, IIIa, q.78, a.4.
[2] *Ibid.*, a.1.

such as are spoken by departing friends, are committed most deeply to memory: since then especially affection for friends is more enkindled and the things which affect us most are impressed the deepest in the soul." [3]

"In order to command more earnestly the depth of this mystery," says St. Augustine, "our Savior willed this last act to be fixed in the hearts and memories of the disciples whom He was about to quit for the Passion." [4] Let us, who are priests, when celebrating Mass, always keep this thought in mind, and remember that the altar is the Lord's Last Supper table. Are not we priests, in some fashion, envious of the apostles who were privileged to be present in the Last Supper chamber? If only we could have leaned against the breast of our Lord like the beloved disciple! And yet, the Lord calls us too to the Last Supper chamber. The Lord calls us to take His very place, to use His very words, to enact, with His authority, what He Himself did, and to imitate His very actions, which have the same effect as His.

The Lord "took bread into His holy and venerable hands." These sacred hands of the divine Master! In order that we, who are priests, may perform this same act of the heavenly Lord, our hands were anointed, blessed, and prayed over by the bishop who ordained us. "Prayed over," that we may pray for, and lay our hands on, the people. "Blessed," that we may confer blessings as the Lord conferred blessings. "Anointed," that we may consecrate as the Lord consecrated. O, that we priests had hands holy and sacred, pure and innocent, like unto the hands of our Lord!

When we compare the words of the liturgical prayer "Qui pridie" with the report of the Last Supper scene, as given us

---

[3] *Ibid.*, q.73, a.5.
[4] Quoted by St. Thomas, *Summa theol., loc. cit.*

by the Synoptics, we will find that the words, ". . . into His holy and venerable hands, and with eyes lifted up towards heaven unto Thee, O God, His heavenly Father," are missing from the Holy Scriptures. To this the Angelic Doctor remarks:

> Our Lord said and did many things which are not written down by the Evangelists; and among them is the uplifting of His eyes to heaven at the supper; nevertheless the Roman Church had it by tradition from the apostles. For it seems reasonable that He who lifted up His eyes to the Father in raising Lazarus to life . . . and in the prayer which He made for the disciples,[5] has more reason to do so in instituting this Sacrament, as being of greater import.[6]

Christ, lifting up His eyes, gave thanks to God His almighty Father. He thanked His heavenly Father that the great moment for the institution of the Sacrifice of the Mass, which he had so eagerly and lovingly longed for during His earthly life, was now at hand. He gave thanks to God that because of the establishment of this sacrament, He was to continue to dwell among men and be with them to the end of time.

And you, O priest, who speak these words in the name of Christ, give thanks, too, for being privileged to perform once more this great Eucharistic offering. For what is more Christlike than being animated at the sacred moment of the Consecration by the same motives and feelings of gratitude that filled the heart of Jesus when He spoke these words in the upper chamber at Jerusalem? Not only should our priestly functions imitate and harmonize with those of Christ at the Last Supper, but also our inward dispositions should be a replica of the inner Christ. The sentiments of our heart should be the sentiments of the divine Model.

[5] John 17:1.
[6] *Summa theol.*, IIIa, q. 83, a. 4, ad 2.

After our Lord had given thanks "to Thee, O God, His almighty Father," He did "bless ✠, break and give [the bread] unto His disciples saying: 'Take and eat ye . . .'" In the liturgy of the Canon, we find preserved the very same order of the words describing the sequence of Christ's actions, as given by the three Synoptics: "took," "blessed," "broke," "gave," "saying." St. Thomas calls attention to the fact that the participle "saying" connects the words spoken by Christ simultaneous with His action, for he says: "It is not necessary for the sequence to be understood only with respect to the last word spoken as if Christ had just then pronounced those words when He gave it to His disciples; but the sequence can be understood with regard to all that had gone before; so that the sense is: While He was blessing, and breaking, and giving it to His disciples, He spoke the words, 'Take ye, . . .'" [7] It is one undivided action. The matter of the Sacrament, the bread, and the form of the Sacrament, the words, are brought into union to effect the transubstantiation.

Simultaneously with the words of the Consecration, our Lord utters His command to all, to take, and to eat His body and blood. The exhortation to partake of the consecrated repast is addressed to all. It seems that the liturgical form, "Take, and eat ye all of this," is taken from the shorter wording of St. Matthew: "Take ye and eat." [8] St. Thomas tells us that, "The additional word, 'all,' is understood in the Gospels, although not expressed; because He had said: 'Except you eat the flesh of the Son of man . . . you shall not have life in you.'" [9] And, indeed, if these words are addressed generally to all the children of the Church, then how much more are they, in particular, addressed to the priests as a command of

[7] *Ibid.*, IIIa, q.78, a.1, ad 1.
[8] Matt. 26:26.
[9] John 6:54; *Summa theol.*, IIIa, q.83, a.4, ad 2.

the Lord to take and accept what He has prepared for us? Take then, O priest, and accept willingly, understandingly, and with gratitude the love gift of your divine Master. The Lord is presenting to you His own sacred self. He urges you to open the door to your innermost being, and in the manner of a willing and happy host, to receive your divine Guest. Take and eat: "He that eateth My flesh and drinketh My blood hath everlasting life: and I will raise him up in the last day. For My flesh is meat indeed: and My blood is drink indeed. He that eateth My flesh, and drinketh My blood, abideth in Me, and I in him." [10]

[10] John 6:55–57.

# CHAPTER 30

# *The Consecration*

Hoc est enim corpus Meum.

IN THE person of Jesus Christ, the priest pronounces distinctly, reverently, and in a subdued voice [1] the words of the Consecration: "For this is My body." Every one of these words is essential except the conjunction "for," which establishes the sequence with the words preceding and which "is set in this form according to the custom of the Roman Church, that derived it from Peter the Apostle." [2] Since "this sentence possesses the power of effecting the conversion of the bread into the body of Christ," [3] it is a matter of duty for us priests to acquaint ourselves with the significance of each and every word.

The first of the sacred words of the Consecration is the word "hoc." Since the word "hoc" is a pronoun, the nature of the word requires that it refer to something. To what does it refer? Does it refer to the term of the conversion, the body of Christ? If this is the case, then the meaning of the sentence would be: the body of Christ is the body of Christ. This sentence, "my body is my body" would express the principle of identity. Christ's body is always Christ's body. The words of the Con-

[1] "Distincte, reverenter et secreto." *Missale Rom.*, "Ritus servandus," VIII, 5.
[2] *Summa theol.*, IIIa, q.78, a.2, ad 5.
[3] *Ibid.*, a.5.

167

secration would not effect any change, but this sentence, "This is My body," possesses the power of effecting the transubstantiation, that is, the conversion of the bread into the Body of Christ. Does the word "this," then, refer to the substance of the bread, which the priest holds in his hands previous to the pronouncement of the last syllable of the words of the consecration? Then the meaning would be: "this bread is My body." But this clearly militates against the teaching of the Church, for, as St. Thomas points out, "the substance of bread never is the body of Christ." [4] What then, we may ask, does the pronoun "this" refer to? In order to get a clear idea of this rather difficult problem, let us follow the reasoning of the Master of the schools. St. Thomas says:

> One must understand the . . . expression [This is My body] with reference to the last instant of the words being spoken, yet not so that the subject may be understood to have stood for that which is the term of the conversion: viz, that the body of Christ is the body of Christ; nor again that the subject be understood to stand for that which it was before the conversion, namely, the bread; but for that which is commonly related to both, i.e., that which is contained in general under those species. For these words do not make the body of Christ to be the body of Christ, nor do they make the bread to be the body of Christ; but what was contained under those species, and was formerly bread, they make to be the body of Christ. And therefore expressly our Lord did not say: This bread is My Body, . . . nor This, My body, is My body, . . . but in general: This is My body, assigning no noun on the part of the subject, but only a pronoun, which signifies substance in common, without quality, that is, without a determinate form. [5]

[4] *Ibid.*, q.75, a.2.
[5] *Ibid.*, q.78, a.5.

In other words, according to St. Thomas, "The term 'this' points to a substance, yet without determining its proper nature." [6] Or, as the saint expresses it again, "The pronoun 'this' does not indicate the accidents, but the substance underlying the accidents, which at first was bread, and is afterwards the body of Christ, which body, although not informed by those accidents, is yet contained under them." [7]

Proceeding to the next word, we again see a word of but one syllable. Short as the word is, it is, nevertheless, a word of great importance and significance. For it is a word that designates the Eternal Being itself. This little word *est* set the world on fire, with the fire of love and charity, when first pronounced by the divine lips at the Supper Table in the upper chamber at Jerusalem, dispelling the coldness and darkness of paganism, and establishing divine worship. And again, it set the world on fire, but with a fire of discord and dissension, when the reformers of four hundred years ago first tried to tear it out of the Christian code and substitute for it various vague and meaningless expressions suiting their fancy, and playing havoc with truth and faith. Yet in spite of the onslaught of the enemy, and the raging of the fires of hell against the Christ-given pronouncement, the word *est* still stands today in the center of the Catholic Church, as it was placed there by Christ Himself. And still, after two thousand years, it has preserved its original meaning, untainted and unchanged by ages or races, and it is as crystal-clear in meaning as when it was first pronounced by the Savior. For, the *est*, which stands for the real existence of Christ in the Holy Eucharist, is the very same *est* that expresses the idea of the aseity of God, the very being of God, the *esse a se*.[8] Existence, being, is the first

[6] *Ibid.*, ad 1.
[7] *Ibid.*, ad 2.
[8] Exod. 3:14.

characteristic of the Divinity. And Christ's real existence in the host is what the *est* of the consecrating words denotes. There is no question of being or of nonbeing, of existence or nonexistence, and any word that does not express the complete existence of a being would be equivalent to nonexistence. Consequently, the reformers who substituted other words and other meanings for the word *est* destroyed the "Real Presence." And again, this presence of Christ, this *est* of the Consecration, is existence at present, as the present tense and the indicative mood, indicate.

The act of Consecration is not an evolving of one state from another state, nor is it a body of Christ being "made out of" the bread, nor is it a "becoming" of the bread into the body of Christ, where the term "whence" is succeeded by the term "whereunto." For, as soon as the last word of the Consecration has been spoken, the conversion instantaneously takes place, and, therefore, the bread is not "becoming" the body of Christ, but what was formerly the substance of bread is, *est*, now the body of Christ, although the accidents of the bread remain. Christ is present, is existent, in the Eucharist. The Real Presence is the great dogma of Christianity.

Christ is really and truly present at the altar. In the statement, "My body," that is, Christ's body, St. Thomas tells us that "the pronoun, My, which implicitly points to the chief person, i.e., the person of the speaker, sufficiently indicates Christ's Person, in whose Person these words are uttered," [9] for, "the priest uses no longer his own words," but "it is Christ's words that perfect this Sacrament." [10]

Christ's body, Christ's Self, is existent in the Eucharist, for, St. Thomas tells us that, "By the power of the sacrament there

[9] *Op. cit.*, IIIa, q.78, a.2, ad 4.
[10] *Ibid.*, a.1.

is contained under it, as to the species of the bread, not only the flesh, but the entire body of Christ, that is, the bones, the nerves, and the like." [11] Here is present, under the appearance of bread, "the body of Christ." But, as the Godhead and the soul of Christ were united with the body of Christ, it follows that also the Godhead and the soul of Christ are contained in this sacrament, though not by the power of the sacrament but concomitantly. "Hence," as the profession of faith of Ephesus [12] reads, "we are made partakers of the body and blood of Christ, not as taking common flesh, nor as of a holy man united to the Word in dignity, but the truly life-giving flesh of the Word Himself." [13]

Christ, with His flesh and blood, His body and soul, His humanity and divinity is present in the Holy Eucharist. "Adore te devote, latens Deitas!" Let us adore the Lord in the Host! Because we priests are only human beings, we are always ready to petition, beg, and plead for our own welfare and concerns. How selfish, how self-centered we are, even in our prayers! Let us, now, at this sacred moment of the Consecration, turn ourselves completely to the Lord. Here, on the altar, a mystery is enacted, which demands more from us than the human senses can supply, for only faith, real and perfect faith, supernatural faith can see, recognize, accept, and comprehend what takes place in the Consecration. All the senses, touch, sight, and taste in Thee are each deceived. Let the word of God reign in our hearts. Let faith rule our inmost selves, and let supernatural truths raise our spirits above the things of this world. With the angels and saints, let us bend our knees before the consecrated Host, before the Lamb of God. Let us worship Christ, prostrate ourselves before Him,

[11] *Ibid.*, q.76, a.1, ad 2.
[12] *PL*, chap. 26.
[13] *Summa theol.*, IIIa, q.76, a.1, ad 1.

adore His divinity and sacred humanity "covered with a sacred veil." [14] How glorious and adorable art Thou, O Eucharistic Christ! To Thee is due all adoration.

As a priest, standing here close to the altar of the Lamb of God, I wish to render to Thy infinite majesty all the service expected from a faithful servant and devoted priest. In my official capacity, as well as in my private devotion, I wish to worship Thee, my Eucharistic Lord and God. With all the powers of my soul I bless and praise Thee, O Christ, in the Sacred Host. Touching with my hands Thy consecrated species, I recollect myself and concentrate on no truth other than Thy Real Presence. I wish, to the utmost of my ability, to adore Thy divine majesty, to magnify and praise Thy infinite greatness, to render to Thy holiness the tribute of a devoted vassal, to pay homage and reverence, allegiance, submission, love, charity, adherence and devotion, respect and worship to Thy divinity and sacred humanity in the Blessed Host. O what can my poor lips utter, in the presence of so august and awful a sacrament, but the words of the Apostle: "My Lord and my God"? [15]

[14] "Preparation for Mass, Sunday."
[15] John 20:28.

# CHAPTER 31

# *The Chalice of My Blood*

Hic est enim calix sanguinis Mei, novi et aeterni testamenti: mysterium fidei; qui pro vobis et pro multis effundetur in remissionem peccatorum.

THE form of the consecration of the chalice is not, in its entirety, reported by the Evangelists. St. Thomas Aquinas says that the Church in using this form "was instructed by the Apostles," [1] and that "the Evangelists did not intend to hand down the forms of the sacraments, which in the primitive Church had to be kept concealed . . . their object was to write the story of Christ." Divus Thomas continues:

> Nevertheless nearly all these words can be culled from various passages of the Scriptures, because the words, "This . . . chalice," are found in Luke [2] and I Cor.,[3] and Matthew says, "This is My blood of the new testament, which shall be shed for many unto remission of sins." [4] The words added, namely, "eternal" and "mystery of faith," were handed down to the Church by the Apostles who received them from our Lord, according to I Cor.,[5] "I have received of the Lord that which also I delivered unto you." [6]

[1] *Summa theol.*, IIIa, q. 78, a. 3.
[2] Luke 22:20.
[3] I Cor. 11:25.
[4] Matt. 26:28.
[5] I Cor. 11:23.
[6] *Summa theol.*, IIIa, q. 78, a. 3, ad 9.

Corresponding to the consecration of the bread, the form for the consecration of the wine would be: This is My blood. Yet our divine Lord employed a different wording in consecrating the wine. Explaining this, St. Thomas remarks correctly when he says: "Drink is not implied under the notion of blood." [7] As our Lord wished to institute this sacrament for our benefit, He offers it to us as the chalice of His blood, saying: "Drink ye all of this." [8]

This chalice of Christ is apt to recall to our minds the bitter Passion of our Savior, for "our Lord Himself spoke of His Passion as a chalice when He said, 'Let this chalice pass from Me.' " [9] Hence the proper form, "This is the chalice of My blood."

These words, duly pronounced by the priest, convert the substance of the wine into the blood of our Lord, leaving the appearance of the wine unchanged. Yet it must be held most certainly that the whole Christ is under this sacramental species of the wine as He is under that of the bread, ". . . yet not alike in each. . . . For the body of Christ is indeed present under the species of bread by the power of the sacrament, while the blood is there from real concomitance, and under the species of wine the blood is present by the power of the sacrament, and His body by real concomitance, as is also His soul and Godhead." [10]

Why, we may ask, did Christ, who is really and truly present under each species, institute this sacrament under the two species of bread and wine? Christ instituted this sacrament in this manner with a specific purpose. "For in the first place this serves to represent Christ's Passion, in which the blood was

[7] *Ibid.*, ad 1.
[8] Matt. 26:27.
[9] Matt. 26:39; *Summa theol.*, IIIa, q.78, a.3, ad 1.
[10] *Summa theol.*, IIIa, q.76, a.2.

separated from the body." [11] "The blood consecrated apart represents Christ's blood more expressively, and therefore mention is made of Christ's Passion and its fruits, in the consecration of the blood rather than in that of the body." [12] "And therefore in this sacrament, which is the memorial of our Lord's Passion, the bread is received apart as the sacrament of the body, and the wine as the sacrament of the blood." [13] Accordingly the form for the consecration of the blood refers to the shedding of Christ's blood. "Secondly, it is in keeping with the use of this sacrament, that Christ's body be shown apart to the faithful as food, and the blood as drink." [14]

In the sacrament of baptism, water is used for the purpose of cleansing, whereas here in the sacrament of the Eucharist wine is used to signify, more appropriately, our spiritual drink and strengthening. [15] "Thirdly, it is in keeping with the effect of this sacrament, for Christ's body is offered under the species of bread for the health of the body, and the blood under the species of wine for the health of the soul." [16] Or as Divus Thomas says in another article of his, "The body is offered for the salvation of the body, and the blood for the salvation of the soul." [17]

The words, "This is the chalice of My blood," effect the change of the wine into Christ's blood. The other words of the form, "of the new and eternal testament" to "unto the remission of sins" are not superfluous, because they "belong to the substance of the form," for by these words there "is

[11] *Ibid.*, ad 1.
[12] *Ibid.*, q.78, a.3, ad 7.
[13] *Ibid.*, q.74, a.1.
[14] *Ibid.*, q.76, a.2, ad 1.
[15] See *Ibid.*, q.74, a.1.
[16] *Loc. cit.*, taken from Ambrose, *Mag. Sent. IV*, d. 11.
[17] *Ibid.*, q.76, a.2, ad 1.

shown the power of the blood shed in the Passion, which
power works in this sacrament." [18]

Christ's blood was shed in His Passion, first and principally,
for securing our eternal heritage, according to the Epistle to
the Hebrews,[19] "Having . . . a confidence in the entering
into the holies by the blood of Christ," and in order to denote
this concept we say the following, "of the new and eternal
Testament." [20] "This testament is a new one by reason of its
showing forth: yet it is called eternal both on account of God's
eternal preordination, and also on account of the eternal
heritage which is prepared by this testament. Moreover,
Christ's Passion is eternal, in whose blood this testament is
appointed." [21]

> A testament is the disposal of a heritage. But God dis-
> posed of a heavenly heritage to men, to be bestowed
> through the virtue of the blood of Jesus. . . . Now
> Christ's blood was exhibited to men in two ways. First
> of all in figure, and this belongs to the Old Testament.
> . . . [and], secondly, it was shown in very truth; and
> this belongs to the New Testament. This is what the
> Apostle promises when he says: "Therefore He is the me-
> diator of the New Testament, that by means of His death
> . . . they that are called may receive the promise of eter-
> nal inheritance." [22] Consequently, we say here, the blood
> of the New Testament, because it is shown now not in
> figure but in truth. . . . [23]

Secondly, the blood of Christ was shed "for justifying by
grace, which is by faith, according to the Epistle to the Romans,[24] 'Whom God hath proposed to be a propitiation,

[18] *Ibid.*, q.78, a.3.
[19] Heb. 10:19.
[20] *Summa theol.*, *loc. cit.*
[21] *Ibid.*, ad 4.
[22] Heb. 9:15.
[23] *Summa theol.*, IIIa, q.78, a.3, ad 3.
[24] Rom. 3:25–26.

through faith in His blood, . . . that He Himself may be just and the justifier of him who is of the faith of Jesus Christ,' and on this account we add, The Mystery of Faith." [25] "The word, 'mystery,' is inserted not in order to exclude reality, but to show that the reality is hidden, because Christ's blood is in this sacrament in a hidden manner." [26]

"It is called [too] the 'Sacrament of Faith,' as being an object of faith, because by faith alone do we hold the presence of Christ's blood in this sacrament. Moreover, Christ's Passion justifies by faith. Baptism is called the Sacrament of Faith because it is a profession of faith. This is called the Sacrament of Charity, as being figurative and effective thereof." [27]

And thirdly, Christ's blood was shed in the Passion "for removing sins which are the impediment to both (our eternal heritage and the justifying by grace) according to the Epistle to the Hebrews,[28] 'The blood of Christ . . . (shall) cleanse our conscience from dead works,' that is, from sins; and on this account, we say: which shall be shed for you and for many unto the forgiveness of sins." [29]

"The blood of Christ's Passion has its efficacy not merely in the elect among the Jews, to whom the blood of the Old Testament was exhibited, but also in the Gentiles; not only in priests who consecrate this sacrament, and in those others who partake of it; but likewise in those for whom it is offered. And therefore He says expressly, for you, the Jews, and for many, namely, the Gentiles; or for you, who eat of it, and for many, for whom it is offered." [30]

And, now that the priest has pronounced the words of the

25 *Summa theol.*, IIIa, q.78, a.3.
26 *Ibid.*, ad 5.
27 *Ibid.*, ad 6.
28 Heb. 9:14.
29 *Summa theol.*, IIIa, q.78, a.3.
30 *Ibid.*, ad 8.

Consecration over the chalice, let us bend our knees in the spirit of true worship and venerate and adore the precious blood of Christ. And as the chalice is lifted up, to be beheld and adored by priest and faithful alike, let us be conscious that this is the memorial of the Passion of Christ. This is the blood shed by the Savior, the price of our eternal salvation, and the memorial of His cruel Passion, which redeemed us from eternal damnation. O Christ, we thank Thee for what Thou didst endure for our sake. On the cross Thy divinity was concealed. Here on the altar Thy body and blood, Thy soul and divinity are hidden away. Yet, let faith pierce the veil. Cleanse and sprinkle us with Thy precious blood, O divine Savior! May the cup filled with drops from Thy sacred side and from Thy adorable veins give spiritual refreshment and strength to our sinful souls, and unite us to Thee in life and in eternity.

# CHAPTER 32

# *In Commemoration of Me*

Haec quotiescumque feceritis, in mei memoriam fa-
cietis.

AFTER our Lord had pronounced the words of the Consecration, He said to His apostles: "Do this for a commemoration
of Me." [1] Let us take notice that these words of our Lord are
not of a general, impersonal nature. They were addressed directly and exclusively to the apostles. It is in virtue of these
words, that the Eucharistic Sacrifice is continued by the
bishops and the priests, the legitimate successors of the
apostles.

Referring to this command of our Lord Jesus Christ, St.
Thomas makes the following remarkable statement: "The
power of consecrating this sacrament on Christ's behalf is
bestowed upon the priest at his ordination, for thereby he is
put upon a level with them to whom the Lord said,[2] 'Do this
for a commemoration of Me.' " [3]

According to the above quotation of St. Thomas, we priests
are on the same level as were the apostles. Therefore let these
words of St. Thomas sink deeply into our hearts. By virtue
of our ordination we possess the same power as did the apos-

[1] Luke 22:19. Cf. I Cor. 11:24, 25.
[2] *Op. cit.*, IIIa, q.82, a.1: "per hoc enim ponitur in gradu eorum quibus
dictum est a Domino."
[3] Luke 22:19.

179

tles; we perform the same acts as did the Twelve. That we are merely priests and have no episcopal consecration does not lower our sacerdotal status. The bishop, though consecrated and enjoying episcopal power and jurisdiction, does not possess greater sacrificial power at the altar than the least of his priests. In like manner, the apostles had no greater power at the altar than we possess, and, on the other hand, with respect to the sacrificial act at the altar, we, who are priests, are not inferior to the apostles. What a dignity the office of priesthood confers on us, and to what spiritual heights we priests have been raised! Yet how far below the apostles we are with regard to piety! Although in our official capacity as priests we are equal to the apostles, in our personal lives, in our zeal and love of Jesus Christ, and in our spiritual accomplishments, of course we can hardly put ourselves on a level with them.

By virtue of this power to consecrate, we priests form a class of our own, a class distinct from the laity. We are men possessing a profession that is placed between heaven and earth, since the priest is the mediator between God and men. The priest, to use the words of the great Apostle St. Paul, ". . . is ordained for men in the things that appertain to God, . . ." [4] That is, the priest is called upon to offer up the Eucharistic Sacrifice, to present a pleasing oblation to the almighty Father in heaven. In order that he may worthily enter upon his dealings with the good God, the priest must be free from sins and sinful attachments. He has the strict obligation to strive seriously and perseveringly after virtue and sanctity. But as priest, he is also "taken from among men" and "ordained for men," [5] to present their petitions and prayers, to work and labor, even

[4] Heb. 5:1.
[5] *Loc. cit.*

to suffer for their salvation's sake, to have pity and compassion on their spiritual infirmities, and aid them in their troubles and difficulties. Though his tasks are laborious and manifold, let us not forget, that in the midst of caring for the salvation of those entrusted to his charge, the priest's first place is at the altar, where as mediator between heaven and earth he stands raised above men, drawing the pleasure of the almighty God down into this valley of tears. Hence it is that St. Ephrem, in consideration of the dignity of the priestly office, cries out in admiration: "O, astounding miracle, O, unspeakable power, O, dread mystery of the priesthood! Spiritual and holy, sublime and immeasurable office, which Christ, after His coming into this world, gave to us without our meriting it! On bended knees, with tears and signs, I beg to consider this treasure of the priesthood! I repeat, the priesthood is a treasure for those who preserve it worthily and holily. Yet, shall I attempt to extol the dignity of the priesthood? It excels all comprehension and all exception. It was, I believe, in consideration of the priesthood, that St. Paul exclaimed: 'O, the depth of the riches of the wisdom and of the knowledge of God!'" [6]

Soon after the divine lips had issued the command to continue the Eucharistic repast, our Lord spoke to His apostles, during the discourse that He delivered following the institution of the Eucharistic Sacrifice, concerning the privileged position and exclusive rank they were to hold in the future, as a reward for their faithful adherence to this His perpetual order: "I will not now call you servants . . . but I have called you friends." [7] "You are My friends if you do the things that I command you." [8] Thus Christ speaks to His apostles, and

[6] Rom. 11:33; St. Ephrem, *The Incomprehensibility of the Son*, chap. 4.
[7] John 15:15.
[8] John 15:14.

in speaking these words to them, so He also speaks to every priest.

To be ordained priest puts you on a level with the apostles, makes you a mediator between God and men, and grants you the privilege to become a friend of Jesus Christ. Do your part, O priest, to be worthy of your high calling.

The mandate given by our Lord, after the Consecration of His body and blood, has another aspect, besides that of the institution of the priesthood. Christ wishes the Mass to be celebrated in commemoration of Him. The exact nature of this commemoration we learn from the first Epistle to the Corinthians, where St. Paul says as follows: "For as often as you shall eat this bread and drink the chalice you shall show the death of the Lord. . . ." [9] The Church has this commemoration of the Passion of our Lord in mind when, on the ninth Sunday after Pentecost, she prays in the Secret: "Whenever the commemoration of this sacrifice is celebrated, the work of our redemption is enacted."

In order that the Mass may become a commemoration of Christ's Passion, there is required an intimate relationship between the Sacrifice of the Mass and the Sacrifice of the Cross. This relationship is brought about by the identity existing between the two sacrifices, for, not only is the sacrificing priest the same at the Mass as at Mount Calvary, but also the sacrificial gift, the Victim, is one and the same in both sacrifices. Only the modes of the sacrifices are distinct. At Mount Calvary, Christ shed His precious blood physically; in the Mass He offers Himself to His heavenly Father in an unbloody, mystical manner. With this specific identity of the two sacrifices, their relationship to each other, however, is not exhausted. We will learn much regarding the interrelation

[9] I Cor. 11:26.

between the Sacrifice of the Mass and that of Calvary if we listen to the explanation given to us by the Council of Trent, for, the twenty-second session [10] of this General Council of the Church tells us that the Mass is "the representation, the memorial, and the application of the sacrifice of the cross." The Mass is more than a dramatic reproduction of the Sacrifice of the Cross. It is the immolation of the body and blood of our Lord under the separated appearances of bread and wine, and this separation of the two species represents, in a mystical manner, the sacrifice that He offered up to His heavenly Father, when He suffered and died on the cross.

As such, the Mass not only represents the Sacrifice of the Cross, but it becomes, in a most perfect way, the memorial of Christ's passion and death. For, let me ask you, where is the bitter suffering and death of our Lord more vividly remembered than during the celebration of the Mass? Under the cross of Golgotha stood only a few faithful souls, witnessing the agony of our Lord. Should the Christian world be deprived of these consoling moments, that is, the moments near the cross? Christ, in His undying love for us, instituted the Holy Eucharist as a memorial of His passion in order that the whole Christian world might be present when He continues to offer Himself to His heavenly Father. Christian people know the desire of the divine Master, for they are animated to attend Mass so that they may be near the Sacrifice.

The meaning of the Mass with reference to the memorial of Christ's Passion, may be brought into better perspective by viewing the Cross and the Mass from another point of view. What has actually happened within those communities that separated themselves from the Mother Church by removing the Mass? As soon as the sacrificial altar was destroyed,

[10] Cap. 1.

the love for the Passion of our Lord grew cold. They remember, it is true, the crucifixion, but it has become merely an historical event, enacted nineteen hundred years ago, as many years removed from the spirit of the present day. The crucifix as the symbol of the original crucifixion has vanished, and all that remains are the two beams forming the cross, so that a bleeding corpus may not offend a sentimental and sensitive people. Likewise, the day of Good Friday is no longer *commemorated* in loving compassion for the bitter suffering of our dear Lord, but is *celebrated* with a certain unconcealed selfishness and pride as the feast day of our redemption. Banish the Mass, and you destroy Mount Calvary. History amply teaches that, in contrast with the interpretation of all other historical events, the perfect understanding of the mysteries of the Crucifixion, together with a correct attitude of Christian people towards all that the cross represents, has been furthered, throughout the course of centuries, only by the Mass in its function as the true memorial of our Lord's Passion.

And finally, the Mass is the application of the effects, or fruits, of Christ's Passion, for, as St. Thomas says: "By this sacrament we are made partakers of the fruits of our Lord's passion," [11] or, as the same universal teacher says in another article of his, "Christ's passion is recalled in this sacrament, inasmuch as its effect flows out to the faithful." [12] Let us marvel how truly the Mass is the commemoration of our Lord's Passion, and let us avail ourselves of its rich and inexhaustible benefits.

[11] *Op. cit.*, IIIa, q.83, a.1.
[12] *Ibid.*, a.2, ad 1.

# CHAPTER 33

# *The Prayer after the Consecration*

Unde et memores, Domine, nos servi tui, sed et plebs tua sancta, ejusdem Christi Filii tui Domini nostri tam beatae passionis, nec non et ab inferis resurrectionis, sed et in caelos gloriosae ascensionis: offerimus praeclarae majestati tuae, de tuis donis ac datis, hostiam ✠ puram, hostiam ✠ sanctam, hostiam ✠ immaculatam, panem ✠ sanctum vitae aeternae, et calicem ✠ salutis perpetuae.

CROWDED indeed have been the precious moments since the priest began the Canon. First of all, his attention has been concentrated in the act of drawing God's blessing down upon the Church. Then, he has made the immediate preparations for the great act. And, now, he has actually re-enacted the Last Supper scene.

All through the sacred prayers of the Canon, the priest has been conscious that he is performing the most sacred act of religion, a sacrifice. By the Consecration, under the two separated species of bread and wine, he has actually, in the name and person of the eternal high priest, Jesus Christ, performed the greatest act of worship, the all-holy sacrifice of the body and blood of the divine Victim, Jesus Christ. In the words of Consecration of the chalice, and particularly in the word "effundetur," the priest has briefly referred to the sacrificial

185

nature of the Mass. But, now that the divine Lamb is slain, so to speak, and has been placed upon the altar, all other considerations give way to the one thought and to the one fact that, here present, the re-enactment of the great Sacrifice of the Cross has taken place. For, as the Council of Trent teaches, the Mass is "a true and real sacrifice," "verum et proprium sacrificium." The consecration is more than the mere bringing about of the sacred species for the purpose of nourishing the lambs and sheep in Holy Communion with the body and blood of Christ. The Mass is a real sacrifice, containing all the elements of a sacrifice.

According to the expressed will of our Lord, as we have previously seen, the Sacrifice of the Holy Mass is performed as a commemoration of His passion. St. Thomas points out, in a few but striking words, the connection between the passion of Christ and the Sacrifice of the Holy Mass when he says: "The celebration of this sacrament is an image representing Christ's passion, which is His true sacrifice. Accordingly the celebration of this sacrament is called Christ's sacrifice." [1]

It is evident that the foremost thought in one's mind, after the Consecration, is the fact that the Mass is a sacrifice. The prayers following the Consecration bear witness to this concept, for, the leading thought of these prayers is that the priest, in the name of Christ and of the Church, is offering a true sacrifice. What has been perfected by the act of the double consecration is now dwelt upon in the words of the prayer, "Unde et memores."

The words of the divine command to do this, to perform this sacrifice, in commemoration of Him are still resounding in the ears of the priest, when he finds himself obliged to continue the sacrificial ritual. What is more natural for the

[1] *Summa theol.*, IIIa, q. 83, a. 1.

priest than to connect the words that just passed his lips with the liturgical prayers which are to follow: "Unde et memores." Conscious of his personal unworthiness, and realizing the high office and dignity that Christ has conferred upon the priest, ". . . he makes excuse for his presumption in obeying Christ's command, saying, 'Unde et memores.' " [2]

To a true Christian, the remembrance of Christ's suffering does not impart embittered and desperate sentiments, for, according to the will of the Savior, His sacrifice is intended to be a holy, loving, compassionate, salutary, and life-giving memorial. Furthermore, Christ conquered and overcame death in His glorious Resurrection. ". . . Christ rising again from the dead, dieth now no more, . . ." wrote the Apostle St. Paul to the Romans.[3] The Sacrifice of the Mass is not the slaying of a corpse, but it is the clean oblation of the body and blood of a victorious and glorious Christ. Hence the priest who was now "calling to mind the blessed passion of the same Christ, Thy Son, our Lord," immediately adds the words, "together with His resurrection from the grave, and also His glorious ascension into heaven."

Christ, in the Eucharistic Sacrifice, offers Himself to His heavenly Father. Christ is the principal celebrant (*offerens principalis*). But Christ, in the excess of His divine bounty, has made the Church His representative on earth and thus, the Church, to whom He committed the keeping of the Holy Eucharist, offers to almighty God the Sacrifice of the Altar. Hence, immediately after the Consecration, the Church hastens to take advantage of her exquisite privilege, and offers to almighty God the gifts of the Eucharistic Victim: "We, Thy servants, and likewise Thy holy people, offer (*offerimus*) unto

[2] *Ibid.*, a.4.
[3] Rom. 6:9.

Thy excellent majesty. . . ." We, Thy "holy priesthood," Thy "kingly priesthood," Thy holy people, Thy "chosen generation," Thy "holy nation," Thy "purchased people," Thy "spiritual house," [4] in brief, we, Thy Church, sanctified by Thy blood, O Savior, offer unto Thy majesty this Eucharistic Sacrifice. Indeed we possess nothing by our own merits, since the Lord exercises dominion over all we have and hold. But we present to "Thy excellent majesty" these Thy gifts and presents, a pure Victim, a holy Victim, an immaculate Victim. This Victim is slain by the two-edged sword of the double consecration, and consequently there is present, here at the altar, "the holy bread of eternal life, and the chalice of everlasting salvation." These are the gifts that we, the Church of Christ, offer up to the eternal majesty of God for our salvation.

This first prayer after the Consecration contains all the elements that constitute a sacrificial prayer. The sacrificial gift (*res oblata*) is named: it is the pure, holy, and immaculate victim; and the offering priest (*minister sacrificii*) is referred to in a double way. By the words "Unde et memores" the connection between this prayer and the preceding words of the Consecration where Christ acts through the priest is established. But the sacrifice is also performed by the Church with a secondary meaning; and the words, "we, Thy servants," make this clear. The sacrificial action (*actio sacrificia, actio sacrificii*) consists in the separate consecration of the body and the blood of our Lord. And the purpose of the sacrifice (*finis sacrificii*) is set forth by the words that speak of our "eternal life" and "everlasting salvation." Thus every act that goes to make up a true sacrifice, is mentioned in this prayer.

And now, O priest, let me ask: What is your own personal offering? As a priest, you hold in your hands the treasure of

4 I Pet. 2:5, 9.

all treasures, the divine Victim. But, now, let me see your personal gifts and presents. Where are the sacrifices you have purchased at the price of your own renunciations and self-denials? Show us your own mortifications, your offerings, your sacrifices. While you are holding the paten and chalice of the Lord in your hands, should your own personal gifts be small and meager? Are you poor and empty-handed when the time arrives for you to produce spiritual gifts and sacrifices? It is true that your personal offerings cannot compare with the Sacrifice of the body and blood of our Lord, which is infinite and immense in value before the eyes of the Almighty. But it is equally true that the smallness of your personal tribute will be noticed, as every soul, truly devoted to the divine Master, hastens to dispose to the divine Lamb during the Sacrifice of the Mass, the flowers cultivated and brought to bloom in the soil of self-denial and mortification. While the flock of pious souls is pressing toward the altar steps to present ". . . an odor of sweetness, an acceptable sacrifice, pleasing to God," [5] must it be the priest who is conspicuous by the meagerness of his personal tribute? Let us not forget that, while we priests are called upon to perform the Eucharistic Sacrifice, we are exhorted, too, to make personal offerings, for, the Apostle St. Paul says: "I beseech you therefore, brethren, by the mercy of God, that you present your bodies a living sacrifice, holy, pleasing unto God, your reasonable service." [6] And in order that we may have no confusion or error, St. Peter makes it clear, in his first Epistle, that we are required ". . . to offer up spiritual sacrifices, acceptable to God by Jesus Christ." [7]

The priest should sanctify himself, and, in matters of morti-

[5] Phil. 4:18.
[6] Rom. 12:1.
[7] I Pet. 2:5.

fication and self denial, he should be an example to his parishioners. Yet these parishioners, seeing in the priest the
representative of Jesus Christ, are the ones who, in the goodness of their hearts, always give their spiritual father the place
of honor and distinction. They make exceptions for his sake.
And the priest, who is only human, must be on guard that he
does not grow accustomed to these privileges of precedence
and take them as a matter of course. In this expectation lies a
grave danger for the spiritual life of the priest. Let us be on
our guard. The good priest accepts these tokens of respect and
refers them to his Lord and Master. Nor does he show any
signs of impatience or annoyance, when they are at times not
so readily forthcoming on account of ignorance. Knowing the
weakness of his own flesh, the ever-ready impulse of his pride,
the many ties of earthly attachments, and the persistency of
his own will, the good and pious priest strives to conquer himself and to offer to the Lord the sacrifice of a renounced and
mortified life. And in the good deeds the priest does for the
benefit of his neighbor, resound the words of the apostle:
"And do not forget to do good and to impart: for by such
sacrifices God's favor is obtained." [8]

And how precious are the good deeds of the priest! They
are not unlike the few drops of water that are added to the
wine in the chalice. For, while the pleasure of the Father almighty rests upon the Eucharistic Victim, the divine Lamb
will be mindful of the nearness of those sacrifices that were
wrought by the sweat and pain of the priest who stands at the
altar.

[8] Heb. 13:16.

# CHAPTER 34

# The Sacrifice of the Old and of the New Testament

*Supra quae propitio ac sereno vultu respicere digneris, et accepta habere, sicuti accepta habere dignatus es munera pueri tui justi Abel, et sacrificium Patriarchae nostri Abrahae; et quod tibi obtulit summus sacerdos tuus Melchisedech, sanctum sacrificium, immaculatam hostiam.*

THE first few words of this prayer indicate that it forms, regarding content and construction, a unit with the preceding prayer. Like the prayer "Unde et memores," it expounds the sacrificial character of the present sacred function. The aim of the prayer, "Supra quae," is to bring out by way of contrast the magnificence and sublimity of the Eucharistic Sacrifice. For, things that in themselves are difficult to comprehend, are made easier to grasp by means of comparison. And what is more becoming than to compare the type with the prototype? When the figure inspires men to admiration, how much more will the original command the respect of men! In this prayer, the priest goes back to the days when the people of Israel were longing and praying for the coming of the promised Redeemer. He recalls the times when, at the expressed order of the Lord, Israel offered bloody as well as unbloody sacrifices, and this order, which was established by the direct command of Jehovah, certainly proved good and pleasing to His eternal

191

Majesty. From the great number of approved sacrifices of the Old Covenant, the priest recalls three particular offerings, which by their unique character prefigured, in a special degree, the Sacrifice of the New Testament and which had merited the pronounced sanction of the Almighty. He recalls to mind "the gifts of Thy just servant Abel, and the sacrifice of our Patriarch Abraham, and that which Thy high priest Melchisedech offered unto Thee." Abel's offering is the first sacrifice mentioned in the Holy Scriptures. Regarding this sacrifice of Abel, the Holy Ghost, in the words of St. Paul, remarks: "By faith Abel offered to God a sacrifice exceeding that of Cain, by which he obtained a testimony that he was just, God giving testimony to his gifts. . . ." [1] To Abraham, who would not have spared his "only-begotten son, Isaac," [2] the Lord, through the mouth of an angel, said: "By My own self have I sworn . . . because thou has done this thing, and hast not spared thy only-begotten son for My sake, I will bless thee. . . ." [3] And, finally, the priest remembers the king-priest of Salem, who suddenly and unexpectedly entered the picture of Holy Scriptures and who disappeared as suddenly as he had appeared. The priest mentions "the priest of the most high God," who offered bread and wine, thus foreshadowing the priest of the New Testament. And on account of this unusual offering of bread and wine, the following words re-echo through the pages of both the Old and the New Testament: "The Lord hath sworn, and He will not repent: Thou art a priest forever according to the order of Melchisedech." [4]

Abel, Abraham, and Melchisedech are figures of the Old

[1] Heb. 11:4.
[2] Gen. 22:2.
[3] Gen. 22:16–17.
[4] Ps. 109:4; cf. Heb. 5:6, 10; 6:20; 7:1.

Testament. Their sacrifices were approved and recommended by the Lord of the heavens. Now, during Mass, the priests of the New Dispensation raise toward heaven a gift that is more precious than the offerings of these holy men. We are presenting to Thy divine Majesty the body and blood of Thy only-begotten Son, Jesus Christ. Thou, O Lord, who accepted with pleasure the lesser gifts of these holy men of the Old Testament, do not be displeased with the true type of all sacrifices. This "holy Sacrifice," this "unspotted Victim," is bound to merit Thy approval, Thy favor, Thy pleasure, O Lord and God!

And, indeed, the prophecies of the Old Law have been fulfilled. The promises have materialized. The types have been replaced by the original. The expectations have become realities, for, what has been foretold by the Old Testament, has become true in the New Covenant: "I have no pleasure in you, saith the Lord of hosts: and I will not receive a gift of your hand. For from the rising of the sun even to the going down, My name is great among the Gentiles, and in every place there is sacrifice, and there is offered to My name a clean oblation: for My name is great among the Gentiles, saith the Lord of hosts." [5]

An interesting interpretation of this prayer, "Supra quae," is found in St. Thomas Aquinas. His explanation has a singularly subjective tone. Let us quote the words of the Angelic Doctor: "Although this sacrament is of itself preferable to all ancient sacrifices, yet the sacrifices of the men of old were most acceptable to God on account of their devotion. Consequently, the priest asks that this sacrifice may be accepted by God through the devotion of the offerers, just as the former sacrifices were accepted by Him." [6]

[5] Mal. 1:10–11.
[6] *Summa theol.*, IIIa, q.83, a.4, ad 8.

For centuries the prophets and patriarchs were separated from the promised Messias, and they, who merited such praise from the Lord, had only "a shadow of the good things to come. . . ." [7] How much more we priests, who are standing on the altar of the fulfillment, should strive to be worthy ministers of the Lord! It is expedient that we, who daily approach the altar, be filled with a living faith and zeal for the glory of God.

This sudden turn of the liturgical prayers from the consideration of the Eucharistic Sacrifice to its types in the Old Testament is certainly more than a dogmatic reflection. This consideration has a most practical meaning, and should stimulate us to never neglect the whole range of theological studies, and in particular the study of the Holy Scriptures, old as well as new. For, as the present prayer, "Supra quae," illustrates, understanding the figures, types, and prophecies of the Old Testament will aid us considerably in penetrating more profoundly the mystery of the Eucharistic Sacrifice, since, to a great extent, it is by means of comparison, as pointed out in the beginning of this chapter, that we may understand the magnitude and beauty of the Eucharistic offering. And what is more beneficial in perfecting our knowledge of the Eucharistic reality than a thorough study of the whole field of theology? It is certainly no coincidence that the greatest teacher of Scholastic theology was, at the same time, the clearest and best exponent of the Eucharistic truths. We refer to the Angelic Doctor, St. Thomas Aquinas. A pursuit of theological studies even after the gates of the seminary have closed behind us will keep us in constant touch with the central idea of all Catholic life, the Holy Eucharist. For, all truths are interrelated, and all branches of the theological

[7] Heb. 10:1.

sciences will lead finally to a more perfect understanding of the center of all Christian truths, the Sacrifice of the Cross and its continuation in the Sacrifice of the Holy Mass, as St. Thomas states.

Moreover, as we advance in years, our knowledge of the Eucharistic mysteries will gain in perfection and profundity, provided that we are making efforts to grow in the wisdom of the Lord. At the seminary, only a brief outline of the most important theological points could be given. On account of our youth we were not always able to grasp even those points in their full significance and importance. But now, that we are more mature, we will be able to penetrate the wealth of theological questions with a greater keeness of mind. May our advancement in years be a real benefit to us in conceiving with greater thoroughness the truths relating to the mysteries of our Eucharistic Lord.

Daily we stand at the altar to celebrate Mass. This is the task of our life, to offer the Eucharistic gifts to almighty God. And we priests perform this duty with great spiritual satisfaction and love. It gives great pleasure to a priest's soul to approach the table of the Lord and to stand in the sanctuary. Now a fundamental principle of psychology may be stated in the following words: the object of our love is also the object of our interest. And interest in a given object consists in a desire to acquire greater knowledge about that certain object. Knowledge and love are, to a great extent, reciprocal. One stimulates the other. Happy is the priest who is interested in acquiring knowledge about the mysteries of the Eucharistic Christ. A priest who celebrates his Mass with love and devotion is bound to be interested in everything that gives his heart a greater and deeper knowledge of his Eucharistic Lord. And again, a true acquaintance with the principles of philosophy and of theology will help us to penetrate deeper into the mysteries of the Sacrifice of the Holy Mass and will, at the same time, inflame in us a greater love and devotion to our Eucharistic Lord, hidden under the veil of the sacramental species.

May we be priests in mind as well as in heart! Let us grow in the wisdom of the Eucharistic Mystery and let us increase our love and veneration for the Eucharistic Sacrifice.

# CHAPTER 35

## The Ministry of the Angel

Supplices te rogamus, omnipotens Deus, jube haec per-
ferri per manus sancti angeli tui in sublime altare tuum,
in conspectu divinae majestatis tuae, ut quotquot, ex hac
altaris participatione, sacrosanctum Filii tui Cor ✠ pus et
San ✠ guinem sumpserimus, omni benedictione caelesti
et gratia repleamur. Per eumdem Christum Dominus
nostrum. Amen.

A BRIEF reading of this prayer, "Supplices te rogamus," will
convince us that here we are face to face with a prayer of
apocalyptical vision, understood more easily by the blessed
and angels in heaven than by us mortals here below. Undoubtedly many attempts have been made to explain heavenly
ideas with earthly words, and some interpreters take one
point of view while others take a different one, but the explanation that gives us probably the best insight into this
mystical prayer is that of St. Thomas Aquinas. With the sole
exception of a brief explanation of the preceding prayer,
"Supra quae," this prayer, of all the prayers of the Canon after
the Consecration, led the Angelic Doctor to give, in his
*Summa,* a more detailed discussion, for the difficulties involved stimulated the Doctor of the Schools to give us a carefully worked out interpretation. He comments as follows:

> The priest does not pray that the sacramental species
> may be borne up to heaven; nor that Christ's true body

197

may be borne thither, for it does not cease to be there; but he offers this prayer for Christ's mystical body, which is signified in this sacrament, that the angel standing by at the divine mysteries may present to God the prayers of both priest and people, according to the Apocalypse, "And the smoke of the incense of the prayers of the saints ascended up before God from the hand of the angel." [1] But God's altar on high means either the Church triumphant, unto which we pray to be translated, or else God Himself, in whom we ask to share; because it is said of this altar, "Thou shalt not go up by steps unto My altar," i.e., thou shalt make no steps towards the Trinity.[2] Or else by the angel we are to understand Christ Himself, who is the Angel of great council,[3] who unites His mystical body with God the Father and the Church triumphant.[4]

In these few words the Angelic Doctor says all that may be said regarding the meaning of this prayer. He leaves us free to favor one or the other interpretation. However, apart from the discussion of the words, this prayer contains a certain aspect that is not easy to express in earthly language, for, its meaning is in the spheres of heaven, far beyond the reach of earthly comprehension. Its meaning approaches the most sacred precincts of the heavenly courts, and penetrates into the regions where angels dwell. Here the blessed spirits hover before the presence of the divine Majesty, singing hymns of praise and adoration to the name of God, and, here in the celestial sanctuary, angels chant the glories of God forever. Here, in the holy of holies, the melodies of the angelic choir re-echo through all eternity.

And, in the course of time, when "the Word was made

[1] Apoc. 8:4.
[2] Exod. 20:26.
[3] Isa. 9:6.
[4] Summa theol., IIIa, q. 83, a. 4, ad 9.

flesh," the blessed inhabitants of heaven were privileged to descend to this earth and to announce the mystery of the Incarnation to the Blessed Virgin, to chant the "Gloria in Excelsis Deo" over the fields of Bethlehem, to strengthen the Savior in His agony in the Garden of Gethsemane, and to announce His glorious resurrection. And, since the angels served the Son of God when He was on earth, we may be sure that they are always at the altar when He continues to be with the sons of men in the Blessed Sacrament. "It is a tradition originating in ancient Christian times," says Father Gihr, "and frequently expressed by the Church, that the angels who participated in the work of the redemption from beginning to end, are also present at, and take part in, the celebration of the holy sacrificial mysteries." [5]

It should suffice to recall the words of St. Chrysostom, as a witness of the Christian tradition. In his writing on the priesthood the saint says: "The priest is himself at that solemn moment surrounded by angels, and the choir of the heavenly powers unite with him; they occupy the entire space around the altar, to honor Him who lies there as a sacrifice." [6] These voices from tradition are in perfect accord with the words of the prayer "Supplices te."

Undoubtedly the angels, who are privileged to surround the altar when Mass is offered, are jubilant and triumphant, since here on the altar the most supreme act of worship and adoration is rendered to God the Father. For, in the Holy Mass, the body and blood of His eternally beloved Son is offered up to the heavenly Father. The more august the priest and the more perfect and valuable the victim, the more acceptable to the divine Majesty is the sacrifice. By this self-

[5] Gihr, *The Holy Sacrifice of the Mass*, p. 662.
[6] *Ibid.*, p. 64.

immolation of Christ, God the Father is adored and praised in the most perfect act of worship.

In this act of worship the angels rejoice. Their celestial hearts are gladdened by the sacrifice of the divine Lamb, who offers to God the Father a superior act of adoration, infinitely more sublime than all the acts of prayer and adoration they are capable of rendering. Hence it is not difficult to see that the angels are always eager to be near the altar, on which so sublime a mystery takes place.

The duty of the angels and blessed in heaven is the obligation, too, of the Church here below, for, there cannot be any difference in the principal tasks performed by the Church triumphant in heaven and those performed by the Church militant on earth. The Church here below, like the Church triumphant, is bound to pay homage and tribute, praise and adoration, thanksgiving and love to the eternal and omnipotent God. But how insignificant even the most precious gifts and the most devoted acts of man are in the sight of an infinite and all-holy God! Christ, in His infinite love, has repaired this natural deficiency, which human beings possess. He has placed Himself, with His body and blood, in the hands of the Church. He has given to His beloved Bride, the Church, the property rights and titles over the Mass, and in His outpouring of love, He has entitled the Church to offer His own body and blood to God the Father as a sacrifice of worship and homage, adoration and jubilation, devotion and respect. Thus due and perfect worship is rendered to the Divinity by the Church. It is a worship perfect indeed, transcending the glories of the heavenly powers. The Sacrifice of the Holy Mass is a service so splendid that it surpasses all efforts and abilities of men in offering worship to God. It is, in itself, an adoration worthy of God, a truly divine worship.

This worship of the divine Lamb renders worth and value to the prayers and good deeds of the Christian world. It is because we join our prayers and pious acts, our personal sacrifices, and good works with the worship of the divine Lamb, or dip them, so to speak, into the blood of the Lamb, that our prayers and pious acts become acceptable to the divine Majesty and make us worthy of heavenly blessings and graces.

We priests, who celebrate Mass daily, perform in the name and by the person of Jesus Christ the greatest act of worship. Let us always be mindful that during these sacred moments the heights of heaven resound with the most perfect act of adoration rendered by Him "in whom [the Father is] well pleased." [7] And while the body and blood of Christ is presented before the throne of God in Christ's name and that of His Church, the saints and blessed join in the praise to God, doubling their efforts to adore the divine Majesty. Choirs of angels soar down to the hallowed spot where an altar stands and two candles burn; on bended knees, with trembling hands, ardent hearts, and fervent lips they adore the Divine. And you, O priest, who stand in the midst of these angelic choirs, beg one of these holy spirits, your guardian angel, to drive away untimely thoughts and distractions, in order that you may perform the sacrificial act devoutly and fully recollected. For is it not shameful that the fervor of your own adoration and worship is withering away while Christ and the Church are adoring the majesty of God the Father in heaven? While you stand there so close to the Lamb, whisper a little prayer into the ear of the "Holy Angel" who carries the sacrificial gift to "the altar on high" and beg him to take your gifts and sacrifices of worship and adoration with him to heaven.

[7] See Matt. 3:17; Mark 1:11; Luke 3:22.

CHAPTER 36

# The Commemoration of the Dead

Memento etiam, Domine, famulorum famularumque
tuarum N. et N., qui nos praecesserunt cum signo fidei,
et dormiunt in somno pacis. Ipsis, Domine, et omnibus
in Christo quiescentibus, locum refrigerii, lucis et pacis,
ut indulgeas, deprecamur. Per eumdem Christum Dominum nostrum. Amen.

IN THE preceding prayer, "Supplices te," the priest was privileged to gaze into the courts of heaven. But now, at the
"Memento etiam," his eyes are lowered to behold in distant
lands an ocean of misery and suffering, for the prayer he is
now saying reminds him of the poor souls in purgatory. These
poor souls are our brethren. But they are separated from us
by the gates of death. These souls are the members of our
spiritual community. They, too, belong to the Church of
Christ, and when the priest ascended the steps of the altar, the
poor souls pressed against the gate of heaven and anxiously
awaited relief from their pains and from their longing for the
hour of release. Surely the priest should hasten to put in the
"Memento" before the precious moments of the sacrificial
act pass away, for it is precisely because the Mass is primarily
a sacrifice that it appeases the justice of God and effects the
condonement of the punishment imposed upon the souls in
purgatory.

In order to conceive the full significance of the value and

of the inner operations of the Mass, let us distinguish, with the Angelic Doctor, between the Eucharist as a sacrifice and the Eucharist as a sacrament. St. Thomas says:

> This sacrament is both a sacrifice and a sacrament; it has the nature of a sacrifice inasmuch as it is offered up; and it has the nature of a sacrament inasmuch as it is received.[1]

> This sacrament is not only a sacrament, but also a sacrifice. For it has the nature of a sacrifice inasmuch as in this sacrament Christ's Passion is represented, whereby Christ "offered Himself a Victim to God," [2] and it has the nature of a sacrament inasmuch as invisible grace is bestowed in this sacrament under a visible species.[3]

Let us stop for a moment and place before our minds the significance of this distinction. As a sacrament, we receive the body and blood of our Lord in Holy Communion, and Christ, in His coming to us, enriches our souls with the treasures of heavenly graces. Now the Church teaches and exhorts us to receive Holy Communion for the sake of the poor souls and to ask God to apply either in whole or in part to the poor souls in purgatory the graces granted us. It is clear that the benefits the suffering souls derive from our pious actions are entirely dependent upon our personal devotion and worthiness. But God, in His infinite wisdom, has designed a mode by which aid and relief is given the poor souls in purgatory in an absolutely direct way, independent of the good will and pleasure of men. For, the body and blood of Christ is also a sacrifice. Because the Mass is a sacrifice of propitiation, it appeases the justice of God and effects the complete or partial remission of punishments.

[1] Summa theol., IIIa, q.79, a.5.
[2] Eph. 5:2.
[3] Summa theol., IIIa, q.79, a.7.

The virtue of justice demands that we give each one his due; the virtue of mercy stimulates acts of kindness, forgiveness, and help to one's neighbor. In the human being there often seems to be a certain inconsistency in harmonizing these two virtues. Yet, what often seems to be contradictory in human nature is perfectly balanced and adjusted in the divine Being. Thus, in God, both the virtues of justice and of mercy are infinite, for they are one with the divine essence.

On account of the sins of men, God's justice would have required full satisfaction. "But if He [God] had willed to free man from sin without any satisfaction, He would not have acted against justice," St. Thomas tells us.

> For a judge, while preserving justice, cannot pardon fault without penalty, if he must visit fault committed against another, for instance, against another man, or against the State, or any Prince in higher authority. But God has no one higher than Himself, for He is the sovereign and common good of the whole universe. Consequently, if He forgives sin, which has the formality of fault in that it is committed against Himself, He wrongs no one: just as anyone else, overlooking a personal trespass, without satisfaction, acts mercifully and not unjustly.[4]

Since God did not choose to forgive man without requiring him to make satisfaction for his sins, He chose this way for infinitely good and wise reasons. Damascene [5] tells us, "He wished to make known to us at once His goodness, His wisdom, His justice, and His power." [6] St. Thomas explains:

> That man should be delivered by Christ's Passion was in keeping with both His mercy and His justice. With

---

[4] *Ibid.*, q.46, a.2, ad 3.
[5] *De fide orthod.*, III, 1.
[6] Quoted by St. Thomas, *Summa theol.*, IIIa, q.1, a.1.

His justice, because by His Passion Christ made satisfaction for the sin of the human race; and so man was set free by Christ's justice; and with His mercy, for since man of himself could not satisfy for the sin of all human nature, God gave him His Son to satisfy for him, according to Romans: "Being justified freely by His grace, through the redemption that is in Christ Jesus, whom God hath proposed to be a propitiation, through faith in His blood." [7] And this came of more copious mercy than if He had forgiven sins without satisfaction.[8]

In no way diminished or neutralized, divine mercy operates in such a perfect way as to bring forth the fullness of the justice of God. And what man could not dream of doing by himself was accomplished by divine wisdom; and because of man's human frailty, he could never have accomplished what was brought about and perfected by the power of God. In the divine plan of the government of the world, divine mercy and divine justice operate harmoniously, for it is due to both the mercy and the justice of God that He did not reject a sinful and rebellious humanity. The sacrifice of His only-begotten Son fully appeased the anger of God, and, at the altar of the cross, the mercy of God was reflected in hitherto unknown vigor and beauty.

God's justice was fully satisfied by Christ's death on the cross. There, on the altar of Mount Calvary, our Lord and Savior paid the price for our redemption. There He offered His body and blood to His heavenly Father as a sacrifice of propitiation.

This sacrifice of our Lord at Calvary was perfect. Inexhaustible in its fullness, the sacrifice of Christ was incapable of being increased or added to by any other factor. His sacri-

---

[7] Rom. 3:24–25.
[8] *Summa theol.*, IIIa, q.46, a.1, ad 3.

fice was perfection itself. It appeased the anger of the heavenly Father, and thenceforth His pleasure descended again upon the children of men. Man was redeemed, heaven was opened.

The cross was the sacrifice of propitiation. The Mass, which is the memorial, the representation, and the application of the Sacrifice of the Cross, is consequently, as the Council of Trent teaches, "a true propitiatory sacrifice." The favor of God, which the Cross procured for the whole human race, is applied to individual man in the Sacrifice of the Holy Mass. Here, in the Sacrifice of the Mass, man is reconciled to God and regains His favor.

The Holy Mass does not remove mortal sin. The sacraments of penance and baptism were instituted by our Lord for this very purpose. But by the Sacrifice of the Mass, the justice of God is disarmed, His anger calmed, His displeasure appeased. Reconciled by the body and blood of His only, beloved Son, God is induced to regard sinful man with mercy. God offers him His graces. God moves him to repentance and prepares the way for the sinner's conversion. God bestows favors on men, and remits, wholly or in part, punishments due to the guilt of man. Thus, after the justice of God has been propitiated by the body and blood of Christ, the divine mercy is imparted to sinful man. From the altar, as from an inexhaustible fountain, a current of the most abundant graces flows to refresh, relieve, and strengthen the soul of man. The mercy of God shines forth most brilliantly in the graces dispensed in the Sacrifice of the Mass; and the wonderful thing is that God dispenses His mercy toward man without doing violence to, or impeding, His justice. In virtue of the propitiatory character of the Mass, the justice of God stands out completely and perfectly. And due to the mercy of God, not the slightest stain is cast upon the justice of God. The divine justice and the divine mercy are infinite and both harmonize perfectly in God. And, in the propitiatory nature of the Holy Sacrifice of the Mass, the mercy of God brings forth, in the greatest possible splendor, His unyielding justice precisely as His justice reveals more perfectly His infinite mercy.

The fact that by its very nature the Mass is a propitiatory sacrifice, becomes evident from the very words of the Consecration, where the priest, in the name of Jesus Christ, pronounces the words, ". . . Calix sanguinis Mei . . . qui pro vobis et pro multis effundetur in remissionem peccatorum." This idea runs through the full length of the Missal. Every prayer breathes this spirit. Nay, it is the keynote of the Mass.

In fact, the propitiatory nature of the sacrifice furnishes the background or foundation stone for every prayer of the Canon. Hence it would be misleading to expound this sin-effacing character of the Eucharistic Sacrifice in connection with any particular prayer because this character is common to all the prayers. But the justice of God, and with it the propitiatory nature of the Mass, reaches not only the regions of the Christian Church on earth, but extends, too, in completeness into the spheres of the departed souls, for, the Church suffering, purgatory, reveals the justice as well as the mercy of God.

"Remember also, O Lord, Thy servants and Thy handmaids, N. and N." How many are they who yesterday were still with us, but are gone today! We promised to remember them. They entrusted themselves to our prayers. They "have gone before us with the sign of faith, and sleep the sleep of peace. To these [our friends and relatives], O Lord, and to all who rest in Christ, grant, we beseech Thee, a place of refreshment, of light, and of peace."

The poor souls in purgatory "sleep the sleep of peace." They are removed from the turmoils and worries of this earthly life. They are beyond all danger of losing forever their eternal destination. They are sure, absolutely sure, of having been saved and they are happy and "in peace," having found mercy before God. They are thankful that the mercy of God visited them. But, though they praise the great mercy of God, they are, at the same time, filled with sorrow, for they have still to suffer, to satisfy the justice of God. "Thy justice is justice forever," [9] they acknowledge with the Psalmist.

Suffering for justice' sake, as do the poor souls, is ennobling. Not that they can gain merits. But God respects human self-respect. He does not wish to degrade the human soul by conferring upon it unearned eternal bliss. For never can man pay in full for the guilt he, a human being, owes to justice. And when the soul has made satisfaction and has been released from the place of pain, it will forever praise the justice of God. ". . . All the judgments of Thy justice are forever." [10]

And while we priests are pronouncing the words of the *Memento*, let us remind ourselves of the justice of God. This divine justice demands that a penalty, at least in part, will have to be paid for all sinful transgressions and all self-indulgence.

Eternal rest grant to them, O Lord, and let perpetual light shine unto them. And while we recite the Church's prayer for the poor souls, the *De Profundis*, let us lift up our minds and praise the infinite mercy and justice of God. His divine mercy gave us His only-begotten Son, who took upon Himself

[9] Ps. 118:142.
[10] Ps. 118:160.

the sins of the world, and His divine justice was appeased by the Sacrifice of the body and blood of His only, beloved Son, dispelling the anger of God, redeeming man, reconciling the human being with the Divine. How grand, how wonderful, to behold the justice and the mercy of God!

# CHAPTER 37

## The Prayer for the Priest

Nobis quoque peccatoribus famulis tuis, de multitu-
dine miserationum tuarum sperantibus partem aliquam
et societatem donare digneris, cum tuis sanctis Apostolis
et Martyribus; cum Joanne, Stephano, Matthia, Barnaba,
Ignatio, Alexandro, Marcellino, Petro, Felicitate, Per-
petua, Agatha, Lucia, Agnete, Caecilia, Anastasia, et omnibus Sanctis tuis: intra quorum nos consortium, non
aestimator meriti, sed veniae, quaesumus, largitor ad-
mitte. Per Christum Dominum nostrum.

STRIKING his breast, the priest interrupts for the first and only
time the solemn silence of the Canon and in a half-loud voice
says these three words: *Nobis quoque peccatoribus.* In the
preceding prayers he has been asking that the Sacrifice find
favor with God, and that those who partake of these sacrificial
gifts "may be filled with all heavenly blessing and grace." He
implored the mercy of God for those "who have gone before
us." And now, in the last prayer of the Canon before the
doxology, the priest petitions heaven not to forget or overlook
"the priests themselves who offer" [1] this Eucharistic Sacrifice.
And in the spirit of humility, with sorrow and compunction in
his heart, and in acknowledgment of his unworthiness, the
priest calls himself and also his brethren in the priesthood by
the name, none other than that, of sinner. In the presence of
the holy and just God, the priest is conscious of his weakness

[1] *Summa theol.*, IIIa, q. 83, a. 4.

and guilt and he confesses himself to be a sinner, yet he is not the hardened, unrepentant, rebellious sinner. There is a tone of trust and confidence in his words, for, immediately he adds: *famulis tuis*. We, who belong to Thy divine household, who are Thy sons and servants; we are the ones "who hope in the multitude of Thy mercy."

Because the Eucharistic Sacrifice is a most holy act, it requires hands of angelic purity to touch the sacred species. Yet, as the Sacrifice is to be performed not by angels, but by men, sinful men, who among them would dare claim absolute innocence and sinlessness? "If Thou, O Lord, wilt mark iniquities: Lord, who shall stand it?" [2]

Though we poor mortals can scarcely hope to attain a life of absolute purity on earth, that is, to be without the slightest stain of sin, we nevertheless are obliged to strive after perfection. To avoid sin and to practice virtue, must be the motto of our lives, and if this law holds good for every human being, without exception, how much more it must apply to us priests, who are the leaders of the people on the way to heaven. The priests, declares Thomas a Kempis, are "bound with a straiter band of disipline, and are obliged to a greater perfection of sanctity." [3] Regarding this persistent striving after perfection, the struggle is not small, trivial, or insignificant. "Who shall stand in His holy place?" asks the Psalmist. And the Holy Ghost answers: "The innocent in hands, and clean of heart." [4] And the great prophet Isaias exhorts the ministers of God: ". . . Be ye clean, you that carry the vessels of the Lord." [5] As early as the book Leviticus, we read: "Whosoever . . . hath a blemish, he shall not offer bread to his God." [6] If the

[2] Ps. 129:3.
[3] *Imitation of Christ*, Bk. 3, chap. 5.
[4] Ps. 23:3–4.
[5] Isa. 52:11.
[6] Lev. 21:17.

Old Testament is so insistent on this point, how much more is expected of the priests of the New Covenant! Of the many exhortations given by the New Testament, let us quote one or two from St. Paul: "It behooveth therefore a bishop to be blameless. . . ." [7] That St. Paul also includes the priest with the bishop in this exhortation, becomes evident from the fact that in his description he passes on directly to the deacons, not mentioning the priesthood especially. In the Epistle to the Corinthians, the selfsame Apostle writes: "In all things let us exhibit ourselves as the ministers of God, in much patience, in tribulation, in necessities, in distresses . . . in chastity, in knowledge, in long suffering, in sweetness, in the Holy Ghost, in charity unfeigned." [8] In the fourth book of the Sentences, St. Thomas insists upon the sanctity of the ministers of God: "Illi qui divinis ministeriis applicantur, adipiscuntur regiam dignitatem, et perfecti in virtute esse debent.": "Those who devote themselves to the divine service, acquire royal dignity and should be perfect in virtue." [9] In the *Summa,* the same Teacher of the Schools writes:

> By holy orders a man is appointed to the most august ministry of serving Christ Himself in the Sacrament of the Altar. For this requires a greater inward holiness than that which is requisite for the religious state, since as Dionysius says: [10] "The monastic order must follow the priestly order, and ascend to Divine things in imitation of them." Hence other things being equal, a cleric who is in holy orders sins more grievously if he does something contrary to holiness than a religious who is not in holy orders.[11]

[7] I Tim. 3:2.
[8] II Cor. 6:4, 6.
[9] St. Thomas, *IV Sent.,* D. XXXIV, q.3, a.1, qw. 3, sol. 1 (ed. 1948, VII, 899 f.).
[10] *Eccles. Hier.,* VI.
[11] *Summa theol.,* IIa IIae, q.184, a.8.

The priest has to remember that when celebrating Mass he is performing not only an act of religion or worship but the most sacred act. "It must be confessed," says the Council of Trent, "that man can perform no action more holy than the celebration of Mass." The priest must bear this in mind, not only when he is actually at the altar or when preparing for Mass in the sacristy or when making his thanksgiving after Mass, but throughout the day: when he is saying the Divine Office, when he is dispensing the sacraments, when he is engaged in pastoral duties, and also when he is recreating and resting. He is a priest, a priest of God. "I, the Lord am holy, and I have separated you from the people, that you should be Mine." [12] Living unto God is the principal task of the priesthood. "They shall be holy to their God," says Leviticus.[13] We are "priests to God," writes St. John in the Apocalypse.[14] And since we are priests of the Most High, living for no purpose other than to serve the Lord, we ask, now that we are standing at the altar engaged in the most sacred actions a man may perform, the dear God of heaven to grant us "some part of fellowship with Thy holy Apostles and Martyrs." We, who are holding in our hands the most sacred Sacrifice, the body and blood of our Lord, Jesus Christ, ask and beseech Thee, O Lord, to admit us into the company of Thy saints. Acting as priests on the altar, let us give "thanks to God the Father, who hath made us worthy to be partakers of the lot of the saints in light." [15] May we priests conduct ourselves in a manner worthy of such high respect; may we earn the high recommendation spoken of in the Book of Wisdom: "Behold, how they are numbered among the children of God, and their lot

---

[12] Lev. 20:26.
[13] Lev. 21:6.
[14] Apoc. 1:6.
[15] Col. 1:12.

is among the saints." [16] Striving seriously and perseveringly
for sanctity, must be the chief task of our lives. No worldly
interest should distract us from this objective. No other occu-
pation should claim us. "No man, being a soldier to God en-
tangleth himself with secular businesses. . . ." [17] Our eyes
should be directed heavenward, and we should be occupied
with things supernatural. We should be interested in eternal
things. The sanctification of our souls should be the greatest
object of our lives. While we are "holy both in body and in
spirit," [18] the hopes and ambitions of our hearts should be
anchored in heaven. God, and nothing but God, should be
the one thought of our life.

My priestly friend, have you ever observed how happy and
pleased the laity are when they have the opportunity of con-
versing a few minutes with the priest? They leave the presence
of the priest feeling holy and as though they had stepped out
of a sanctuary. The laity see the spiritual and the supernatural
reflected in the good and holy priest, and they cleave to his
words as if they were a message from heaven. The laity have
an appreciation for sanctity. Do not disappoint them with
worldly remarks or by an unpriestly spirit. Give them the milk
of truth, the bread of life, the wine of spiritual joy. And now,
ask yourself this question, my dear friend: Is this same fine
feeling, this same delicate sense for the spiritual, for that
which breathes the spirit of sanctity and supernatural perfection, highly cultivated by me and developed in me? Surely,
spiritual souls are not queer, old-fashioned, or one-sided. I
know, my friend, you have an appreciation for every delicate
virtue which blossoms in the garden of sanctity. You have an
understanding of saintly souls. You, surely, enjoy the com-

[16] Wisd. 5:5.
[17] II Tim. 2:4.
[18] I Cor. 7:34.

pany of pious people, of solid characters, of religious minded friends. Well then, if the companionship of saintly souls is your delight here in this world, you may be sure that the Lord will lead you to join the legion of saints in the world to come.

St. John, describing with delight the countless numbers of the saints in heaven, says:

> . . . I saw a great multitude, which no man could number, of all nations, and tribes, and peoples, and tongues, standing before the throne, and in sight of the Lamb, clothed with white robes, and palms in their hands. And they cried with a loud voice, saying: Salvation belongs to our God, who sitteth upon the throne, and to the Lamb. And all the angels stood round about the throne, and the ancients and the four living creatures: and they fell down before the throne upon their faces and adored God, saying: Amen. Benediction and glory, and wisdom, and thanksgiving, honor, and power, and strength to our God forever and ever. Amen.[19]

[19] Apoc. 7:9–12.

# CHAPTER 38

# *The Doxology*

Per quem haec omnia, Domine, semper bona creas, sancti ✠ ficas, vivi ✠ ficas, bene ✠ dicis, et praestas nobis.

Per ip ✠ sum, et cum ip ✠ so, et in ip ✠ so, est tibi Deo Patri ✠ omnipotenti, in unitate Spiritus ✠ Sancti, omnis honor et gloria.

THE prayer "Per quem" forms the conclusion of the sacrificial part of the Mass, or, as it is most commonly called, the Canon proper. Hence, we may listen with renewed interest to its wording, for here the priest sums up the purpose and end of Christ's sacerdotal mission. In a few profound words, the liturgy outlines the work of Christ. By Him all good things are created, sanctified, and blessed. The Sacrifice of the Mass bestows on man countless fruits, blessings, and benefits. And through Christ, and with Christ, and in Christ, the Divine Majesty is glorified and honored, and praise and adoration are given to the triune God in heaven.

It is by Christ Jesus, "per quem," that "these good things" are bestowed on us. "These good things" are the Eucharistic gifts, the body and blood of our Lord, Jesus Christ. By the power of Christ these Eucharistic good things were brought to us in the act of the Consecration. And it is by this same Lord that the sacrificial gifts are "sanctified," "vivified," and "blessed."

Why, we may ask, does the Canon not call the body and blood of our Lord, Jesus Christ, by a term that is more specific than the general expression of "all good things"? "These good things," which are here present on the altar, are the center of all good things, of all sacraments and of sacramentals, of all graces and spiritual benefits and blessings. "These good things" on the altar are the keystone to all good things in the kingdom of God. They are "the" good things. They are the aim and end for which all the other sacraments were instituted. All other sacraments lead the soul up to the union with the Eucharistic Lord. Again, the sacraments and sacramentals receive their life, vigor, and power by, through, and in the Eucharistic good things. Take away "these good things" and you take away all good things in the kingdom of God. The whole sacramental life in the Church rests and depends upon "these good things," for in them all graces are given to us, receive their sanctifying power, transform our spiritual being, bring life to our soul, bless us, and bestow upon us all spiritual good things. The Sacrifice of the Mass is the channel of all graces and spiritual benefits. The Holy Eucharist forms the center of the whole and supernatural life of the Church.

Yet our spiritual welfare is not the only purpose or the exclusive reason for the existence of these good things. The Eucharistic Presence has a much higher purpose, one that is far nobler than to be merely the spiritual nourishment for men. The Eucharistic Presence has an end beyond men, beyond the reach of creatures. "Through Him and with Him and in Him (our Lord, Jesus Christ), is unto Thee, God the Father almighty, in the unity of the Holy Ghost, all honor and glory." The glorification of the Blessed Trinity is the aim and end of the Eucharistic Sacrifice.

The conclusion of the Canon forms the most magnificent and glorious doxology.

Great is the praise and honor given to God by all creatures. "And every creature," writes St. John in the Apocalypse, "which is in heaven, and on the earth, and under the earth, and such as are in the sea, and all that are in them: I heard all saying: To Him that sitteth on the throne, and to the Lamb, benediction and honor, and glory, and power, forever and ever." [1]

But all glory and jubilation of creatures is excelled by the praise and adoration given to the Godhead by the Word incarnate, Jesus Christ. Through, by, and in our Lord, Jesus Christ, the Church offers her tribute of praise to almighty God. In this sense, St. Paul writes to the Ephesians, when he says: "To Him [God] be glory in the Church, and in Christ Jesus unto all generations, world without end." [2] And also St. Jude glorifies the name of God in a similar way, when he writes: "To the only God our Savior, through Jesus Christ, our Lord, glory and magnificence, empire and power, before all ages and now, and for all ages of ages." [3] And this selfsame idea is brought out, most significantly, in the prayer "Per quem." Christ Himself performs the greatest of all adorations. He offers Himself as a sacrifice of adoration to His heavenly Father. A more sublime act of worship is not possible. A more perfect adoration of the Divinity is inconceivable.

Who, while reading this doxology of the Canon, is not reminded of a similar one, which St. Paul wrote to the Romans: "For of Him, and by Him and in Him are all things. To Him be glory forever"? [4]

[1] Apoc. 5:13.
[2] Ephes. 3:21.
[3] Jude 1:25.
[4] Rom. 11:36.

In order to get a clear conception of the doxology in the
Canon, let us study the meaning of the three prepositions,
"per," "cum," and "in." In his treatise on the Blessed Trinity,
St. Thomas tells us that the Latin meaning of the "preposition
through (by) points out . . . some cause or principle." [5] Accordingly, the Eucharistic Christ is the cause by which glory
and honor are rendered to the Divinity. By the Sacrifice of the
body and blood of our Lord, Jesus Christ, God is sublimely
honored and glorified. In another question of the same
treatise, the Angelic Doctor calls attention to the fact that
"the preposition through (by) sometimes designates an inter-
mediate cause." [6] In accordance with this interpretation of
St. Thomas, all honor, praise, and jubilation of the Church
and of creatures goes through the mediatorship of Jesus
Christ, to be presented by Him before the high courts of the
Divinity. The Sacrifice of the Mass, which the Church offers
as a worship of praise and adoration, receives its value through
Christ. The power of Christ "sanctifies" and "vivifies" the
Eucharistic oblation and offers it up to almighty God as a
worship of adoration and praise. Christ is the mediator, who
places His sacrificial body and blood before the throne of
God. And, as we may read a twofold aspect into the preposition "per," so we may also regard the word "cum" in the same
manner. Christ is true God and, therefore, together with Him
the other divine Persons receive the homage and praise of
the Eucharistic Sacrifice. And "cum Christo," the Church
offers the good deeds and meritorious works of the saints and
faithful as a sacrifice of adoration to the Blessed Trinity.

Coming to the third of the prepositions, the holy Doctor
states: "The preposition 'in' strictly denotes the habitude of

[5] *Summa theol.*, Ia, q.36, a.3.
[6] *Ibid.*, Ia, q.39, a.8.

one containing." [7] Just as the Eucharistic Christ is true God
and is separably united in the Godhead with God the Father
and God the Holy Ghost, so the glory and honor which is
Christ's is also in the other divine Persons. All honor and glory
of the Eucharistic Christ is the worship and adoration of every
one of the divine Persons. The Teacher of the Schools continues: "In another sense things are contained in God foras-
much as He in His goodness preserves and governs them, by
guiding them to a fitting end." [8] Christ continually abides
with His beloved Bride, the Church, and guides her to her
fitting place of destination in the glories of heaven. All the
glories and honors of the mystical Christ, the Church, are,
too, the praise and jubilation of the Son of man, and in Him
the blessed Trinity receives the highest possible acts of worship and adoration.

Thus, the Sacrifice of the Holy Mass gives us poor human
beings an insight into the economy of God's graces and His
divine activities. Here we behold the intimate relations between Christ and His Bride, the Church. And here we conceive ideas regarding the mysteries that operate within the
Godhead. In the Sacrifice of the Mass, we see reflected, as in
a mirror, the operations and activities, the relations and con-
nections, of the Church, of Christ, and of the Blessed Trinity.
Here Christ and the Church glorify and praise, unending,
eternally, each one of the divine Persons. In the Mass, the
Church, Christ, and the Divinity meet to perfect a sacrifice,
which is a worthy worship and a pleasing adoration of the
Blessed Trinity. And here in the concluding prayer "Per
quem," the full depth of revealed truth, the height of theological speculation, the wealth of Christian thought, and the

[7] *Loc. cit.*
[8] *Loc. cit.*

beauty and harmony of inspired wisdom culminate to form the final prayer, the crowning praise of the Canon, the sacrificial part of the Mass.

And we priests who are pronouncing these words should join our hearts to our divine Lord's in His praise of the Blessed Trinity. And since the Eucharistic Sacrifice is the center of all worship, the celebration of the Mass should form the focal point of our daily life. The Mass is not a thing to be "through with" in the morning, so that we may be free to commence the great tasks of the day. The Mass, and nothing else, is the great task of the day. The Mass is the central point of our daily occupations. The priest should have, perpetually, before his mind the fact that all other priestly works, that is, his whole sacred ministry, derive their vigor and strength from the Mass. As the sun gives life, light, and warmth to the earth, so the Mass gives vitality to the priest's work in the ministry. If the Mass is not offered piously by the priest, where will he derive blessings and graces? If the Mass is celebrated with devotion, divine assistance is secured for the labors of the day. If the Mass really forms the center of the priest's life, the right proportions and the correct values will be given by him to all the works in the ministry. A good and pious priest, in whose life the Mass is the high point, the principal task, of the day, glorifies and praises God the Father almighty in unity with the Holy Ghost, through, with, and in our Lord, Jesus Christ.

# CHAPTER 39

## *The Lord's Prayer*

V. Per omnia saecula saeculorum.

R. Amen.

OREMUS

Praeceptis salutaribus moniti, et divina institutione formati, audemus dicere:

Pater Noster, qui es in caelis, sanctificetur nomen tuum: adveniat regnum tuum: fiat voluntas tua sicut in caelo, et in terra. Panem nostrum quotidianum da nobis hodie: et dimitte nobis debita nostra, sicut et nos dimittimus debitoribus nostris. Et ne nos inducas in tentationem. R. Sed libera nos a malo. Amen.

THE life of our dear Lord, Jesus Christ, was dedicated to a threefold purpose. His mission was to be the teacher of man. He was to be, too, the great high priest who was to sacrifice His own sacred self for the redemption of the world; and, finally, He was to be the king of Israel, the leader of men, the shepherd of souls.

Our Lord Himself referred to His threefold mission, when He said: "I am the way, and the truth, and the life." [1] And these words were uttered on a most solemn occasion during our Lord's earthly life. They are part of His farewell discourse, delivered immediately following the institution of the Blessed Sacrament. They are, so to speak, the keynote to the purpose and nature of our Lord's mission on earth.

[1] John 14:6.

He is to be the way that we must follow in pursuing our final destiny, that is, He is to be our leader, our shepherd, and our king. Christ is to be the truth, which we must accept and believe, that is to say, Christ is to be our teacher. And, finally, Christ is to be the life, the source and principle of our spiritual life; the priest who sacrificed His own flesh and blood that we may have life and that we may live by, through, and in Him. And this, in brief, was the task of His earthly mission, to be priest, teacher, and king.

With the institution of the Holy Eucharist, Christ continues His earthly life, in a sacramental manner. In the Holy Eucharist, His being is not essentially changed. He is the selfsame Christ, under the sacramental veil. Nor is it logical that, under the sacramental form, He would abandon His mission, forget His care for men, or grow unconcerned regarding the spiritual welfare of the human race. Christ, now, as in the days of His earthly life, is "the way, the truth, the life." He is ever the priest, prophet, and king of men. In the liturgy of the Eucharistic Sacrifice, we see incorporated these three offices of our Lord. Christ is the truth, the prophet, and the teacher. In the Sacrifice of the Mass the divine truth speaks to us, first, through the mouth of the prophets, when the Epistle is read or sung, and then, directly, by His own sacred words, when the Gospel is read or sung. In fact, the first part of the Mass through the Creed represents the teaching office of our Lord. Christ is the life, the principle of our spiritual vitality. At the altar, He offers His body and blood that we may have life everlasting. That part of the Mass extending from the Offertory up to the prayer "Per quem," preceding the "Pater Noster," represents the priestly office of Christ. And, finally, He is the way, the way which leads heavenward. He is the shepherd of our souls. He enters our hearts to take possession of us. He is our divine king, who rules the kingdom of our souls. In the third part of the Mass, the part which begins with the "Pater Noster," we recognize the kingship of Christ when He enters our hearts in Holy Communion, and takes possession of the kingdom of human souls.

Beginning with the "Our Father," a change in the nature of the liturgical prayers may be noticed. Up to now, every prayer has been directed and centered in the one great idea that the body and blood of our Lord is offered up to almighty God as a sacrifice of praise, adoration, thanksgiving, and petition. But, now that due service has been rendered to the Divinity, man, in his misery, is permitted to think of his own needs. To help the poor human creature in his struggle for spiritual and material health and strength, the sacrifice, which was offered up to God, becomes food and nourishment for our soul and body. God's altar becomes the supper table of men. "The chalice of benediction, which we bless, is it not the communion of the blood of Christ? And the bread, which we break, is it not the partaking of the body of the Lord?" [2]

Furthermore, in the Eucharistic Sacrifice, Christ is the priest who offers, and the high priest who performs, the sacrificial act. Does His function come to an end with the Communion? No, the priest of the Eucharistic Sacrifice becomes the king of His communicants. He takes possession of their hearts and thus establishes His throne in them. For without a dominion there is no kingdom, and without a kingdom there is no king. But Christ is a real king. Not merely by title and dignity and prerogatives, but by the real exercise of His royal power over the souls of men. Christ is king because He reigns over those who approach His table.

Here we must not lose sight of the fact that the part of the

[2] I Cor. 10:16.

Mass in which Christ exercises His royal office, His kingship, holding sway over the souls of His faithful in Holy Communion, is ushered in by the Lord's Prayer. For, the "Our Father," of all the prayers, is most suited to open the Communion service. This prayer of the Lord contains, in brief, all the prayers and concerns of a Christian soul. The royal Shepherd, the divine King, indeed, lends an attentive ear to the prayers of His flock, for He knows our worries, needs, and necessities. In Holy Communion, Christ is to reign in the hearts of men. Due to the fact that Christ, in the completeness of His sacred being, in His divinity and humanity, enters the heart of man, so also He wishes to take possession of man, the whole man, with all his concerns, worries, and troubles. Whatever ails our soul, whatever our concerns may be, whatever our hearts may desire, whatever conditions of life we may wish to be delivered from, and whatever our aspirations and pious wishes may be, "if we pray rightly and fittingly, we can say nothing else, but that which is contained in the Lord's Prayer." [3] It is only right that this prayer should be our first prayer when Christ is about to enthrone Himself in the midst of our human hearts. Tertullian observed that the Our Father "contains almost the whole sum of the doctrine and law of Christ." [4] Yet, we do not intend to insinuate that hereby the perfection of the Lord's Prayer was exhausted. St. Thomas Aquinas makes another observation, which, on account of its beauty, is worth noting. He says: "In the Lord's Prayer not only do we ask for all that we may rightly desire, but also in the order wherein we ought to desire them, so that this prayer not only teaches us to ask, but also directs all our affections." [5]

[3] St. Augustine, *ad Probam,* ep. 130, 12; quoted by St. Thomas, *Summa theol.,* IIa IIae, q. 83, a. 9.
[4] *De Orat.,* chap. 1.
[5] *Loc. cit.*

Now let us ask, What is this order of desire? The Angelic
Doctor answers this question, when he says: "Since prayer
is the interpreter of desire, the order of the petitions corre-
sponds with the order, not of execution, but of desire, or intention, where the end precedes the things that are directed
to the end, and attainment of good precedes removal of
evil." [6]

Because this is a perfect prayer, a prayer containing wonderful wealth and depth of thought, as well as possessing great
simplicity and conciseness, it is obvious that the Our Father
is that "common prayer of the congregation," [7] for the Our
Father is said in a loud voice by the priest in order that the
people may join in the recitation of its sevenfold petitions.
Therefore this prayer, in the eyes of the Church, is best fitted
to prepare the people for Communion.

The Church in arranging her liturgy followed the advice
of the Lord Himself, who said expressly: "Thus, therefore,
shall you pray. . . ." [8] Hence the priest, regarding the exalted
dignity and origin of the words he is going to pronounce,
prefaces the Pater Noster with a preamble, saying: "Taught
by Thy saving precepts, and following the divine directions,
we presume to say: Our Father."

"Our Father who art in heaven." By these very first words
"confidence is excited in us chiefly by the consideration of His
[God's] charity in our regard, whereby He wills our good.
Wherefore we say: Our Father; and of His excellence,
whereby He is able to fulfill it. Wherefore we say: Who art in
heaven." [9]

We wish to see the name and honor of our heavenly Father

[6] *Ibid.*, ad 2.
[7] *Ibid.*, IIIa, q.83, a.4.
[8] Matt. 6:9.
[9] *Summa theol.*, IIa IIae, q.83, a.9, ad 5.

treated as a holy thing by men, and therefore we say: "Hallowed be Thy name."

We desire the diffusion of God's glory among men. We pray that "Thy kingdom come"; "Thy will be done." "May Thy commandments be obeyed on earth as in heaven, i.e., by men as well as by angels." [10]

And now that we have professed our confidence in God and our zeal for His glory, we are permitted to think of our own human needs and wants. Hence we say: "Give us this day our daily bread, whether we understand this of the sacramental bread, the daily use of which is profitable to man, and to which all the other sacraments are ordained, or of the bread of the body so that it denotes all sufficiency of food . . . since both the Eucharist is the chief sacrament, and bread is the chief food." [11]

And now that we have prayed for our spiritual and material wants, we ask our heavenly Father to forgive us our guilt. "And forgive us our trespasses." Our trespasses are forgiven under one condition, namely, that we forgive them that trespass against us. "And lead us not into temptation, that is, to be not conquered by temptation." [12] "But deliver us from evil, Amen."

St. Matthew reports the Our Father in connection with our Lord's Sermon on the Mount shortly after the enumeration of the eight beatitudes. And, indeed, there exists a striking analogy between the petitions of the Our Father and the beatitudes, an analogy deserving a moment of reflection.

In quoting from a sermon of St. Augustine, St. Thomas says:

[10] St. Augustine, *Ad Probam*, "De serm. Dom. in monte," II, 5; quoted by St. Thomas in *Summa theol.*, IIa IIae, q.83, a.9, ad 1.

[11] *Summa theol.*, IIa IIae, q.83, a.9.

[12] *Ibid.*

If it is fear of God whereby blessed are the poor in spirit, let us ask that God's name be hallowed among men with a chaste fear. If it is piety whereby blessed are the meek, let us ask that His kingdom may come, so that we become meek and no longer resist Him. If it is knowledge whereby blessed are they that mourn, let us pray that His will be done, and thus we shall mourn no more. If it is fortitude whereby blessed are they that hunger, let us pray that our daily bread be given to us. If it is counsel whereby blessed are the merciful, let us forgive the trespasses of others that our own may be forgiven. If it is understanding whereby blessed are the pure in heart, let us pray lest we have a double heart by seeking after worldly things which are the occasion of our temptations. If it is wisdom whereby blessed are the peacemakers for they shall be called the children of God, let us pray to be delivered from evil: for if we be delivered we shall by that very fact become the free children of God.[13]

It is to the beatitudes, begun here on earth and perfected in eternity, that the prayer of the Our Father and the whole Eucharistic service should lead us. Let this consideration become reality in us!

[13] *Ibid.*, ad 3.

# CHAPTER 40

## *Deliver Us from Evil*

Libera nos, quaesumus, Domine, ab omnibus malis, praeteritis, praesentibus, et futuris: et intercedente beata et gloriosa semper Virgine Dei Genitrice Maria, cum beatis Apostolis tuis Petro et Paulo, atque Andrea, et omnibus Sanctis, da propitius pacem in diebus nostris: ut ope misericordiae tuae adjuti, et a peccato simus semper liberi, et ab omni perturbatione securi.

AFTER the "Pater Noster" has been sung or said in a loud voice, the priest continues to reflect at greater length on its last petition. Yes, it may be said that the last words of the "Pater Noster" form the antiphon to the "Libera." "Sed libera nos a malo." "Libera nos, quaesummus, Domine, ab omnibus malis." O Lord, break the chains which hold us in the bondage of sin and deliver us from its dreadful consequences. Preserve us, O merciful Father, from impending miseries. We beseech Thee, O Lord, to free us from all sins and evils which continue to abide with us, all evils that surround us at present, and from all evils that may assail us in the future. O Lord, deliver us from all evils of the body, from all sufferings and pains, and from an unprovided death. Protect us against the evils that may burden the soul: worries, troubles, and, especially, the greatest of all evils, sin. "Many are the afflictions of the just; but out of them all will the Lord deliver them." [1] "Have mercy

[1] Ps. 33:20.

on me, O Lord, for I am weak: heal me, O Lord, for my bones
are troubled." [2]

Evil is a word everyone knows, no one loves, and all hate.
All flee when evil approaches. No one can escape it altogether. Everyone knows evil by experience, but few of us
understand its meaning. The wise men of ancient Greece and
of Rome pondered over the nature of evil, and they failed to
find a satisfactory explanation. Evil, in fact, regardless of how
common it may be, is so puzzling that it took the keenest
minds among Christian philosophers to analyze and explain
its nature.

Nowhere does the superiority of Christian philosophy become more evident, than when tested on the crucial problem
of evil.

Hence, let us follow the prince of the Schools in his analysis
of evil. St. Thomas says that "there is no one first principle
of evil." [3] This thesis combats all those pagan philosophies
that divide the world into two opposing camps, one directed
by a supreme power of good, the other under the irresistible
control of a supreme evil being. There is no room for this
dualism in Christian thought. Nor may evil be explained by
saying it comes from God. "God is not the author of evil." [4]
For "every creature of God is good," [5] and "God is the greatest
good, therefore every being is good." [6] Let us keep this thesis
before our mind: "Every being is good."

How, then, may we explain evil? No one will deny that evil
is the opposite of good. St. Thomas remarks: "One opposite
is known through the other, as darkness is known through

[2] Ps. 6:2.
[3] *Summa theol.*, Ia, q.49, a.3.
[4] *Ibid.*, a.2.
[5] I Tim. 4:4.
[6] *Summa theol.*, Ia, q.5, a.3.

light. Hence also, what evil is must be known from the nature of good." [7] Now the question is simply this, what is good or what is goodness? If we can find in what goodness consists, we shall have the answer to what evil is.

The philosophers have defined goodness as that which is desirable, or "goodness is what all desire." [8] Now the aim of our desire must be directed towards an object or a being that arouses our delight or satisfaction on account of its perfection. "For," St. Thomas says, "a thing is desirable only in so far as it is perfect, for all desire their own perfection. But everything is perfect so far as it is actual. Therefore, it is clear that a thing is perfect so far as it exists; for it is existence that makes all things actual. . . . Hence it is clear that goodness and being are the same really. . . . They differ only in idea. . . . Goodness presents the aspect of desirableness, which being does not present." [9]

Since we have established the fact that goodness and being are really the same, it will be easy to demonstrate what evil consists in.

"We have said," St. Thomas continues, "that good is everything appetible; and thus, since every nature desires its own being and its own perfection, it must be said also that the being and the perfection of any nature is good. Therefore it cannot be that evil signifies being, or any form or nature. Hence it must be that by the name of evil is signified the absence of good." [10] Or "evil consists in the fact that a thing fails in goodness." [11] "Evil is . . . a privation." [12] Evil, in brief, is the absence or lack of good.

[7] *Ibid.*, q.48, a.1.
[8] *Ibid.*, q.5, a.1.
[9] *Loc. cit.*
[10] *Ibid.*, q.48, a.1.
[11] *Ibid.*, a.2.
[12] *Ibid.*, ad 1.

Having established the thesis that goodness and being are
the same, and that evil is not a being but the absence of good,
it is easy to see that "evil exists only in good," or that "the
subject of evil is good," [13] or "that there is no possible source
of evil except good." [14] St. Thomas says:

> It must be said that every evil in some way has a cause.
> For, evil is the absence of the good which is natural and
> due to a thing. But that anything fail from its natural and
> due disposition, can come only from some cause drawing
> it out of its proper disposition. For a heavy thing is not
> moved upwards except by some impelling force, nor
> does an agent fail in its action except from some impedi-
> ment. But only good can be a cause, because nothing can
> be a cause except inasmuch as it is a being, and every
> being, as such, is good.[15]

Consequently good is the cause of evil.

There is still another conclusion that we may arrive at without meeting considerable difficulties, as long as we keep before our minds the guiding principle that goodness and being
are the same, and that evil is the absence of some good. And
this conclusion is that "there can be nothing essentially
bad," [16] for, "evil cannot wholly consume good." [17] The reason
for this conclusion is evident, for, if evil, which is the absence
of good, would increase to such an extent as to consume the
good, the good would cease to be a being. There would be
sheer nothingness.

Now let us remember that God is the Creator of all good
things. He is supreme and all-powerful; and, if He permits
evil, it is only for good and wise reasons. Nay, in virtue of His

[13] *Ibid.*, a. 3.
[14] *Ibid.*, q. 49, a. 1.
[15] *Loc. cit.*
[16] *Ibid.*, a. 3.
[17] *Ibid.*, q. 48, a. 4.

infinite wisdom He has the power to make good out of evil. "God is so powerful," observes St. Thomas, "that He can even make good out of evil. Hence many good things would be taken away if God permitted no evil to exist; . . . the life of a lion would not be preserved unless the ass were killed. Neither would avenging justice nor the patience of a sufferer be praised if there were no injustice." [18]

What we have said so far may seem to our readers highly metaphysical, and it is; but regardless of this fact the above philosophical problem has the most practical bearing on our daily life. We do not need to fear an all-powerful evil principle, as the pagans did. God is the Creator of the whole world and of every single being. There is nothing essentially bad in this world. The common expression "this or that is not good," or "he or she is not good" is lacking in the Christian spirit, unless understood relatively. There is not a being, much less a human being, on earth in whom some good is not found. It is, therefore, wise and prudent to withhold all criticism. Let us rather make an effort to see the good in others. As priests, let us appeal to the good side in our fellow men. There is no human being so perverse as to lack all good qualities. Let us draw out the good that dwells in the breast of our fellow men. Our priestly vocation is to lead and guide men towards what is good and true. Good, or goodness, is not a foreign article that has to be introduced to our fellow men. There is some good in every man. The zealous priest who possesses prudence and wisdom and who is a master in the art of psychology knows how to obviate the less desirable qualities in a human being. He appeals to the "higher instinct" in man, he draws out of man what is good. He helps his fellow man to prefer good to evil, to foster goodness in himself and others, to

[18] *Ibid.*, a.2, ad 3.

strengthen all of the better tendencies and higher aspirations that may still be dormant in his human heart; and he enkindles in men the flame of noble ambition to do what is good and virtuous. And in doing this, he converts evil into good. That, indeed, is the blessed task of the priesthood, to combat evil by making good out of evil. But let us priests not forget that we require aid from heaven in our efforts to make good out of evil. We need, as the "Libera" prays, "the intercession of blessed and glorious Mary ever Virgin, Mother of God, together with Thy blessed Apostles Peter and Paul, and Andrew, and all Thy Saints."

If we priests will faithfully do all in our power and will cooperate willingly with God's graces to become worthy instruments, or agents, of God in combating sin and evil, there is no doubt that our heavenly Father will lend a merciful ear to our supplications; and we will "graciously be given peace in our days; that aided by the help of His [Thy] mercy, we may be always free from sin, and secure from all disturbance. Through the same Jesus Christ, Thy Son our Lord, who liveth and reigneth with Thee in the unity of the Holy Ghost, one God, world without end. Amen."

# CHAPTER 41

## *The Lamb of God*

Per eumdem Dominum nostrum Jesum Christum Filium tuum, qui tecum vivit et regnat in unitate Spiritus Sancti Deus.

V. Per omnia saecula saeculorum.

R. Amen.

V. Pax ✠ Domini sit ✠ sempter vobis ✠ cum.

R. Et cum spiritu tuo.

Haec commixtio et consecratio corporis et sanguinis Domini nostri Jesu Christi fiat accipientibus nobis in vitam aeternam.

Amen.

Agnus Dei, qui tollis peccata mundi, miserere nobis.

Agnus Dei, qui tollis peccata mundi, miserere nobis.

Agnus Dei, qui tollis peccata mundi, dona nobis pacem.

IN THE "Libera" we prayed to be delivered from all evils. When the dangers, arising from evils, are held back by the hand of God and do not threaten us, peace, the blessed gift of heaven, descends upon us.

"Peace, peace be to thee, and peace to thy helpers. For thy God helpeth thee." [1] "Peace from God our Father, and from the Lord Jesus Christ." [2] This prayerful Apostolic salutation, which we read so often in the Epistles, is heard anew during the celebration of Mass. And once more Christ stands in the midst of us and says: "Peace be to you." [3]

[1] I Par. 12:18.
[2] Rom. 1:7.
[3] John 20:21.

"Pax Domini sit semper vobiscum."

As soon as the response, "Et cum spiritu tuo," has been given, the priest, while dropping into the chalice a particle of the host, says: "May the mingling and the consecration of the body and blood of our Lord Jesus Christ be unto us who receive it effectual unto life everlasting. Amen."

The host, that is, the sacramental species, but not Christ's very body, is broken.[4]

> Breaking arises from the division of that which has quantity. But nothing having quantity except the sacramental species is broken here, because neither Christ's body is broken, as being incorruptible, nor is the substance of the bread, because it no longer remains. . . . The breaking is in the dimensive quantity of the bread, as in a subject, just as the other accidents. And as the sacramental species are the sacrament of Christ's true body, so is the breaking of the species the sacrament of our Lord's Passion, which was in Christ's true body.[5]

In other words, "The breaking of the consecrated host, and the putting of only one part into the chalice, regards the mystical body." [6]

"The breaking of the host denotes three things: First, the rending of Christ's body, which took place in the Passion; secondly, the distinction of His mystical body according to its various states; and thirdly, the distribution of the graces which flow from Christ's Passion; . . . hence this breaking does not imply severance in Christ." [7]

And who, when breaking the host, is not reminded of the first "fregit, deditque" as it took place in the Last Supper chamber? By the sign of the breaking of the bread, the two

---

[4] *Summa theol.*, IIIa, q77, a.7, ad 3.
[5] *Ibid.*, a.7.
[6] *Ibid.*, q.83, a.6, ad 6.
[7] *Ibid.*, a.5, ad 7.

apostles on their way to Emmaus recognized their risen Lord. By this same sign we should remind ourselves that we are about to receive into our hearts the divine food, prepared by our Lord and Master Himself. "The bread that I will give is My flesh, for the life of the world." [8]

Humbly and affectionately, the priest, conscious of his own unworthiness and mindful of the meek and immaculate Eucharistic victim, strikes his breast three times, while he says:

"Lamb of God, who takest away the sins of the world, have mercy on us."

"Lamb of God, who takest away the sins of the world, have mercy on us."

"Lamb of God, who takest away the sins of the world, grant us peace."

The Lamb of God. This cry has been heard through the ages. Seven hundred years before the coming of the Messias, the great prophet Isaias with a heart longing for the speedy advent of the promised Redeemer, cried out: "Send forth, O Lord, the Lamb, the ruler of the earth." [9] And when explaining the mission of the future Messias, Isaias prophesied the passion of the divine Lamb in these impressive words: "The Lord hath laid on him the iniquity of us all. He was offered because it was his own will, and he opened not his mouth; he shall be led as a sheep to the slaughter, and shall be dumb as a lamb before his shearer, and he shall not open his mouth." [10]

The prophet Jeremias speaks in a similar language of Christ, when he says: "And I was as a meek lamb, that is carried to be a victim." [11] And also when Christ had come into this world

---

[8] John 6:52.
[9] Isa. 16:1.
[10] Isa. 53:6–7.
[11] Jer. 11:19.

and was about to begin His mission, another prophet, the
greatest of them all, stood near the Jordan River and pointing
to the One in whom the prophets were fulfilled, and employing a language understandable by all people, cried: "Behold
the Lamb of God, behold Him who taketh away the sin of the
world." [12] This cry remained in the memories of the apostles. And many years after they had received the gift of the
Holy Ghost, St. Peter wrote the following words: ". . . The
precious blood of Christ as of a lamb unspotted and undefiled." [13] In his Apocalypse, St. John gives unending praise
and adoration to "the Lamb that was slain." [14]

To symbolize Christ as the lamb requires a more striking
illustration than the mere meekness and patience of the
animal. In the Temple of Jerusalem, a lamb was the daily
sacrifice offered up morning and evening. This sacrificial victim of the Temple of the Old Law foreshadowed the Lamb
that was slain on the altar of the cross.

Apart from being offered up as a daily sacrifice, a lamb was
the victim that served as a solemn sacrifice on certain feast
days, and especially during the Paschal celebration. This
paschal lamb foreshadowed, as St. Thomas Aquinas teaches,
the Eucharistic sacrifice in three ways:

> First of all, since it was eaten with unleavened loaves,
> according to Exodus: 'They shall eat flesh . . . and un-
> leavened bread.' [15] As to the second, because it was im-
> molated by the entire multitude of the children of Israel
> on the fourteenth day of the moon; and this was a figure
> of the Passion of Christ, who is called the Lamb on ac-
> count of His innocence. As to the effect, because by the
> blood of the paschal lamb the children of Israel were

[12] John 1:29.
[13] I Pet. 1:19.
[14] Apoc. 5:12.
[15] Exod. 12:8.

preserved from the destroying Angel, and brought from the Egyptian captivity; and in this respect the paschal lamb is the chief figure of this sacrament, because it represents it in every respect.[16]

The Lamb of God!

Jesus Christ the incarnate Son of the eternal God the Father in heaven. Jesus Christ, to whom all power is given in heaven and on earth. Jesus Christ, who overcame sin and death. This same Jesus Christ is the ever-meek, humble, and patient Lamb of God. What a lesson in patience and meekness! "Behold the Lamb of God." See, how even in the early days of His preaching mission in Galilee, long before the days of the Passion, He is the model of meekness and patience. See, how the throngs continuously follow Him, surround Him, press on Him, and push Him; call Him hither and thither to cure this sick person and that afflicted man and woman. Notice how the crowd talks and chats, always demanding to see new miracles, but never thinks of giving Him any rest or relaxation. Think of this continuous annoyance. Observe this multitude, these curious onlookers, these men who take no lesson to their hearts and never profess any faith in Him. See this crowd, today applauding Him, dispersing tomorrow, and turning against Him on a later day. Witness the watchful Pharisees, full of ill will and malicious designs, asking questions to trap Him in order that they may denounce Him before the people and the high court. And the Lamb of God subjects Himself to all these trials and provoking situations. He undergoes these hardships, permitting all of them, to be all to all. What heroic patience! What meekness! What charity! "Behold the Lamb of God!"

And what a lesson to us priests!

It may be trying at times to have to listen to the heartbreak-

[16] *Summa theol.*, IIIa, q. 73, a. 6.

ing stories of some poor caller at the rectory. It may be wearisome to spend your time with people who are ignorant and boring. It may be tiresome to attend to so many matters that, in themselves, are trifles, or, at least, of no great importance. One's nerves are put to a severe test under the strain of having to bear unpleasant situations and of coping with responsibility. Should you stand all this? Yes, remember, one unkind or imprudent word to a person may undo many weeks and months of labor, whereas charity, patience, and meekness, persevering to the last, gain the victory. How these virtues win the confidence of the people! What an asset they are in the life of a priest! Make it your aim to possess them, and to perfect yourself in them. Acquire the patience and meekness of a lamb; and "let this mind be in you, which was also in Christ Jesus." [17] "Take up My yoke upon you, and learn from Me, because I am meek, and humble of heart. . . ." [18]

[17] Phil. 2:5.
[18] Matt. 11:29.

# CHAPTER 42

# *The Prayer for Peace*

Domine Jesu Christe, qui dixisti Apostolis tuis: Pacem relinquo vobis, pacem meam do vobis: ne respicias peccata mea, sed fidem Ecclesiae tuae; eamque secundum voluntatem tuam pacificare et coadunare digneris. Qui vivis et regnas Deus per omnia saecula saeculorum. Amen.

THE "Domine Jesu Christe" is a prayer for peace. The idea of peace does not come suddenly upon the celebrant. After he had prayed to be delivered from all evils, the very first word of the priest was a salutation of peace. "Pax Domini sit semper vobiscum." A few seconds later, when the priest for the third time struck his breast at the "Agnus Dei," he again prayed for peace, "dona nobis pacem." Now that he has put all his trust in the Lamb of God and implored His mercy, the priest reminds our Lord, Jesus Christ, of the promise He Himself made, that is, to give peace, His peace, to His apostles. "O Lord Jesus Christ, who didst say to Thy apostles: Peace I leave with you, My peace I give to you: look not upon my sins, but upon the faith of Thy Church: and vouchsafe to her that peace and unity which are agreeable to Thy will: who livest and reignest God, world without end. Amen."

The prophet Isaias announced the Messias as prince of peace: "For a child is born to us, and a son is given to us, and the government is upon his shoulder: and his name shall be,

Wonderful, Counsellor, God the Mighty, the Father of the world to come, the Prince of Peace. His empire shall be multiplied, and there shall be no end of peace. . . ." [1] The prophet Zacharias revealed that the promised Redeemer "shall speak peace to the Gentiles." [2] When our Lord was born, angels carried the message of peace to men of good will. At the birth of our Lord, peace actually reigned, an unprecedented thing indeed. St. Thomas Aquinas, in quoting St. Jerome, says: "If we search the pages of ancient history, we shall find that throughout the whole world there was discord until the twenty-eighth year of Augustus Caesar: but when our Lord was born, all war ceased; according to Isaias: [3] 'Nation shall not lift up sword against nation.' " [4]

The mission of Christ was peace: "God sent the word to the children of Israel, preaching peace by Jesus Christ. . . . " [5] "And coming, He preached peace to you that were afar off, and peace to them that were nigh." [6] "These things I have spoken to you that in Me you may have peace." [7] "Peace I leave with you, My peace I give unto you. . . ." [8]

Now, what is peace? Though we may be acquainted with the definition given by St. Augustine, "peace is the tranquillity of order," [9] it will be of little use to us unless we know the sequence of considerations and the train of ideas that lead up to this definition.

The best way to arrive at a clear conception of peace is to approach the subject from its negative side. When is man not

[1] Isa. 9:6–7.
[2] Zach. 9:10.
[3] Isa. 2:4.
[4] *Summa theol.*, IIIa, q.35, a.8, ad 1.
[5] Acts 10:36.
[6] Eph. 2:17.
[7] John 16:33.
[8] John 14:27.
[9] *Summa theol.*, IIa IIae, q.29, a.2.

at peace? "Man's heart is not at peace so long as he has not what he wants, or if having what he wants, there still remains something for him to want, something he cannot have at the same time." [10] From this concept of peace, we conclude that peace has something to do with desire. And, in fact, peace is attained when desire finds rest in an object.

> From the very fact that a man desires a certain thing it follows that he desires to obtain what he desires, and, in consequence, to remove whatever may be an obstacle to his obtaining it. Now a man may be hindered from obtaining the good he desires by a contrary desire either of his own or of some other, and both are removed by peace. . . . Hence it follows of necessity that whoever desires anything desires peace, in so far as he who desires anything desires to attain, with tranquillity and without hindrance, to that which he desires, and this is what is meant by peace which Augustine [11] defines, 'the tranquillity of order.' [12]

Now follows the second question. Where is this tranquillity of order found, or what is the object of our desire? There can be no doubt that the ultimate end of all human desire must be God. In Him the soul finds perfect peace. "It consists in the perfect enjoyment of the sovereign good, and unites all one's desires by giving them rest in one object. This is the last end of the rational creature, according to the Psalms: 'Who hath placed peace in thy borders.' " [13] This is the peace St. Augustine wrote of: "Fecisti nos [Domine] ad te, et inquietum est cor nostrum, donec requiescat in te." [14] This is "the peace of God which surpasseth all understanding." [15]

[10] *Ibid.*, a. 1.
[11] *De Civ. Dei*, XIX, 13.
[12] *Summa theol.*, IIa IIae, q. 29, a. 2.
[13] Ps. 147:3; *Summa theol.*, IIa IIae, q. 29, a. 2, ad 4.
[14] *Confessions*, I, 1.
[15] Phil. 4:7.

Pointedly the Apostle of the Gentiles calls the supreme good "the God of peace." [16]

Besides this perfect peace, there is also an imperfect peace "which may be had in this world, for though the chief movements of the soul find rest in God, yet there are certain things within and without which disturb that peace." [17] This imperfect peace therefore consists in "freedom from outward disturbance; for it is impossible to rejoice perfectly in the beloved good if one is disturbed in the enjoyment thereof." [18] Hence the correct idea of peace implies two things, "namely, that we be not disturbed by external things, and that our desires rest altogether in one object." [19] This conception of peace in its completeness and fullness is in the mind of the Church when, in Mass, the priest prays for peace.

Let us ask once more, What is peace? Is it a virtue we can acquire or practice? No, peace is not a virtue,[20] but peace is the effect of a virtue, namely, charity. Charity means loving God, and loving our neighbor. And if we love God and our neighbor, peace will be the result. In explaining peace, the Angelic Doctor says as follows:

> Peace implies a twofold union. . . . The first is the result of one's own appetites being directed to one object, while the other results from one's own appetite being united with the appetite of another, and each of these unions is effected by charity; the first, in so far as man loves God with his whole heart by referring all things to Him, so that all his desires tend to one object; the second, in so far as we love our neighbor as ourselves, the result being that we wish to fulfill our neigh-

[16] Rom. 15:33; 16:20.
[17] *Summa theol.*, IIa IIae, q.29, a.2, ad 4.
[18] Ia IIae, q.70, a.3.
[19] *Ibid.*
[20] See *Summa theol.*, IIa IIae, q.29, a.4.

bor's will as though it were ours, hence, it is reckoned a
sign of friendship if people make choice of the same
things,[21] and Tully [22] says: "That friends like and dislike
the same things." [23]

Charity effects peace. Be charitable, and you will spread
the blessings of peace. Dionysius says: "Peace is the cause of
consent and of connaturalness." [24] St. Paul writes to the same
effect: ". . . Pursue justice, faith, charity, and peace." [25]
Charity creates union and peace among men: ". . . Brethren,
rejoice, be perfect, take exhortation, be of one mind, have
peace; and the God of peace and of love shall be with you." [26]

As priests, it is our particular mission to spread the kingdom of truth and peace. "Only love ye truth and peace!" [27]
Again and again the great Apostle St. Paul sends this message
to the faithful: "Follow peace with all men." [28] "Let us follow
after the things that are of peace." [29]

In this valley of tears, conditions are frequently contrary
to peace. It behooves us priests to be messengers of peace.
And ". . . God hath called us in peace." [30] As priests and
leaders of the faithful, it is our duty not to become involved
in petty quarrels, or to take part in discords. It is true that not
all persons we have to deal with are congenial. The ways of
some of our neighbors are provoking to us. Some people are
of an irritable disposition. Some can only be described by the
term "cranks," but the truth is that this cranky disposition is

[21] *Ethic.*, IX, 4.
[22] *De amicitia.*
[23] Sallust, *Catilin.; Summa theol.* IIa IIae, q.29, a.3.
[24] *Ibid.*, IIa IIae, q.29, a.2, ad 1.
[25] II Tim. 2:22.
[26] II Cor. 13:11.
[27] Zach. 8:19.
[28] Heb. 12:14.
[29] Rom. 14:19.
[30] I Cor. 7:15.

frequently caused by sickness or by adverse conditions, which the poor sufferer tries to hide from the eyes of the world. Let us realize that if we were in his place, we might be less jolly and less disposed to good humor. But no matter how difficult one may be to approach, no matter how easily one becomes "cross," there are some lovable features in every human being. It is the art of the wise and prudent guide of souls to appeal to the better side of men, to touch those finer chords in the character of men, regardless of the depth at which they may be buried or hidden under a crude and raw exterior. Have not we ourselves touchy spots, sensitive points, which are better left alone? The pastor who has some insight into the psychology of souls refrains from antagonizing irritable natures. He does not provoke the anger of those less well-disposed, for he has an understanding of the weaknesses of certain characters. He is a master in the art of governing his subject in such a way as to avoid the sore spots. An allusion to these difficulties is found in Holy Scripture. In the Psalms, we read these remarkable words: "With them that hated peace I was peaceable." [31] And in the Epistle to the Romans we read is a sentence from which we may draw a similar inference: "If it be possible, as much as is in you, having peace with all men." [32] A true spirit of charity conquers these difficulties, and plants its seed even in soil that was not deemed favorable by those less filled with the spirit of Christian charity.

To "seek after peace and pursue it," [33] is the spirit of the zealous priest. His task, as pastor and shepherd of souls, consists frequently in straightening out misunderstandings and in settling discords. When disputes arise, his charity dissolves them. To bring to a sinful world the fruits of the Holy Ghost,

[31] Ps. 119:7.
[32] Rom. 12:18.
[33] Ps. 33:15.

"charity, joy, peace, patience, benignity, goodness, longanimity" is the task of the one who stands daily at the altar and prays for peace and unity, while his hands hold the sacred Host. And our Lord will hear this pre-Communion prayer, and He will bless the priest's efforts to promote peace and concord among His people, for as St. Thomas so truly and so beautifully says: "The Mass is the sacrament of unity and peace." [34]

[34] *Summa theol.*, IIIa, q. 83, a. 4.

# CHAPTER 43

## The Magnificent Summary

Domine Jesu Christe, Fili Dei vivi, qui ex voluntate
Patris, cooperante Spiritu Sancto, per mortem tuam
mundum vivificasti: libera me per hoc sacrosanctum
corpus et sanguinem tuum ab omnibus iniquitatibus
meis, et universis malis: et fac me tuis semper inhaerere
mandatis, et a te numquam separari permittas: qui cum
eodem Deo Patre et Spiritu Sancto vivis et regnas Deus
in saecula saeculorum. Amen.

THE prayers following the Consecration are, in content, principally dogmatic. It is true that they contain many moral lessons, but the dogmatic aspect is more pronounced, more emphasized. When we come to the "Pater Noster," a complete change takes place. The first part of the "Pater Noster" is still a dogmatic lesson, the great doctrine of Monotheism, but the second part of the "Our Father," beginning with the petition for bread, consists pronouncedly in moral applications. And due to this change in the "Pater Noster," the prayers following the "Our Father" are, for the greater part, of a moral character. However, the dogmatic foundation is not missing from these prayers. But the second part of the "Our Father" as well as the prayer, "to be delivered from evil," and the prayers whose leading note is that for peace, are of the moral order. And now that the priest is approaching the moment of union with Christ in Holy Communion, he makes a great summary of all the prayers preceding this one, summing up in a few, clear, and distinct words, first, the dogmatic principles on which the doctrine of the Eucharistic Sacrifice is based, and secondly, the moral applications that proceed from the dogmatic foundation, and that were thought of by him at greater length in the prayers he just finished.

And, while we glance at the "Domine Jesu Christe," we cannot help noticing its great likeness to the "Pater Noster," with regard to its construction, yet with the marked distinction that the "Pater Noster" is addressed to God, "Our Father who art in heaven," whereas the second prayer in preparation for Communion is directed to "our Lord Jesus Christ, Son of the living God."

The Holy Eucharist has its foundation in the divinity of Christ. In accordance with the rules of logic, we see that the profession in the divinity of Jesus Christ forms the beginning and the head of the prayer "Domine Jesu Christe." The confession of St. Peter: "Thou art Christ, the Son of the living God,"[1] which was spoken in the name of the Apostolic College, and consequently in the name of the whole Church, is repeated individually by every priest when he celebrates Mass. "Domine Jesu Christe, Fili Dei vivi." This confession in the divinity of Christ, establishing the activity of God the Father and God the Holy Ghost in the work of the Redemption, is solemnly declared. "Qui ex voluntate Patris, cooperante Spiritu Sancto." The work of the Redemption consisted in the death of our Savior, the death which gave life to the world. "Per mortem tuam mundum vivificasti." For, the Eucharistic Sacrifice is in an unbloody manner the continuation and memorial of our Savior's death on the cross.

By this most sacred body and blood of our Lord, we are

[1] Matt. 16:16.

delivered from all iniquities and from all evils. "Libera me per hoc sacrosanctum Corpus et Sanguinem tuum ab omnibus iniquitatibus meis, et universis malis." Evidently the petitions of the "Libera nos quaesumus," which the priest said just a moment ago, come back to his mind. Now that he has referred to all things negative, "malis, iniquitatibus," the priest presents two positive petitions. He pleads to heaven that the Lord by His graces will make him adhere always to God's commandments, "et fac me tuis semper inhaerere mandatis." He knows that he will attain the bliss of heaven only by faithful obedience to God's will. Finally, in order that there will be no doubt about his heart's desires, the priest, in the most affectionate and sweetest way, adds the petition and desire never to be separated from his Lord and Savior, "et a te numquam separari permittas." Is there a holier, more beautiful thought than the wish to be united with Christ? After the struggle in this life is over, the soul, created and sustained in its very existence by the hand of God, longs for, and cries out to return to, its Lord and Maker.

And, indeed, the eating and drinking of the body and blood of our Lord is, according to Christ's sacred words, a pledge of everlasting union with Him, for He solemnly declared: "If any man eat of this bread, he shall live forever." [2] Or to put this thought into Thomistic language, we read: "The attaining of glory is an effect of this sacrament." [3]

The reason for this sacrament is most evident. Christ Himself is contained in the Sacrament and this in itself is sufficient to assure us union with Him here, in this life, and in the life to come. But let us add some further reflections, given by the Angelic Doctor:

[2] John 6:52.
[3] *Summa theol.*, IIIa, q.79, a.2.

Because it was by His Passion that Christ opened to us the approach to eternal life, according to Hebrews: "He is the Mediator of the new testament; that by means of His death . . . they that are called may receive the promise of eternal inheritance." [4] Accordingly in the form of this sacrament it is said: This is the chalice of My blood, of the new and eternal testament. In like manner the refreshment of spiritual food and the unity denoted by the species of the bread and wine are to be had in the present life, although imperfectly; but perfectly in the state of glory. Hence Augustine says on the words, My flesh is meat indeed: [5] "Seeing that in meat and drink, men aim at this, that they hunger not nor thirst, this verily naught doth afford save only this meat and drink, which maketh them who partake thereof to be immortal and incorruptible, in the fellowship of the saints, where shall be peace and unity, full and perfect." [6]

This effect is not accomplished immediately. Let us hear the words of Aquinas: "As Christ's Passion, in virtue whereof this sacrament is accomplished, is indeed the sufficient cause of glory, yet not so that we are thereby forthwith admitted to glory, but we must first suffer with Him that we may be also glorified with Him,[7] so this sacrament does not at once admit us to glory, but bestows on us the power of coming unto glory." [8]

Now, the one thing that is an obstacle to the working of Christ's graces in the soul, and to man's attaining eternal glory, is sin. To subdue sin, to save man from falling further into sin; or in short, to preserve man from future sins, is the

[4] Heb. 9:15.
[5] John 6:56.
[6] Summa theol., IIIa, q.79, a.2.
[7] Rom. 8:17.
[8] Summa theol., IIIa, q.79, a.2, ad 1.

effect of this sacrament. For, the Angelic Teacher gives us
the following exposition:

> Our Lord said, "This is the bread which cometh down
> from heaven; that if any man eat of it, he may not die," [9]
> which manifestly is not to be understood of the death of
> the body. Therefore it is to be understood that this sacra-
> ment preserves from spiritual death, which is through
> sin. Sin is the spiritual death of the soul. Hence man is
> preserved from future sins in the same way as the body
> is preserved from future death of the body; and this hap-
> pens in two ways, first of all, in so far as man's nature is
> strengthened inwardly against inner decay, and so by
> means of food and medicine he is preserved from death.
> Secondly, by being guarded against outward assaults,
> and thus he is protected by means of arms by which he
> defends his body. Now this sacrament preserves man
> from sin in both of these ways. For, first of all, by uniting
> man with Christ through grace, it strengthens his spir-
> itual life, as spiritual food and spiritual medicine, ac-
> cording to the Scriptures: "[That] bread strengthens
> [Vulg., may strengthen] man's heart." [10] Augustine like-
> wise says: "Approach without fear, it is bread, not poi-
> son." [11] Secondly, inasmuch as it is a sign of Christ's
> Passion, whereby the devils are conquered, it repels all
> the assaults of demons. Hence Chrysostom [12] says: "Like
> lions breathing forth fire, thus do we depart from that
> table, being made terrible to the devil." [13]

As we have seen, the Holy Eucharist is a pledge of eternal
glory, and preserves us against future sins. Certainly our Lord
could not extend more generous gifts to a human being in this
earthly life. To go further in His bestowal of graces would

[9] John 6:50.
[10] Ps. 103:15.
[11] Tract. 26, *In Joan.*
[12] Hom. 46, *In Joan.*
[13] *Summa theol.*, IIIa, q.79, a.6.

necessitate that He take man entirely out of this world; but such a course was not planned by divine Providence. While the priest celebrates his daily Mass, our Lord Himself, like a noble knight with a strong arm and an indestructible shield, does His best to guard His faithful servant at the altar against future pitfalls and against sins that he could commit some day out of human weakness. Our Lord pledges His faithful servant the reward of eternal life. Could He do more? Certainly not. He has done everything necessary, on His part, in assisting us to gain this eternal life. And all He expects in return from the priest is one single thing, the priest's cooperation with His graces. Will you, who are standing at the altar of the Eucharistic Lord, hesitate? It is difficult to imagine. Promise your cooperation anew to our Lord, my priest friend, you, the servant and friend of Christ. In a few seconds hence, you are going to consume the sacred species. You will be united with Christ Himself. And this union of yourself with His sacred self, under the appearance of bread and wine, is already half a step into heaven. This union will be perfected some day, when this material life comes to an end, for, it is to become a reality, an irrevocable reality, when the course of life will be continued in eternity in the perfect union with Christ, our Lord and Master.

# CHAPTER 44

## *The Eucharistic Union*

Perceptio Corporis tui, Domine Jesu Christe, quod ego indignus sumere praesumo, non mihi proveniat in judicium et condemnationem; sed pro tua pietate prosit mihi ad tutamentum mentis et corporis, et ad medelam percipiendam. Qui vivis et regnas cum Deo Patre, in unitate Spiritus Sancti Deus per omnia saecula saeculorum. Amen.

THIS prayer, "Perceptio Corporis tui," is distinct from the preceding prayer, "Domine Jesu Christe," in that the former is addressed to Christ, the Son of God and the Redeemer of the world, whereas the latter is directed to the Eucharistic Christ, "Perceptio Corporis tui, Domine Jesu Christe."

In just a moment, now, the priest will consume the sacred species. "Quod ego indignus sumere praesumo." According to the laws of justice, no human being has the right to unite himself with God, for, the distance between the divine and the human is too great. But the priest presumes to receive God in Holy Communion. He takes, by the divine command, the liberty to receive Christ's body and blood. The priest recognizes his unworthiness, "Ego indignus." Not that he would consciously approach the table of the Lord in the state of mortal sin. This thought is out of the question. But who is so holy and so sinless that he is worthy to receive the sacrament? Who possesses the personal sanctity that measures up to the dignity of the Eucharist? We are always the inferior, the debtor; therefore the priest prays that the receiving of this sacrament may not turn to his judgment and condemnation. "Non mihi proveniat in judicium et condemnationem." No one reads these words without being reminded of St. Paul's warning to the Corinthians: "For he that eateth and drinketh unworthily, eateth and drinketh judgment to himself, not discerning the body of the Lord." [1] Fittingly we may add the reflection of St. Thomas regarding the unworthy reception of this sacrament. "Just as Christ's Passion has not its effect in them who are not disposed towards it, as they should be, so also they do not come to glory through this sacrament who receive it unworthily. Hence Augustine,[2] expounding the same passage, observes: 'The sacrament is one thing, the power of the sacrament another. Many receive it from the altar . . . and by receiving die. . . . Eat, then, spiritually the heavenly bread, bring innocence to the altar.' " [3]

Unworthy Communion is not in the mind of the celebrant. The words of his prayer rather reflect a certain fear and awe in consuming a sacrament as holy as the Eucharist. The priest is fully conscious of his unworthiness, for, although the priest's preparations for Communion are made as thoroughly as human weakness will permit, he is never worthy to approach the Divine. Not by my personal strength or virtue, which would merit only judgment and condemnation, but by Thy condescension, by Thy goodness and mercy, "pro tua pietate," will this sacrament become profitable to me, to the protection and health both of body and soul and to my salvation; "prosit mihi ad tutamentum mentis et corporis, et ad medelam percipiendam."

[1] I Cor. 11:29.
[2] Tract. 26, *In Joan.*
[3] *Summa theol.*, IIIa, q.79, a.2, ad 2.

"To the protection and health of soul and body." The Holy
Eucharist, being a spiritual food, gives nourishment and
strength to the soul, yet the body, being united to the soul,
participates in the graces of this sacrament. For, thus the
Angelic Doctor teaches: "Although the body is not the immediate subject of grace, still the effect of grace flows into the
body while in the present life we present our [Vulg.: your]
members as instruments of justice unto God,[4] and in the life
to come our body will share in the incorruption and the glory
of the soul." [5]

"Prosit mihi ad tutamentum mentis et corporis, et ad medelam percipiendam." How is this beneficial effect achieved,
and to what extent is it achieved? This is a question which
requires some consideration. The Holy Eucharist is, as we
have said repeatedly, a spiritual food or nourishment. What
is meant by this? What place in our spiritual life is assigned
to the Eucharistic food? A correct answer to this question will
teach us the value of Holy Communion in our spiritual life.
The *Summa* says:

> The Church's sacraments are ordained for helping
> man in the spiritual life. But the spiritual life is analo-
> gous to the corporal, since corporal things bear a re-
> semblance to the spiritual. Now it is clear that just as
> generation is required for corporal life, since thereby
> man receives life; and growth, whereby man is brought
> to maturity, so likewise food is required for the preser-
> vation of life. Consequently just as for the spiritual life
> there had to be Baptism, which is spiritual generation,
> and Confirmation, which is spiritual growth; so there
> needed to be the Sacrament of the Eucharist, which is
> spiritual food.[6]

[4] Rom. 6:13.
[5] *Summa theol.*, IIIa, q.79, a.1, ad 3.
[6] *Ibid.*, q.73, a.1.

The Holy Eucharist is spiritual food, nourishment, for the preservation of the life of the soul. Just as corporal food holds body and soul together, so Holy Communion brings spiritual life to the soul, that is, the Holy Eucharist is the life principle for the spiritual activities of the soul. In explaining the meaning of this concept, let us follow the approved teacher of the Church. St. Thomas says:

> Damascene [7] compares this sacrament to the burning coal which Isaias [8] saw, "For a live ember is not simply wood, but wood united to fire; so also the bread of Communion is not simply bread, but bread united with the Godhead." But as Gregory observes in a homily for Pentecost, "God's love is never idle; for wherever it is, it does great works." And, consequently, through this sacrament, as far as its power is concerned, not only is the habit of grace and of virtue bestowed, but it is furthermore aroused to act, according to Corinthians: "The charity of Christ presseth us." [9] Hence it is that the soul is spiritually nourished through the power of this sacrament by being spiritually gladdened, and is inebriated with the sweetness of the divine goodness according to Canticles,[10] "Eat, friends, and drink, and be inebriated, my dearly beloved." [11]

In another article St. Thomas observes: "In our pilgrimage He [Christ] does not deprive us of His bodily presence, but unites us with Himself in this sacrament through the truth of His body and blood. Hence He says: 'He that eateth My flesh, and drinketh My blood, abideth in Me, and I in him.' [12] Hence this sacrament is the sign of supreme charity, and the uplifter

[7] *De fide orthod.*, IV.
[8] Isa. 6:6.
[9] II Cor. 5:14.
[10] Cant. 5:1.
[11] *Summa theol.*, IIIa, q.79, a.1, ad 2.
[12] John 6:57.

of our hope, from such familiar union of Christ with us." [13]

When charity rules our hearts supremely, a twofold union is established: first, a union, through Christ, with our fellow men who eat from the same table of the Lord. And secondly, a union of the soul with Christ Himself. Continuing the Thomistic thought, the sacrament "has the meaning . . . of ecclesiastical unity, in which men are aggregated through this sacrament, and in this respect it is called Communion or Synaxis. For Damascene [14] says that 'it is called Communion because we communicate with Christ, through it, both because we partake of His flesh and Godhead, and because we communicate with and are united to one another through it.' " [15]

In Holy Communion, Christ unites us with Himself, takes us to Himself, or, so to speak, absorbs us unto Himself.

> The difference between corporal and spiritual food lies in this, that the former is changed into the substance of the person nourished, and consequently it cannot avail for supporting life except it be partaken of, but spiritual food changes man into itself, according to that saying of Augustine [16] that he heard the voice of Christ, as it were, saying to him: "Nor shalt thou change Me into thyself, as food of thy flesh, but thou shalt be changed into Me." [17]

What an infinitely intimate relationship the soul will experience in union with the Eucharistic Christ! This relationship is, indeed, so extraordinary that only gradually are we human beings able to conceive Christ's beautiful designs and experience His ardent and profound love for us.

[13] *Summa theol.*, IIIa, q.75, a.1.
[14] *De fide orthod.*, 4.
[15] *Summa theol.*, IIIa, q.73, a.4.
[16] *Confessions*, 7.
[17] *Summa theol.*, IIIa, q.73, a.3, ad 2.

First, the Lord, as a reward for the faithful reception of His sacred flesh and blood, has promised eternal life: "If any man eat of it, he may not die." [18] "If any man eat of this bread he shall live forever." [19] In the great goodness of His loving heart, the divine Master was not satisfied with this great and wonderful promise, for He goes further and lifts, as it were, the veil which envelops our mortal eyes with earthly things, and permits us a glance into the mysteries of heaven. For He tells us: "He that eateth My flesh, and drinketh My blood, abideth in Me and I in him." [20] "And I live, now not I: but Christ liveth in me." [21] And to St. Augustine, the profoundest exponent of Christian thought in early Christian times, the divine Lord gives still a deeper insight into the truth and beauty of Eucharistic union: "Thou shalt be changed into Me." [22] St. Peter, in his second Epistle, alluded to this above thought when he wrote: ". . . You may be made partakers of the divine nature." [23] Certainly, mere earthly man is not able to enter deeper into the mysteries of a soul in Eucharistic union.

In every worthily celebrated Mass, this Eucharistic union between Christ and the priest is renewed. Daily, at the altar, the priest is made once more a "partaker of the divine nature." Every morning in the sanctuary, he, anew, is "changed into Him," his Eucharistic Lord and Savior. As the weeks, months, and years of the priest's earthly life pass by, the daily Eucharistic union is renewed, strengthened, and perfected. When, at last, his bodily strength fails, the curtain of his life on earth falls, and the eve of his reward draws near, death to the good

[18] John 6:50.
[19] John 6:52.
[20] John 6:57.
[21] Gal. 2:20.
[22] *Summa theol.*, IIIa, q.73, a.3, ad 2.
[23] II Pet. 1:4.

priest is but the continuation in heaven of what he celebrated here on earth, the continuation of this sacred relationship, this holy intimacy, this perfect union with his Lord and Savior, his God and all. Henceforth, unveiled, released from earthly bondage, and discarding all appearances of material forms, the true priest lives face to face with his Lord and Master in celestial reality, uninterrupted, everlasting, throughout all eternity.

# CHAPTER 45

## Holy Communion

Panem caelestem accipiam, et nomen Domini invocabo.

Domine, non sum dignus ut intres sub tectum meum; sed tantum dic verbo, et sanabitur anima mea.

Corpus Domini nostri Jesu Christi custodiat animam meam in vitam aeternam. Amen.

WITH regard to the Communion prayers, we notice a change in the technique of the Missal, for, with the "Perceptio Corporis tui," the well-constructed prayers have come to an end. Henceforth the priest utters only short sentences, or a few words. Is it because the priest's spirit has been transported to heavenly regions that he now prays in few words, or is it due to the fact that his heart is pulsating more rapidly due to the sacredness and awe of Holy Communion? Yes, the Church herself is so overwhelmed with feelings of holy fear, sacred love, humility, spiritual joy, and celestial happiness, that she can place only ejaculations, so to speak, in the mouth of the priest.

Holy Communion is at last at hand. Where is the pen that can adequately describe the union of the soul with its Eucharistic Lord? A union so sublime, so spiritual, cannot be described on paper by pen and ink. Celestial relationships cannot be cast into material forms.

It would be presumptuous to attempt to describe the love

of the divine Bridegroom for a human soul, nor can the ardent desires and the holy feelings of a true spouse of the Lord be fully related by the human tongue. Let us listen to our Lord's own words, or to what the writers of the Old and of the New Testaments have to say. We will also consult two outstanding masters of spirituality, Thomas a Kempis and St. Thomas Aquinas. These two privileged friends of the Lord will tell us, better than we ourselves can, of the joy and love that fills a holy soul at the moment of Holy Communion.

"With desire I have desired to eat this pasch with you." [1] At last this sacred moment is at hand. The divine Master stretches forth His hand, saying: "Take ye and eat. This is My body." [2] "Drink ye all of this." [3] Obeying the summons of the Lord, the priest, before taking the Host into his hands, says: "I will take the bread of heaven, and I will call upon the name of the Lord." With King David, the priest says: "I will sacrifice to thee the sacrifice of praise, and I will call upon the name of the Lord." [4] "I will praise Thee, O Lord, my God, with my whole heart, and I will glorify Thy name forever." [5] "But who am I, O Lord, that I should presume to approach unto Thee?" [6]

"Behold the heaven of heavens cannot contain Thee, and Thou sayest: Come ye all to Me." [7] "How shall I dare to approach, who am conscious to myself of no good on which I can presume?" "How shall I introduce Thee into my house, who have too often offended Thy most benign countenance?" "The angels and the archangels stand in reverential awe; the

[1] Luke 22:15.
[2] Matt. 26:26.
[3] Matt. 26:27.
[4] Ps. 115:17.
[5] Ps. 85:12.
[6] *Imitation,* Bk. IV, chap. 1, par. 2.
[7] *Ibid.*

saints and the just are afraid; and Thou sayest: Come ye all to Me." [8] "But whence is this to me, that Thou shouldst come to me? Who am I, that Thou shouldst give to me Thyself." [9]

With this thought in mind, the priest takes the Host and paten into his hand and strikes his breast, saying three times: "Lord, I am not worthy that Thou shouldst enter under my roof: but only say the word, and my soul shall be healed."

> Almighty, everlasting God look down in mercy upon me, Thy servant, who now again draws near to the most holy sacrament of Thine only-begotten Son, our Lord Jesus Christ. I approach, as one who is sick, to the physician of life; as one unclean, to the fountain of mercy; as one blind, to the light of eternal brightness; as one poor and needy, to the Lord of heaven and earth. I implore Thee, therefore, out of the abundance of Thy boundless mercy, Thou wouldst vouchsafe to heal my sickness, to wash away my defilement, to give sight to my eyes, to enrich my poverty, and to clothe my nakedness; that I may receive the bread of angels, the King of kings, the Lord of lords, with such reverence and humility, such contrition and devotion, such purity and faith, such purpose and intention, as may tend to the salvation of my soul.[10]

"When I consider Thy dignity, O Lord, and my own vileness, I am affrighted exceedingly, and am confounded within myself." [11] "Whatever is wanting to me, O good Jesus, most holy Savior, do Thou in Thy bounty and goodness supply for me." [12]

Strengthened by these thoughts, the priest blesses himself

[8] *Ibid.*, par. 3.
[9] *Ibid.*, chap. 2, par. 1.
[10] Prayer of St. Thomas Aquinas: "Praeparatio ad Missam."
[11] *Imitation*, Bk. IV, chap. 6, par. 1.
[12] *Ibid.*, chap. 4, par. 4.

with the Host while saying: "May the body of our Lord Jesus Christ preserve my soul unto life everlasting. Amen." The priest dares to pronounce these words, for he is reminded of the repeated promise of Christ:

"I am the bread of life." [13]

"This is the bread which cometh down from heaven; that if any man eat of it, he may not die.

"I am the living bread which came down from heaven.

"If any man eat of this bread, he shall live forever: and the bread that I will give is My flesh, for the life of the world."

"He that eateth My flesh and drinketh My blood hath everlasting life: and I will raise him up in the last day."

"For My flesh is meat indeed: and My blood is drink indeed.

"He that eateth My flesh and drinketh My blood abideth in Me, and I in him.

". . . He that eateth Me, the same also shall live by Me."

"This is the bread that came down from heaven."

"He that eateth this bread shall live forever." [14]

Visibly our Lord makes every effort possible to set forth His promise in unmistakable language. He employs every conceivable phrase, using clear but simple construction of words in order to exclude all errors in the interpretation of His meaning. He repeats Himself to emphasize His idea. Again and again He brings out the same idea in different forms. He throws light upon His promise from different angles, that He may be understood by all men.

Indeed, the wisdom of the Old Testament finds its fulfillment in the Holy Eucharist. ". . . Thou didst feed Thy people with the food of angels, and gavest them bread from heaven

[13] John 6:48.
[14] John 6:50–59.

prepared without labor; having in it all that is delicious, and the sweetness of every taste." [15]

"Taste, and see that the Lord is sweet." [16]

"How lovely are Thy tabernacles, O Lord of hosts!" [17]

"My heart and my flesh have rejoiced in the living God." [18]

"The poor shall eat and shall be filled: and they shall praise the Lord that seek Him: their hearts shall live forever and ever." [19]

Fittingly we may add the words of St. John, who wrote, in the Apocalypse, the following lines: "Blessed are they who are called to the marriage supper of the Lamb." [20]

"O Sacrament most holy!

O Sacrament divine!

All praise and all thanksgiving be every moment Thine."

Let us continue with the Church chanting the O Sacram Convivium.

O sacred banquet, in which Christ is received, the memory of His passion is renewed, the mind is filled with grace, and a pledge of future glory is given to us.

V. Thou hast given them bread from heaven.

R. Replenished with all sweetness and delight.

O God, who in this wonderful sacrament hast left us a memorial of Thy passion; grant us, we beseech Thee, so to reverence the sacred mysteries of Thy body and blood, that we may ever perceive within us the fruit of Thy redemption, who livest and reignest, world without end. Amen.

Grant to me, I beseech Thee, not only to receive the sacrament of the body and blood of the Lord, but to

[15] Wisd. 16:20.
[16] Ps. 33:9.
[17] Ps. 83:2.
[18] Ps. 83:3.
[19] Ps. 21:27.
[20] Apoc. 19:9.

profit by its substance and virtue. O God, most merciful, grant me the grace to receive the body of Thine only-begotten Son, Jesus Christ, our Lord, which He took of the Virgin Mary, in such wise, that I may be found worthy to be incorporated into His mystical body, and forevermore to be numbered among His members.

O Father, most loving, I am about to welcome into my heart Thine only beloved Son, hidden under His sacramental veil. May it, in Thy great goodness, be mine, in the end, for all eternity face to face to gaze upon Him: who with Thee liveth and reigneth, in the unity of the Holy Ghost, God, world without end. Amen.[21]

O Godhead hid, devoutly I adore Thee,
Who truly art within the forms before me;
To Thee my heart I bow with bended knee,
As failing quite in contemplating Thee.

Sight, touch, and taste in Thee are each deceived;
The ear alone most safely is believed:
I believe all the Son of God has spoken,
Than truth's own word there is no truer token.

God only on the cross lay hid from view;
But here lies hid at once the manhood too;
And I, in both professing my belief,
Make the same prayer as the repentant thief.

Thy wounds, as Thomas saw, I do not see:
Yet Thee confess my Lord and God to be.
Make me believe Thee ever more and more;
In Thee my hope, in Thee my love to store.

O Thou memorial of our Lord's own dying!
O living bread, to mortals life supplying!
Make Thou my soul henceforth on Thee to live:
Ever a taste of heavenly sweetness give.

[21] St. Thomas Aquinas, "Praeparatio ad Missam."

O loving Pelican! O Jesus Lord!
Unclean I am, but cleanse me in Thy blood!
Of which a single drop, for sinners spilt,
Can purge the entire world from all its guilt.

Jesu! whom for the present veiled I see,
What I so thirst for, oh, vouchsafe to me:
That I may see Thy countenance unfolding,
And may be blest Thy glory in beholding.[22]

[22] Translation by Father Coswall; taken from Father Lasance's *Blessed Sacrament Book.*

# CHAPTER 46

## Consuming the Chalice

Quid retribuam Domino pro omnibus quae retribuit mihi? Calicem salutaris accipiam, et nomen Domini invocabo.

Laudans invocabo Dominum, et ab inimicis meis salvus ero.

Sanguis Domini nostri Jesu Christi custodiat animam meam in vitam aeternam. Amen.

AFTER consuming the sacred Host, the priest for a moment remains speechless. Only with difficulty can he find words to express his feelings. "What shall I render to the Lord for this grace, for charity so remarkable?" [1] "Oh, how admirable is Thy work, O Lord, how mighty is Thy power, how infallible Thy truth!" [2] "O most sweet and most benign Jesus, how great reverence and thanksgiving, with perpetual praise, are due to Thee for the receiving of Thy sacred body, whose dignity no man can be found to unfold!" [3]

While similar thoughts of thanksgiving, charity, praise, and adoration inflame his soul, the priest begins to recite the "Quid retribuam Domino." "What shall I render to the Lord for all the things that He hath rendered to me?"

I offer my entire self to Thee, O Lord.

The priest prays with St. Ignatius, "Take, O Lord, and re-

[1] *Imitation*, Bk. IV, chap. 13, par. 3.
[2] *Ibid.*, chap. 2, par. 4.
[3] *Ibid.*, par. 2.

ceive all my liberty, my memory, my understanding, and my whole will. Thou hast given me all that I am and all that I possess; I surrender it all to Thee that Thou mayest dispose of it according to Thy will. Give me only Thy love and Thy grace; with these I will be rich enough, and will have no more to desire." [4]

Gratitude, charity, and adoration consume the soul of the pious priest. "Oh, how sweet, O Lord, is Thy spirit, who, to show Thy sweetness towards Thy children, vouchsafe to refresh them with that most delicious bread which cometh down from heaven!" [5] "How sweet and delightful this banquet wherein Thou hast given Thyself for our food!" [6]

"Rejoice, O my soul, and give thanks unto God for so noble a gift, and so singular a solace left to thee in this valley of tears." [7]

"Why, then, am I not inflamed in seeking Thy adorable presence?" [8]

Taking the chalice and consuming the sacred blood, the priest says: "I will take the chalice of salvation and I will call upon the name of the Lord."

"O Lord, in the simplicity of my heart, with a good and firm faith, and at Thy command, I come to Thee with hope and reverence; and I believe truly that Thou art here present in the sacrament, both God and man." [9]

After making this short act of faith, let us continue with the priest: "Praising I will call upon the Lord, and I shall be saved from my enemies."

[4] "Suscipe" by St. Ignatius of Loyola.
[5] *Imitation*, Bk. IV, chap. 13, par. 2.
[6] *Ibid.*, chap. 2, par. 4.
[7] *Ibid.*, par. 6.
[8] *Ibid.*, chap. 14, par. 1.
[9] *Ibid.*, chap. 4, par. 2.

"Give joy to the soul of Thy servant, for to Thee, O Lord, I have lifted up my soul." [10]

Praising, singing, joyful, and jubilant, I will call upon the Lord.

"I praise Thee, O my God, and I extoll Thee forever; I despise myself, and cast myself down into the depth of my own vileness." [11]

All ye works of the Lord, bless the Lord: praise and exalt Him above all forever.

O ye angels of the Lord, bless the Lord: praise and exalt Him above all forever.

O ye heavens, bless the Lord: praise and exalt Him above all forever.

O ye sons of men, bless the Lord: praise and exalt Him above all forever.

O ye priests of the Lord, bless the Lord: praise and exalt him above all forever.

O ye servants of the Lord, bless the Lord: praise and exalt him above all forever.

O ye spirits and souls of the just, bless the Lord: praise and exalt Him above all forever.

O ye holy and humble of heart, bless the Lord: praise and exalt Him above all forever.[12]

Praise ye the Lord in His holy places.
Praise ye Him in the firmament of His power.
Praise ye Him for His mighty acts.
Praise ye Him according to the multitude of His greatness.
Praise Him with sound of trumpet.
Praise Him with psaltery and harp.
Praise Him with timbrel and choir.

[10] Ps. 85:4.
[11] *Imitation*, Bk. IV, chap. 2, par. 2.
[12] Dan. 3:57–59, 82, 84–87.

Praise Him with strings and organs.
Praise Him on high sounding cymbals.
Praise Him on cymbals of joy.
Let every spirit praise the Lord, Alleluia.[13]

Before consuming the chalice, while his soul is still filled with praises of the holy name of the Lord, the priest recites these few words: "The blood of our Lord Jesus Christ preserve my soul unto life everlasting. Amen."

Soul of Christ, sanctify me.
Body of Christ, save me.
Blood of Christ, inebriate me.
Water from the side of Christ, wash me.
Passion of Christ, strengthen me.
O good Jesus, hear me.
Within Thy wounds hide me.
Permit me not to be separated from Thee.
From the malignant enemy defend me.
In the hour of my death call me.
And bid me come to Thee,
That with Thy saints I may praise Thee
Forever and ever. Amen.[14]

The soul of man united with his God and Lord, verily, this union is heavenly!

Thou, the Lord of all things, who standest in need of no one, art pleased by this sacrament to dwell in us.[15]

For this I pray, this I desire, that I may be wholly united to Thee, and that I may withdraw my heart from all things created.
Thou in me, and I in Thee, and thus grant us both equally to continue in one.[16]

[13] Ps. 150.
[14] "Aspirations" of St. Ignatius.
[15] *Imitation*, Bk. IV, chap. 2, par. 5.
[16] *Ibid.*, chap. 13, par. 1.

There is not anything that I can present to Him more acceptable than to give up my heart entirely to God, and closely unite it to Him.

This is my whole desire, that my heart may be united to Thee.[17]

Verily, Thou art my beloved, the choicest among thousands, in whom my soul is well pleased to dwell all the days of its life.

Verily, Thou art my peacemaker, in whom is sovereign peace and true rest, and out of whom is labor and sorrow and infinite misery.[18]

I receive Thee, and unite myself to Thee in charity.[19]

"O, how great is the multitude of Thy sweetness, O Lord, which Thou hast hidden for them that fear Thee!" [20]

O, that with Thy presence Thou wouldst totally inflame, consume, and transform me into Thyself, that I may be made one spirit with Thee by the grace of internal union, and by the melting of ardent love! [21]

O Lord my God, my Creator and Redeemer, I desire to receive Thee this day with such affection, reverence, praise, and honor; with such gratitude, worthiness, and love; with such faith, hope, and purity, as Thy most holy Mother, the glorious Virgin Mary, received and desired Thee, when to the angel announcing to her the mystery of the Incarnation, she humbly and devoutly answered: Behold the handmaid of the Lord, be it done unto me according to thy word.[22]

O my God, eternal Love, my whole good and never ending happiness, I desire to receive Thee with the most

[17] *Ibid.*, par. 3.
[18] *Ibid.*, par. 2.
[19] *Ibid.*, chap. 4, par. 2.
[20] Ps. 30:20.
[21] *Imitation*, Bk. IV, chap. 16, par. 3.
[22] *Ibid.*, chap. 17, par. 2.

vehement desire and most worthy reverence that any of the saints have ever had, or could experience.[23]

I offer and present to Thee the joys of all devout hearts, their ardent affections, their ecstasies, supernatural illuminations, and heavenly visions; together with the virtues and praises that are, or shall be, celebrated by all creatures in heaven and earth, for myself and all such as have been recommended to my prayers; and thus by all Thou mayest be worthily praised and glorified forever.[24]

Receive my vows, O Lord my God, and my desires of infinite praise and boundless blessing, which, according to the multitude of Thy unspeakable greatness, are most justly due to Thee.[25]

Be Thou merciful to me, O good Jesus, sweet and gracious, and grant Thy poor mendicant to feel, sometimes at least, in the sacred Communion some little of the cordial affection of Thy love, that my faith may be more strengthened, my hope in Thy goodness increased; and that charity, once perfectly enkindled, and having tasted the manna of heaven, may never die away.[26]

I give Thee thanks, eternal Father, for having out of Thy pure mercy, without any deserts of mine, been pleased to feed my soul with the body and blood of Thy only Son, our Lord Jesus Christ. I beseech Thee that this Holy Communion may not be to my condemnation, but prove an effectual remission of all my sins. May it strengthen my faith; encourage me in all that is good; deliver me from my vicious customs; remove all concupiscence; perfect me in charity, patience, humility, and obedience, and in all other virtues. May it secure me against all the snares of my enemies, both visible and invisible; perfectly moderate all my inclinations, closely

[23] *Ibid.*, par. 1.
[24] *Ibid.*, par. 3.
[25] *Ibid.*, par. 4.
[26] *Ibid.*, chap. 14, par. 2.

unite me to Thee, the true and only good, and obtain for me the grace of a happy death. Do Thou, O heavenly Father, vouchsafe one day to call me, though an unworthy sinner, to participate in that ineffable banquet, where Thou with Thy Son and the Holy Ghost, art to Thy saints true light, fullness of content, everlasting joy, and perfect happiness.[27]

[27] St. Thomas Aquinas, "Gratiarum actio post Missam."

# CHAPTER 47

# The Thanksgiving Service

Quod ore sumpsimus, Domine, pura mente capiamus:
et de munere temporali fiat nobis remedium sempiternum.

Corpus tuum, Domine, quod sumpsi, et Sanguis, quem
potavi, adhaereat visceribus meis: et praesta; ut in me
non remaneat scelerum macula, quem pura et sancta refecerunt sacramenta: Qui vivis et regnas in saecula saeculorum. Amen.

Communio.

Post-Communio.

AFTER the priest has consumed the precious blood, the acolyte
pours wine into the chalice while the priest recites the "Quod
ore sumpsimus." Then the fingers of the celebrant are cleansed
with wine and water. While this takes place the priest says the
"Corpus tuum Domine."

St. Thomas remarks that, "Wine, by reason of its humidity
is capable of washing . . . and this is done in order to rinse
the mouth, after receiving this sacrament lest any particles
remain." [1] "It is a matter of reverence," [2] to rinse the mouth
with wine and water and this applies, also, to the pouring of
wine and water over the fingers of the priest, since they have
touched the sacred body of Christ.

"Quod ore sumpsimus, Domine, pura mente capiamus: et

---

[1] Summa theol., IIIa, q. 83, a. 5, ad 10.
[2] Loc. cit.

de munere temporali fiat nobis remedium sempiternum." In this prayer, the priest states the fact that he received with his mouth the sacrament of the Holy Eucharist; that he consumed the sacred species; that he brought to an end the Eucharistic Sacrifice. Now, that the temporal sacrificial gifts have been presented to almighty God, the priest's wish and prayer is that, with the grace of heaven, he may have received this oblation with a pure mind, and that it will, consequently, become a pledge of everlasting salvation to him.

The concept of the temporal leading to the eternal dwells in the mind of the celebrant when he proceeds to recite the next prayer: "Corpus tuum, Domine, quod sumpsi, et Sanguis, quem potavi, adhaereat visceribus meis: et praesta, ut in me non remaneat scelerum macula, quem pura et sancta refecerunt sacramenta: Qui vivis et regnas in saecula saeculorum. Amen." Yes, may the body and blood of Christ, which I have consumed cleave to my bowels, that is, cleave unto my inmost parts, become one with my whole being, take possession of my very soul. Grant us, O Lord, that the power of the Eucharistic sacrament may wash away all impurities and corruptions, so that no stain of sin may remain in the soul of Thy happy priest, who was granted the privilege of being refreshed by these pure and holy mysteries. Yes, the priest prays that his soul may be clothed in the garment of sanctifying grace, and become an immaculate object, pleasing to the eyes of the heavenly Father. May the visible Eucharistic species "sanctify the Lord Christ in your hearts." [3] May the priest cry out with St. Paul: "I live, now not I, but Christ liveth in me." [4]

With this thought in mind, the celebrant turns to a verse

[3] I Pet. 3:15.
[4] Gal. 2:20.

from the Scriptures which constitutes the reading of the "Communion." Then he recalls the mystery of the day, saying the "Postcommunion." This prayer is, in construction and content, identical and harmonious with the Collect and the Secret. These three prayers, Collect, Secret, and Communion, express and state the purpose for which the Sacrifice of the Holy Mass is celebrated.

At first sight it would seem that the thanksgiving service of the Church is rather brief. To the laity the thanksgiving service may appear abbreviated, yet let us remember that the Holy Mass is not, as the Protestant service actually is, a Communion service, but is in the full and strictest sense a sacrifice. Holy Mass is first, and principally, a sacrifice. Holy Communion is not the high point of Mass, but merely the completion of the Sacrifice. The Sacrifice having been consumed, the Mass logically comes to an end.

St. Thomas has this in mind, too, when he declares that "the entire celebration of Mass ends with the thanksgiving, the people rejoicing for having received the mystery [and this is the meaning of the singing after the Communion] and the priest returning thanks: by prayer, as Christ, at the close of the supper with His disciples, said a hymn." [5]

The priest has fulfilled his sacerdotal duty when he steps down from the altar and, although in his official capacity as priest, or sacrificer, he has finished his action, as a spiritual man he is bound to nourish his own soul in the spirit of prayer and contemplation. The priest is supposed to kneel in the sanctuary or in the church, and his soul should offer thoughts and feelings of gratitude to God. Now that the priest is *corporaliter* united with Christ through the sacred species, it is most becoming to his soul to dwell on this divine union, and to

[5] *Summa theol.,* IIIa, q. 83, a. 4.

become one with his divine Master. The prayer a soul breathes forth during these precious moments is of particular value. St. Alphonsus says: "There is no prayer more agreeable to God, or more beneficial to the soul, than the one which is offered to God during the thanksgiving after Communion." [6]

If we desire the laity to make appropriate thanksgivings after Holy Communion, should not the priest himself set the example? The priest certainly becomes a shining light to his congregation, and an outstanding example to his parishioners, if, after Holy Mass, he devoutly kneels on the prie-dieu to make his thanksgiving. Is there a more forceful contradiction of the old Protestant slander that in the Catholic Church all is liturgy and ceremonies, with no time left free for lifting up the mind to heaven, than to see the priest devoutly praying in the sanctuary or church? The priest who is seen by his people making his thanksgiving after Holy Communion, is a source of edification and inspiration to them.

An unhurried and devout thanksgiving after Holy Communion should be made by every priest. The Canon Law lays down this norm: "The priest should not omit to prepare his soul by pious prayer for the oblation of the Eucharistic Sacrifice, and upon its conclusion give thanks to God for such a great benefit." [7] All theologians and spiritual writers agree that the thanksgiving should last until the sacred species have been dissolved, or approximately ten to twenty minutes.

The best prayer is the one which pours spontaneously from the soul. Every priest, at least for a few moments, should make a serious effort to speak from the bottom of his heart to his divine Lord and Master. Yet the Church knows the weaknesses and deficiencies of human nature, so she comes to our

---

[6] E. Grimm, *The Ascetical Works*, VI, 75.
[7] Canon 810.

aid assisting us with the beautiful prayers that we find in the Missal under the heading of "Orationes ante et post Missam." They are, as the Missal expresses, "pro opportunitate sacerdotis dicendae." To omit these prayers would not constitute a sin, yet one who neglects to make an adequate preparation before Mass as well as a sufficient thanksgiving after Mass would certainly not be devoid of fault. If the priest does not wish to say all these prayers, he could at least say a part of them.

The laity often think that the best and surest time to see the pastor, or the assistant priest, is immediately after Mass. Nevertheless, in well-regulated parishes, other priests will be appointed to take house calls until the celebrant returns from the sacristy. If the people have been well instructed, they will gladly cooperate with the pastor and afford him the time to make his thanksgiving after Holy Communion.

The priestly life is a Eucharistic life. The whole life of the priest, all his activities and official functions, are related in some way to the Eucharistic Sacrifice. The priest's life, so to speak, is one sacerdotal action after the other; hence, in his mind and reflections, the priest ought to think frequently of what he possesses, what he is, and what he must perform daily, and, during the busy hours of the day, he should find a few moments to return, in holy contemplation, to the Sacrifice of the Holy Mass. It is good and wholesome for him to dedicate a few minutes each day to a short meditation on his priestly functions. This can easily be done, let us say, before supper, or during the last ten or twenty minutes of the day before retiring, or when he has finished his Breviary. Any time during the day, meditation on the prayers, "before and after Mass," are advantageous. For, although the priest may thank his Eucharistic Lord for the Mass celebrated that morning, he may, in the interim, prepare himself by saying the prayers before Mass, in anticipation of the ascent to the altar the next morning; since the pious priest lives principally for the altar.

# CHAPTER 48

# *The Blessing*

Ite, missa est.

Placeat tibi, sancta Trinitas, obsequium servitutis meae, et praesta; ut sacrificium, quod oculis tuae majestatis indignus obtuli, tibi sit acceptabile: mihique et omnibus pro quibus illud obtuli, sit, te miserante, propitiabile. Per Christum Dominum nostrum. Amen.

Benedicat vos omnipotens Deus, Pater et Filius ✠ et Spiritus Sanctus. Amen.

THE Sacrifice of the Mass has come to an end. "Ite, missa est." "And from this," the Angelic Doctor says, "the Mass derives its name (missa); because the priest sends (mittit) his prayers up to God through the angel, as the people do through the priest. Or else because Christ is the victim sent (missa) to us; accordingly the deacon on festival days dismisses the people at the end of the Mass, by saying: 'Ite, missa est,' that is, the victim has been sent (missa est) to God through the angel, so that it may be accepted by God." [1]

"Ite, missa est." By these words the congregation is, officially, told that it is dismissed, it may go. Yet, the people are not sent away precipitately, for they are sent home in a becomingly Christian way, with the blessing of the Church. Before the priest imparts his blessing over the people, one thought that still holds his attention must be expressed, for, his mind is still occupied with the desire that the Eucharistic

---

[1] *Summa theol.*, IIIa, q. 83, a. 4, ad 9.

Sacrifice may be acceptable to God. So the priest bends down slightly at the middle of the altar and says the "Placeat tibi."

We may ask, to whom should this prayer be addressed? It should be addressed to the Blessed Trinity, since the Mass was begun in the holy name of the Blessed Trinity when the priest signed himself with the cross at the foot of the altar, and the Mass is brought to a close in the same manner, that is, in the name of God the Father and God the Son and God the Holy Ghost. "May the homage of my bounden duty be pleasing to Thee, O holy Trinity." The Eucharistic Sacrifice was the "obsequium servitutis sacerdotis," and upon this sacerdotal service the priest implores the good pleasure of the Blessed Trinity. "Et praesta, ut sacrificium, quod oculis tuae majestatis indignus obtuli, tibi sit acceptabile." The foremost concern of the priest is, indeed, the honor and glory of the Blessed Trinity, together with the desire that God's pleasure and complacency may graciously extend to himself, the celebrant, and to all those for whom the sacrifice was offered. "Mihique et omnibus pro quibus illud obtuli, sit, te miserante, propitiabile. Per Christum Dominum nostrum. Amen."

". . . Because thou hast done this thing, and hast not spared thy only begotten son for My sake: I will bless thee. . . ." [2] Yes, because we have offered up the Sacrifice of the Holy Mass, and have not spared the sacred body and blood of His only-begotten Son for the greater glory of the Blessed Trinity, we will now receive the blessings of the Eucharistic Sacrifice. Accordingly, the priest says: "May almighty God bless you, the Father, the Son, and the Holy Ghost." Surely, "salvation is of the Lord: and Thy blessing is upon Thy people." [3]

[2] Gen. 22: 16, 17.
[3] Ps. 3:9.

The act of blessing is not an invention of Christianity, for the act of blessing is itself as old as the creation of the objects that are blessed. In the history of the creation of the world, as early as the fifth day, before the creation of man, God blessed the animals, and said: "Increase and multiply. . . ." The Creator repeated this blessing on the sixth day, after He had created man.[4] From then on, we find the act of blessing well established in the history of the children of Israel. God blessed the patriarchs and the prophets, and He commanded His priests, as His special envoys, to bless the people "in His name." [5] We read regarding Moses that "stretching forth his hands to the people, he blessed them." [6] The blessing of God was explained at great length to the Jewish people:

> And the Lord spoke to Moses, saying:
> Say to Aaron and his sons: Thus shall you bless the children of Israel, and you shall say to them:
> The Lord bless thee, and keep thee.
> The Lord show His face to thee, and have mercy on thee.
> The Lord turn His countenance to thee, and give thee peace.
> And they shall invoke My name upon the children of Israel, and I will bless them.[7]

> Now if thou wilt hear the voice of the Lord thy God, to do and keep all His commandments, which I command thee this day, the Lord thy God will make thee higher than all the nations that are on the earth.
> And all these blessings shall come upon thee and overtake thee: yet so if thou hear His precepts.
> Blessed shalt thou be in the city, and blessed in the field.

[4] Gen. 1:22, 28.
[5] Deut. 21:5.
[6] Lev. 9:22.
[7] Num. 6:22–27.

Blessed shall be the fruit of thy womb, and the fruit of
thy ground, and the fruit of thy cattle, the droves of thy
herds, and the folds of thy sheep.
Blessed shall be thy barns and blessed thy stores.
Blessed shalt thou be coming in and going out.

The Lord will send forth a blessing upon thy store-
houses: and upon all the works of thy hands: and will
bless thee in the land that thou shalt receive.[8]

Blessings, or the invocation of divine favors, are so profoundly rooted in the conscience of the people and are so
beneficial and salutary to the good and just, that the New
Covenant could not ignore such blessings.

We read about blessings all through the pages of the New
Testament. The child Jesus, together with His Blessed Mother
and St. Joseph, were blessed by Simeon. Christ blessed the
people, especially the sick and the children. "And embracing
them [the children] and laying His hands upon them, He
blessed them." [9] In like manner our Lord departed from His
beloved disciples, when He ascended into heaven: ". . . and
lifting up His hands, He blessed them. And it came to pass
while He blessed them, He departed from them and was carried up to heaven." [10] As the Sacrifice of the Holy Mass comes
to an end, it could not be that our Lord or His representative,
the priest, would act in a different way, for it is in keeping
with the spirit of Christ that the priest, at the end of Mass,
raises his hand and imparts the blessing upon the congregation soon to disperse. "Benedicat vos omnipotens Deus, Pater
et Filius, ✠ et Spiritus Sanctus. Amen."

What is a "blessing," we may ask? The word "blessing" has
a variety of meanings. The Psalmist uses the word, when he

[8] Deut. 28:1–6, 8.
[9] Mark 10:16.
[10] Luke 24:50, 51.

says: "Blessed be the Lord, my God," [11] or "Bless the Lord, O my soul," [12] to express his wish for the praise and glory of God. Another meaning of this word manifests a desire to see good fortune or earthly, as well as spiritual, benefits and favors bestowed upon a person. King David had this in mind, when he chanted: "Blessed are all they that fear the Lord . . . blessed art thou, and it shall be well with thee." [13] The term "blessing," furthermore, may become a synonym for the sanctification or dedication of an article (or person), as when St. Matthew, describing the actions of our Lord at the Last Supper, said: ". . . Jesus took bread, and blessed, and broke, and gave it to His disciples." [14] Finally, a blessing may also, as in the liturgy of the Church—and this is its most restricted sense—be a ritual act, or a sacramental, by which in the name and by commission of the Church, a priest by an official liturgical act confers upon the members of the Church graces and benefits, merited by the Passion and death of our Lord, Jesus Christ. As there is no place or time when the graces merited by Christ are more abundantly released, diffused, and shed upon the faithful than in Holy Mass, it is evident that the liturgical blessing at the end of the Eucharistic Sacrifice is of a most effective, powerful, fruitful, and abundant nature. Yes, in Mass, we may say that "His blessing hath overflowed like a river." [15] These graces will not depart from the people, but will rest upon them and aid them in the struggle of life. It may be that these gifts are not released at once by divine Providence, but only later in life, when they will be more profitable and salutary. Yet it is absolutely certain that

[11] Ps. 143:1.
[12] Ps. 102:1; 103:1.
[13] Ps. 127:1, 2.
[14] Matt. 26:26.
[15] Ecclus. 39:27.

these graces are not lost, provided that the recipient is in the right disposition and cooperates with these graces.

Fortified by the blessing received at the end of Mass, the Christian, confident in the divine assistance, may step into a world hostile to the salvation of his soul. The graces of God will protect him, guide him through the perils of life, and assist him in his needs. "He shall receive a blessing from the Lord, and mercy from God his Savior." [16] "Blessed be the God and Father of our Lord Jesus Christ, who hath blessed us with spiritual blessings in heavenly places in Christ." [17] With God's help, there will be re-established "all things in Christ, that are in heaven and on earth." [18] "For unto this are you called that you may inherit a blessing." [19]

[16] Ps. 23:5.
[17] Eph. 1:3.
[18] Eph. 1:10.
[19] I Pet. 3:9.

# CHAPTER 49

# *The Last Gospel*

Initium sancti Evangelii secundum Joannem.
R. Gloria tibi, Domine.
In principio erat Verbum, et Verbum erat apud Deum;
et Deus erat Verbum. Hoc erat in principio apud Deum.
Omnia per ipsum facta sunt, et sine ipso factum est nihil
quod factum est: in ipso vita erat, et vita erat lux homi-
num; et lux in tenebris lucet, et tenebrae eam non com-
prehenderunt. Fuit homo missus a Deo, cui nomen erat
Joannes. Hic venit in testimonium, ut testimonium perhiberet de lumine, ut omnes crederent per illum. Non
erat ille lux; sed ut testimonium perhiberet de lumine.
Erat lux vera quae illuminat omnen hominen venientem
in hunc mundum. In mundo erat, et mundus per ipsum
factus est, et mundus eum non cognovit. In propria venit,
et sui eum non receperunt. Quotquot autem receperunt
eum, dedit eis potestatem filios Dei fieri, his, qui credunt
in nomine ejus, qui non ex sanguinibus, neque ex voluntate carnis, neque ex voluntate viri, sed ex Deo nati sunt.
Et Verbum caro factum est, et habitavit in nobis; et
vidimus gloriam ejus, gloriam quasi Unigeniti a Patre,
plenum gratiae et veritatis.
R. Deo gratias.

THE last prayer of the Mass is taken from the Gospel of St.
John. With the reading of the first fourteen verses of this
Gospel, the Mass comes to an end. Why, we may ask, is this
Gospel read at the end of Mass? This Gospel is a splendid re-
capitulation of the principal dogma, the foundation upon

which the Sacrifice of the Mass is established. The divinity of Christ forms the basis upon which the sacrifice of the New Covenant rests. All Christianity stands or falls on the dogma of the divinity of Christ. And the Mass, the center of all Christian worship, has a meaning only in virtue of the divinity of Christ. Deny this foremost dogma and you will destroy the altar in every Catholic Church. Profess your belief in the truth that Jesus Christ is the Son of God, and it will not be difficult to bend your knee in adoration before the Blessed Sacrament.

In the early age of Christianity, the errors of Cerinthus, a Gnostic heretic, demanded a public refutation. At this time, St. John the Evangelist had been turning over in his mind the idea of writing a history of the life of his divine Master, Jesus Christ, with the special intent of refuting the heresies of his contemporary. Men who denied Christ to be the Son of God had to be put to shame for all times. The dogma of the divinity of Christ had to be set before all men and had to be established by proofs so powerful as not to leave open any room for doubts or questioning. When, at last, St. John took the pen into his hand to begin the work he had in mind, it was as if the pent-up energy of the great thinker and lover of our Lord were suddenly released, and he burst forth and gave language to the most profound reflections regarding the divinity of our Lord, Jesus Christ. With this intent in mind, to refute the heresies of his time, St. John the Evangelist first speaks of the second Person of the Blessed Trinity in His relation to the first divine Person, God the Father. In his Gospel, St. John shows us the Son of God in His eternal being, eternally generated in the bosom of God the Father. He tells us of the second Person of the Blessed Trinity as He existed before the world was made and before time was created. In other words, the beloved disciple reveals to us the mystery of the Son of God as He dwells in the Godhead. Then the Evangelist goes on and speaks to us of the role the second Person of the Blessed Trinity fulfills when, in the beginning of time, all things were made through Him. And again, St. John unfolds to us the mystery of the Incarnation when, in the course of time, the Word was made flesh. None of the Synoptics had ever reported to us so much of the inner working of the Blessed Trinity.

St. John shows himself to be a master in composition and style. He writes verses with a delightful rhythm. Beginning the verse with exactly the same word that he had used as the last word, or as the most important word of the preceding line, he gives his strophes a certain poetical swing, effecting vivacity and delightfulness. There are harmony and diversity in his writing; there are beauty and simplicity in his composition, and he accomplishes all of this in spite of the fact that he writes about the most profound mysteries ever penned by a human hand.

In the beginning of this prologue to his Gospel, St. John speaks, as we have seen, of the eternal Word within the Godhead; he ends his discourse by referring to the Incarnation, of which fact he himself was a living witness. He tells us of the Word of God and His relation to God the Father, to the world, and to man. He relates the mystery of the Incarnation and its effect upon humanity. The word of God becomes the light of men. Most of the men reject this divine light, but those who receive it become sons of God. In order to show this concept in greater relief and to bring out more forcefully the contrast between the mission of St. John the Baptist and that of Christ, St. John, in master fashion, puts the divine Word, so to speak, in contrast to His precursor. St. John the Baptist was sent by God, but he himself was not the light, but was to bear witness to the divine light.

St. John the Evangelist starts his Gospel with the very word used by Moses to open the books of the Old Testament, but whereas the great prophet of Israel beheld only the world whose creation he relates, St. John dwells upon the very being of God and unfolds to us the mystery of the Blessed Trinity.

"In the beginning was the Word." In the language of our days, this means that the Word was in existence before the creation of the world. The Word was from all eternity. "And the Word was with God and the Word was God." The Word is uncreated. If He was in the beginning, we may ask with St. Basil, when was He not? [1] The only answer can be that He is always. Eternity is a mark of the Divinity. "The Word was God." Yet the Word was distinct from God the Father, for "the Word was with God." The Word from eternity was within the Godhead; united with God the Father. The Word is the Son of God, the second Person of the Blessed Trinity.

Why does St. John call the second Person of the Blessed Trinity "the Word"? He names the Son of God this way because the word which proceeds from the mouth of men resembles in a certain way, though imperfectly, the generation of God the Son from the bosom of God the Father. A word is the reflex of man's thoughts, proceeds from his intellect without passion or carnal sentiments, and is a being owing its existence to the activity of another being. In like manner, God the Son was begotten in eternity by God the Father. He is the image of God the Father. He proceeds from God the Father through the divine intellect. God the Son is of the same divine substance as is God the Father; hence the second Person of the Blessed Trinity is truly divine. He is truly God, yet

[1] *De Div.*, Hom. 16, 82.

not forming a second God, but in a living union with God the Father. "The Word was with God and the Word was God." The divine Word, or the Son of God, is, according to this verse of St. John, coeternal with God the Father, but possesses His own distinct personality. Yet the Son of God, the second divine Person, with the first divine Person, forms one divine substance. God the Son forms with God the Father one essential unity. With a few striking words, the beloved disciple has outlined the high points of the doctrine of the Blessed Trinity.

The dogma of the divinity of our Lord, Jesus Christ, is today just as hotly denied by the enemies of Christianity as it is severely and faithfully defended and proved by the teachers and writers of the Catholic Church. So it was when St. John wrote his Gospel. So it was when St. Thomas worked on his *Summa,* and so it is at the present time. So it will be in times to come. Hence it is useful and appropriate to recall the arguments brought forth by the Angel of the Schools in favor of the divinity of Christ. St. Thomas sees in the miracles the proof for Christ's divinity. In particular he analyzes the argument as follows:

> The miracles which Christ worked were a sufficient proof of His Godhead in three respects. First, as to the very nature of the works, which surpassed the entire capability of created power, and therefore could not be done save by divine power; . . . secondly, as to the way in which He worked miracles, namely, He worked miracles as though of His own power, and not by praying, as others do . . . whereby it is proved, as Cyril says, ". . . that He did not receive power from another, but being God by nature, He showed His own power over the sick; . . ."[2] thirdly, from the very fact that He

[2] *Comment. in Lucam.*

taught that He was God; for unless this were true it
would not be confirmed by miracles worked by divine
power. Hence it was said "What is this new doctrine?
For with power He commandeth even the unclean spirits, and they obey Him." [3]

[3] Mark 1:27; *Summa theol.*, IIIa, q.43, a.4.

# CHAPTER 50

## *The Word, Creator*

WITH a few vigorous strokes of his pen, St. John built up the basis for all further discussions regarding the divinity of Christ. He put on a firm foundation the doctrine of the divinity of the Son of God. Now he proceeds to speak of the relations of the divine Word to the universe. "All things were made through Him, and without Him was made nothing that has been made." A few verses further the Evangelist repeats this idea when he says: "And the world was made through Him." The world was created according to God's ideas. St. Thomas says: "God makes nothing except through the conception of His intellect, which is the Wisdom from eternity conceived; and this, in turn, is the Word of God or the Son of God. Accordingly, it is impossible that God makes anything unless it is through His Son." [1] Though the creation of all things is the work of the three divine Persons, we may, for the reason stated, attribute this work to the second divine Person and say that the creation of the world was accomplished through God the Son.

The Word of God is not an abstract idea but a living being: "In Him was life." The second divine Person is full of life, as is the first divine Person. "And the life was the light of men." The Word, through whom all created things came into exist-

[1] St. Thomas, *Commentary on the Gospel according to St. John*, Moretti edition, chap. 1, sect. 2, towards the end of the first subdivision, p. 21, column 2.

ence, extends His life-conferring operation to the soul of man. The Word is the source and originator of man's faith. The second divine Person, through whom man was created, enlightens us spiritually. "And the light shines in the darkness and the darkness grasped it not." In his sin and unbelief, man did not see the light. Man did not recognize the Word. Man was told of the coming of the Word. The light was announced to man. "There was a man, one sent from God, whose name was John." The Baptist's mission was to herald the coming of the Word. His life's task consisted in becoming a witness to the light. "This man came as a witness, to bear witness concerning the light, that all might believe through him." He was not himself the Messias, but His precursor. He was not himself the light, but was to bear witness to the light. St. John the Baptist was not the uncreated light. He was, nevertheless, set up by heaven to give testimony of the true, eternal light. "It was the true light that enlightens every man who comes into the world." The Messias was the true light. Every human creature was expected to benefit from the rays of graces and blessings that radiate from the divine light, yet the world closed its eyes against the envigorating rays from this divine light. "He was in the world." The Word of God, the divine light, was in the world sustaining "and upholding all things by the word of His power. . . ." [2] "And the world was made through Him and the world knew Him not." The world did not and would not recognize its Creator. When, in the course of time, the Word assumed human flesh, was born of the Virgin Mary, "He came unto His own, and His own received Him not." His own rejected Him and turned away from His doctrine and nailed Him to the cross. Many of the Jewish people were guilty of this crime, but, on the other hand, there were

[2] Heb. 1:3.

"many who received Him," who accepted His teaching, "who believed in His name." And to these, His followers, "He gave the power of becoming sons of God." These followers of Christ received His graces and power, which enabled them to triumph over sin and unbelief. Thereby they became His children, His sons, that is, they became the sons and daughters of God. These sons of God were, indeed, "born not of blood, nor of the will of the flesh, nor of the will of man, but of God." The fact that the Jewish people were of the seed of Abraham, Jacob, and Isaac would not avail them anything, for they were to be regenerated in the Spirit of God. "And the Word was made flesh and dwelt among us." St. Thomas says:

> When we say the Word was made flesh, "flesh" is taken for the whole man, as if we were to say, the Word was made man, as Isaias says: "All flesh together shall see that the mouth of the Lord hath spoken." [3] And the whole man is signified by flesh, because, . . . the Son of God became visible by flesh; hence it is subjoined: and we saw His glory. Or, because, as Augustine [4] says: ". . . in all that union the Word is the highest, and flesh the last and lowest. Hence, wishing to commend the love of God's humility to us, the Evangelist mentioned the Word and flesh, leaving the soul on one side, since it is less than the Word and nobler than flesh." [5]

The Word assumed human flesh and lived among the children of men. And, indeed, "we," the apostles, and the eye-witnesses of His miracles and wonderful deeds, "saw His glory." This glory belongs to the second divine Person, yet in Him and through Him, God the Father was glorified. It was the "glory as of the only-begotten of the Father, full of grace

[3] Isa. 40:5.
[4] Q. 83, qu. 80.
[5] *Summa theol.*, IIIa, q.5, a.3, ad 1.

and of truth." "I am the way and the truth and the life." [6] The divine Word is the source of all graces, because in Him and through Him and by Him we are redeemed, justified, and sanctified. He is our guide and teacher. For, in Him are there not "hid all the treasures of wisdom and knowledge"? [7] "Neither is there salvation in any other. For there is no other name under heaven given to men, whereby we must be saved." [8]

Could there be a more appropriate ending of Holy Mass? The Sacrifice of the Mass was made possible and perfected in virtue of the divinity of Christ. And now, with this great truth still ringing in our ears, we leave behind church and altar, to return to our daily tasks and to resume our ordinary life; however, not as the pagans who are occupied exclusively with the things of this world. No, we Catholics are animated by the spirit of Jesus Christ even in the midst of the performance of our daily duties. Throughout the day we remain in union with Him, our Lord and God. In the midst of the world we live in a supernatural life. "Our conversation is in heaven." [9] "And I live, now not I, but Christ liveth in me. And that I live now in the flesh: I live in the faith of the Son of God. . . ." [10]

"Deo Gratias."

Glory be to the Father and to the Son and to the Holy Ghost. As it was in the beginning, is now, and ever shall be, world without end. Amen.

[6] John 14:6.
[7] Col. 2:3.
[8] Acts 4:12.
[9] Phil. 3:20.
[10] Gal. 2:20.